# Middle Eastern Security, the US Pivot and the Rise of ISIS

### Edited by Toby Dodge and Emile Hokayem

# Middle Eastern Security, the US Pivot and the Rise of ISIS

Edited by Toby Dodge and Emile Hokayem

IISS The International Institute for Strategic Studies

# The International Institute for Strategic Studies

Arundel House | 13–15 Arundel Street | Temple Place | London | WC2R 3DX | UK

First published December 2014 by **Routledge**
4 Park Square, Milton Park, Abingdon, Oxon, OX14 4RN

for **The International Institute for Strategic Studies**
Arundel House, 13–15 Arundel Street, Temple Place, London, WC2R 3DX, UK
www.iiss.org

Simultaneously published in the USA and Canada by **Routledge**
270 Madison Ave., New York, NY 10016

*Routledge is an imprint of Taylor & Francis, an Informa Business*

© 2014 The International Institute for Strategic Studies

DIRECTOR-GENERAL AND CHIEF EXECUTIVE Dr John Chipman
EDITOR Dr Nicholas Redman
EDITORIAL Chris Raggett, Carolyn West, Dr Matthew Harries
CONTRIBUTORS Dr Dana H. Allin, Dr Henri J. Barkey, Dr Samuel Charap,
Dr Toby Dodge, Ben Fishman, Emile Hokayem, Charles Lister, Alexander Neill,
Dr Pierre Noël, Rahul Roy-Chaudhury, Adam Ward, Becca Wasser
COVER/PRODUCTION John Buck, Kelly Verity
COVER IMAGE US-led coalition forces hit ISIL targets in Kobani (Photo by Rauf
Maltas/Anadolu Agency/Getty Images)

**The International Institute for Strategic Studies** is an independent centre for research, information and debate on the problems of conflict, however caused, that have, or potentially have, an important military content. The Council and Staff of the Institute are international and its membership is drawn from almost 100 countries. The Institute is independent and it alone decides what activities to conduct. It owes no allegiance to any government, any group of governments or any political or other organisation. The IISS stresses rigorous research with a forward-looking policy orientation and places particular emphasis on bringing new perspectives to the strategic debate.

The Institute's publications are designed to meet the needs of a wider audience than its own membership and are available on subscription, by mail order and in good bookshops. Further details at www.iiss.org.

Printed and bound in Great Britain by Bell & Bain Ltd, Thornliebank, Glasgow

British Library Cataloguing in Publication Data
A catalogue record for this book is available from the British Library

Library of Congress Cataloging in Publication Data

ADELPHI series
ISSN 1944-5571

ADELPHI 447-448
ISBN 978-1-138-90778-2

# Contents

CONTRIBUTORS

**Dana H. Allin**      Editor of *Survival* and Senior Fellow for US Foreign Policy and Transatlantic Affairs at the IISS.

**Henri J. Barkey**      Bernard L. and Bertha F. Cohen Professor of International Relations at Lehigh University.

**Samuel Charap**      Senior Fellow for Russia and Eurasia at the IISS.

**Toby Dodge**      Professor of International Relations at the London School of Economics and Political Science, and Consulting Senior Fellow for the Middle East at the IISS.

**Ben Fishman**      IISS Consulting Senior Fellow for the Middle East and North Africa. He worked for four years on the US National Security Council staff, including as Director for North Africa and Jordan from 2012 to 2013.

**Emile Hokayem**      Senior Fellow for Middle East Security at the IISS.

**Charles Lister**      Visiting Fellow at Brookings Doha Center.

**Alexander Neill**      Shangri-La Dialogue Senior Fellow for Asia-Pacific Security at the IISS.

**Pierre Noël**      Sultan Hassanal Bolkiah Senior Fellow in Economic and Energy Security at the IISS.

**Rahul Roy-Chaudhury**  Senior Fellow for South Asia at the IISS.

**Becca Wasser**      Program Officer and Research Analyst at the IISS.

## Adam Ward, Director of Studies, IISS

For one crucial weekend each December, the Kingdom of Bahrain becomes the fulcrum of regional defence and security diplomacy in the Gulf, when ministerial delegations from over two dozen countries converge on the IISS Manama Dialogue. Outwardly, the Manama Dialogue has all of the appearances of a conventional conference. But its purpose and its function is the provision of a de facto regional security institution, with at least three very particular characteristics. Firstly, it combines all of the advantages of a formal intergovernmental summit – that is, the ability of ministers to meet in many combinations to advance policy objectives, plan for contingencies and respond to crises – with none of the inconveniences often associated with such overly choreographed occasions, such as communiqués and joint statements that are laboriously precooked well in advance of a ministerial meeting, and that therefore lend the actual encounter a somewhat unspontaneous, ritualistic feel. The Manama Dialogue provides a more flexible, businesslike approach for ministerial interaction. Secondly, while the Manama Dialogue is a meeting of the Gulf and for the Gulf, it is not only that. The region is beset by a range of local security challenges whose actual or potential consequences carry far and wide. It is for that reason that the Manama Dialogue features strong representation from the Americas, Europe, Eurasia and the Asia-Pacific: parts of the world that see themselves as stakeholders in the security of the region. Finally, the Manama Dialogue provides a venue not only for intergovernmental action, but for experts, defence and security professionals, business and elements of civil society. The value of the Manama Dialogue, then, is both the specific policy outcomes that it can achieve, and something at once intangible and concrete: the development of the sense of a regional security community in a part of the world where such a thing has been conspicuously absent for far too long.

December 2014 marks the tenth anniversary of the Manama Dialogue process.

To mark this tenth anniversary and to capitalise on the new light it has shed on security issues in the Gulf and the wider Middle East, the IISS decided to convene two workshops in its Middle East office in Manama to examine the most important geostrategic issues facing the region. The IISS assembled nine of its own analysts, all recognised world experts in their own right, from their network of global offices in London, Washington DC and Singapore. In addition, it invited a number of outside experts, to complement this process. The workshops set out to discuss the myriad security challenges in the Middle East. At the end of the process, the IISS decided to publish the results of these forums in a set of interlinked papers, focusing on the two most important geostrategic challenges now faced by the Middle East: the regional ramifications of the civil war in Syria and the effects of the United States changing posture in the Middle East.

The first set of papers examines the symbiotic crisis that has engulfed Syria and Iraq, driving them both into civil war. Emile Hokayem (Senior Fellow for Middle East Security, IISS–Middle East) argues that the contest between Iran, Saudi Arabia and Qatar over Syria has exacerbated the fault lines in societies across the

Levant. While the struggle over Syria has been immensely costly and remains inconclusive, Iran's commitment has helped secure President Bashar al-Assad's survival and guaranteed that Tehran will be central to any future settlement. Examining the rise of the Islamic State of Iraq and al-Sham (ISIS), Charles Lister (Visiting Fellow at Brookings Doha Center) argues that jihadist movements will be central to the future of Syria and Iraq, and also to the broader jihadist–Salafist and Islamist universe. At the core of this conflict, ISIS has proven highly adaptable to the complex environment it operates in. As a result of this, Lister argues, Syria has become the hub for the next generation of transnational jihadists. Henri Barkey (Bernard L. and Bertha F. Cohen Professor of International Relations at Lehigh University) highlights the shortcomings and predicaments facing Turkey as it seeks to lead the effort to depose Assad, contain the repercussions for its own Kurdish dilemma and manage its relationship with the US. The ambitions of the leadership in Ankara have been frustrated, exposing enduring weaknesses in Turkish regional and security policy. Toby Dodge and Becca Wasser (Consulting Senior Fellow for the Middle East, IISS; and Research Analyst, IISS–US) trace the roots of ISIS's rise, and the collapse of the Iraqi army units fighting it, to the decline of the Iraqi state since 2003. They argue that successive post-regime-change governments in Baghdad recovered neither the authority nor the legitimacy lost after the invasion. This resulted in debilitating institutional and operational weaknesses that led to ISIS's dominance of northwest Iraq. Ben Fishman (Consulting Senior Fellow for the Middle East and North Africa, IISS–US) looks at how Jordan, a fragile country surrounded by powerful or failing states, is managing the multidimensional spillover from Syria, which ranges from massive refugee inflows to renewed threats of Islamist militancy.

The second set of papers published in this volume examines the other geostrategic issue that dominates the concerns of decision-makers in the Gulf: the ramifications of the US 'pivot' to Asia under the Obama administration. Emile Hokayem and Becca Wasser open this section of the book by arguing that the new security posture of the US in the region has been the culmination of a series of long-running trends in American policy, global politics and within the region itself. This has compelled various Gulf states to diversify their political and security relationships, and to dilute the perception of their dependence on the US. The strategy was driven forward by an awareness in the region and in Washington that the centre of global economic activity was moving east. Dana Allin (Senior Fellow for US Foreign Policy and Transatlantic Affairs, IISS) argues that the aim of the Obama administration's Middle East policy was to balance its continued regional responsibilities against the limited resources and capabilities it had access to after the debilitating wars in Afghanistan and Iraq and the 2008 financial crisis. However, this strategic balancing act has been thrown into doubt by the rise of ISIS, its increasing dominance of the Syrian civil war and its seizure of Mosul. The administration's use of air power in combination with the empowerment of local allies is its attempt to limit its exposure to the Middle East while attempting to deal with the ISIS threat. Pierre Noël (Sultan Hassanal Bolkiah Senior Fellow for Economic and Energy Security, IISS–Asia) examines the changing patterns of both supply and demand in the world's oil market, and concludes by arguing that America's declining need for Middle East oil will not, by itself, lead to a reduction in its commitment to the region's security. Alexander Neill (Shangri-La Dialogue Senior Fellow for Asia-Pacific Security, IISS–Asia), Rahul Roy-Chaudhury (Senior Fellow for South Asia, IISS) and Samuel Charap (Senior Fellow for Russia and Eurasia, IISS–US) then examine the roles that China, Russia and India are playing in a Gulf concerned with what is widely perceived to be a declining US commitment. All three papers conclude that these three outside powers are neither willing nor, indeed, able to fill a security vacuum that may be created by a reduction in America's commitment to the region. Instead, China, Russia and India are intent on pursuing policies that are primarily shaped by economic interest.

The aim of this volume is to both highlight and develop the ongoing discussions and debates about Gulf security that have taken place in the Manama Dialogue over the previous decade, and that will continue to do so over the next ten years. As such, it has capitalised on the IISS's global reputation not only as the world leader in convening para-diplomatic events, but also as a provider of the best possible objective information and analysis on global military and political developments.

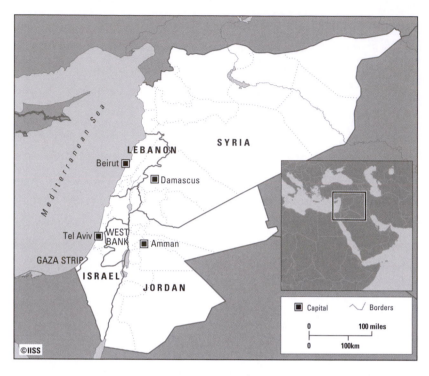

# CHAPTER ONE

# The Crisis of the Iraqi State

Toby Dodge and Becca Wasser

The new and severe crisis that has engulfed Iraq became apparent on 10 June 2014, when the Islamic State of Iraq and al-Sham (ISIS) took control of Mosul, the country's second-largest city. There were estimated to have been only 3,000 ISIS fighters in Iraq during 2013–14, yet forces aligned with the rebellion overwhelmed and defeated a garrison in Mosul believed to contain more than 30,000 Iraqi government troops.[1] The rebels then fought their way out of Nineva Province, heading down the main highway towards Baghdad. They pushed into Diyala Province, which borders Iran to the east, while simultaneously consolidating their position in Anbar Province, bordering Syria. The coordination and alacrity of the ISIS expansion not only demonstrated that the operation had been well planned, but also highlighted the profound failings of the Iraqi state.

Clearly, the violence that engulfed Iraq in June was more akin to a multifaceted and widespread uprising than the actions of one terrorist group. The gravity of the present crisis, with the Iraqi army quickly losing control of large tracts of territory to the north of Baghdad following the fall of Mosul, casts doubt upon the sustainability of the country's post-invasion political settlement, the security of the whole nation and the future of Iraq itself.

However, this crisis originated long before June 2014. It is the outcome of much more than just the cumulative mistakes made by former Prime Minister Nuri al-Maliki during his eight years in office. The crisis has its roots in the profound failings of Iraq's post-war political system. The rebellion that swept into Mosul and then spread down the Tigris towards Baghdad reflects far more than the ambitions of ISIS. It is illustrative of a wider comparative dynamic of violence brought on by a reduction in state power, and social alienation caused by discriminatory political, economic and social systems.

## The three pillars of state survival

What, exactly, does a state need to do to survive, and what has brought the Iraqi state to the brink of collapse? In order to assess these requirements, it is important to understand the drivers that can lead a state to failure or collapse. According to William Zartman, the absence of 'structure, authority (legitimate power), law and political order' contributes to state failure.[2] At the heart of this lies the power of the state (or the lack of it). The stability of a state is dependent on its ability to project power over the population through its institutions, functions and actions.[3] Therefore, the state relies on three main elements to guarantee its survival: firstly, it must control coercion across its territory; secondly, it must deliver the services that citizens need in their day-to-day lives and develop the infrastructure to do so; and, thirdly, it must ideologically bind the population together and to itself.

In order to achieve the level of coercion needed for survival, a state must impose order on the population and maintain a monopoly on the use of force in its territory. As Max Weber notes, the state must strive to become the sole source of legitimacy for adjudication and the use of violence across its territory.[4] This coercive power compels the population to conform to the requirements of the state, but also justifies the state's role as the guarantor of law and order. Zartman goes further, contending that a state must act as a security guarantor for both its population and its territory.[5]

Once a state has successfully imposed and guaranteed order, it then seeks to build its legitimacy through infrastructural power and the ability to deliver services within its territory.[6] The strengthening of infrastructure and institutions has multiple benefits, as a state's coercive capacity also relies on high levels of organisation.[7] Developing the capacity of coercive institutions such as the military and the police reinforces the state's ability to hold a monopoly on coercion.

Without the state to act as a central authority, general lawlessness is likely to prevail, as individuals are freed from the threat of coercion and institutional restraint. An individual's motives for action become more complex as the state's capacity to guarantee order decreases. As a result, individuals focus on survival, profit or a mixture of both, sometimes leading to war or a free-for-all.[8]

A state must also develop the second element of survival: the institutions and infrastructure used to deliver public goods and services throughout its territory and thus engender legitimacy among its population. Michael Mann terms this distributional capacity 'infrastructural power', defining it as the ability of the state to 'penetrate and centrally coordinate the activities of civil society through its own infrastructure'.[9] To ensure their sustainability, states must provide services that are central to the population's 'strategies of survival'.[10] These include a number of functions, with an emphasis on welfare delivery.[11] Examples include the delivery of electricity and water, the establishment of institutions such as ministries and police forces, and the development of communications and transportation infrastructure. By ensuring that basic services reach the population, the state accrues legitimacy and the support of the population within its territory.

Furthermore, the state requires infrastructure such as maintained roads and reliable energy networks to retain political control and enforce the rule of law.[12]

During times of insecurity, the state rarely, if ever, provides the basic social services and infrastructure required by the population. When a state fails, the population struggles to locate the public goods that it traditionally provides. In such a scenario, individuals turn to informal channels to obtain these goods and services, further eroding state authority and legitimacy.[13]

The competition for resources in the face of state collapse can strengthen secondary identity traits, particularly those that stem from religion and ethnicity. This is partly due to the fact that, in such a situation, the provision of stability, goods and ideational bonds is often more easily delivered at the community level. During times of insecurity, individuals will align with the political or religious grouping, or militia, that provides them with the greatest chance of survival.[14] These identities can be used by local leaders or 'ethnic and religious entrepreneurs' to mobilise segments of the population for political, economic or violent aims.

Hence, a state must successfully employ a mixture of coercive and administrative power in order to ensure its survival.[15] States with weak institutional power, in terms of both security and service delivery, create space for sub-state violence to flourish. According to James Fearon and David Laitin, 'financially, organisationally, and politically weak central governments render insurgency more feasible and attractive due to weak local policing or inept and corrupt counterinsurgency practices'.[16]

The last element of state stability is the development of an ideology that binds the population to the state. Linked closely to this is its ability to harness, sustain or create a unitary nationalism within its own borders. According to Andrea Kathryn Talentino, an operating state is a precondition for 'the development of a civic identity that can incorporate group identities and create a shared sense of community'.[17] Michael Billing adds that a state's existence is naturalised or 'flagged' in the everyday lives of its population through its institutional presence or references to it in the media.[18] The state takes the lead role in producing and manipulating 'a set of foundational myths that define and institutionalise a particular nationalist imaginary'.[19] In short, the rise of a sustainable nationalism follows the establishment of the state. Once created, the ideology of a state seeks to separate itself from, amalgamate and then rise above the tribal, religious, ethnic and class identities that it competes with for the loyalty of the population.[20]

A unified national identity is thus an essential component of state power. Societal cohesion empowers the state, which uses it to develop legitimacy and authority through ideology. Commitment to the state and belief in the legitimacy of its actions are key factors in building a national identity.[21] This identity is strengthened by the population's connection to the state and acknowledgement of a central, rather than local, power structure as the dominant authority.[22] The collapse of the state removes a central point of identity. Politics, economics and identity quickly become localised without a national identity to act as a force for social cohesion.[23]

## State power in Iraq from 1920 to 2014

With the rise in politically motivated violence following regime change and the ISIS advance of 2014, the Iraqi state's sustainability has been called into question. Yet has the Iraqi state ever managed to build the pillars of stability?

Its evolution can be broken down into five historical periods. The first of these occurred under the Ottoman Empire, before the British Army's 1914 invasion of what would become Iraq. The second is the era of British colonial domination, from 1920 until the removal of the Iraqi monarchy in 1958. The third is the tumultuous post-revolution period, which lasted until 1968. The penultimate era began with the Ba'ath Party's seizure of power that year, and ended with its removal by US forces after the invasion of 2003. The final period continues to this day.

It is important to examine how the area under Ottoman rule became Iraq, as there is an increasingly influential argument that blames the problems the country currently faces on the establishment of a modern state.[24] Leslie Gelb argues that the Ottomans presided over a stable and harmonious region because they 'ruled all the peoples of this land as they were: separately'.[25] But the truth of Ottoman rule is more complex than Gelb would have us believe. Although the Ottoman Empire first conquered what would become Iraq in the early sixteenth century, it was not until the nineteenth century that it brought the area into a centralised administrative system.[26] In stark contrast to Gelb's depiction, the empire did not govern along sectarian lines, but instead recognised a territorial entity called Iraq, which it ruled from Baghdad.[27] Indeed, Reidar Visser argues that nineteenth-century literature produced in the territory under Ottoman rule shows clear signs of a proto-political identity focused on the area that would become Iraq.

The establishment of the Iraqi state was formally declared in Baghdad in May 1920, with the announcement that the League of Nations had awarded Britain a mandate to build the state. This process was completed in October 1932, when the mandate ended and Iraq entered the League of Nations as a sovereign state. Throughout this period, with Britain still suffering from the debts incurred during the First World War, comparatively little money was expended on building state institutions. That said, the 'centralised unitary state model in Iraq is a heritage of the British mandate period', as Visser argues.[28] The building of the formal institutions of the state, with Baghdad as its capital and the integration of Iraq into the world economy that transformed the country, took place under British rule. By 1930, this process had resulted in 32% of Iraq's population living in urban areas.[29] However, the coercive and infrastructural power of the state remained weak under the mandate. At its creation in 1921, the core of the Iraqi army consisted of 640 former Ottoman officers.[30] The slow speed with which Iraq's armed forces were built left the country heavily dependent upon the British air force, not only to defend the country's borders but also to suppress its population.

*Hakumat al tayarrat*, or government by aircraft, had a number of negative consequences for the Iraqi state. Firstly, it meant that when Iraq gained entry into the League of Nations, it could not defend its own borders, let alone claim a monopoly on the collective use of violence across its territory. More importantly, the use of aircraft to police the population directly undermined the capacity of the government to expand its infrastructural power – the delivery of services and authority to the population. Air control, or the strafing of recalcitrant sections of the population, was easier and cheaper than building civil institutions.[31] This lack of infrastructural power was exacerbated by governmental instability, with the average lifespan of a cabinet being eight months in the first 16 years of the state.[32]

From 1920 to 1932, two divergent ideologies evolved within Iraq, one linking sections of the population to the state while the other mobilised citizens around a commitment to the inter-state political unit of the Arab nation. The main Iraqi proponents of Arab nationalism during this time were those in the circle of King Faisal I. Many of these individuals had served in the Ottoman army and followed him to Syria in his short-lived role there, before forming a core group within Iraq's new ruling elite.[33] Eric Davis contends that, during this period, Iraqi nationalism had a much wider and stronger base within society than Arab nationalism. The Iraqi revolt against the British, which started in July 1920 and was finally put down in February 1921, led to an estimated 131,000 people across Iraq fighting against the occupation. Davis convincingly argues that an 'Iraqist nationalist vision' played a major role in mobilising the revolutionaries. He concludes that the bulk of politically active Shi'ites were Iraqi nationalists, who adopted the battle cry '*al-istiqlal al-tamm*' (unconditional independence).[34] The power of this movement forced the British to replace the mandate with a treaty in 1923, and to begin negotiations for full Iraqi sovereignty by the late 1920s.[35]

The legacy of British state-building was mixed, to say the least. At the end of British rule, the coercive and institutional capacity of the Iraqi state was very low. But the presence of a foreign occupier had helped create and develop a powerful Iraqi nationalism. This state weakness facilitated the bloody coup of 1958, which removed the British-installed monarchy and replaced it with a military government. The state itself remained economically weak, but was run, from 1958 to 1963, by the charismatic Brigadier Abd al-Karim Qasim.[36] Qasim attempted to unite Iraq's population by rallying them around a socialist vision of Iraqi nationalism. Although he was popular, especially with Iraq's growing urban working class, the ideological divide between Qasim's Iraqi nationalism and the Arab nationalism of other military figures triggered his removal in another violent coup, in 1963. The instability that followed lasted until the 1968 seizure of power by the Ba'ath Party.

Led by Hassan al-Bakr from 1968–79 and subsequently by Saddam Hussein, the Ba'athist dictatorship built a state of unprecedented coercive and infrastructural power. By fully nationalising Iraq's oil industry in 1972, the state was in a position to accrue great wealth during the oil-price rises of 1973–74. Oil revenue rose from $488 million in 1968 to $21.4 billion in 1979. The number of government employees doubled in the same period.[37] From 1979 onwards, Saddam Hussein maintained the stability of the regime by effectively utilising a mixture of coercion, nationalist ideology and patronage funded by Iraq's oil wealth. The Ba'athist regime bypassed, destroyed and then rebuilt elements of civil society. It used these methods, as well as the employment of large swathes of the population by the state, to create a dependence on the government and hence perpetuate support for Saddam Hussein.[38] Before 1990, the regime was effective at using the institutional capacity and resources of the state to secure the quiescence of Iraqi society.

The state's ability to deliver services and maintain institutional capacity under Saddam Hussein's rule was constrained by the Iran–Iraq War and the First Gulf War, as well as the harsh international sanctions on the country that followed. While the sanctions regime successfully broke the government's ability to deliver basic services to the population, the state still managed to maintain power through the deteriorating infrastructure that it had built during the 1970s.[39] The government rationing system, which provided food to approximately 60% of the population, was yet another means of securing the loyalty of the population.[40]

In spite of war and sanctions, the Ba'athist dictatorship continued to dominate Iraqi society by using high levels of state-sanctioned violence. The coercive power of the state was reinforced by the Ba'athification of the military and the prevalence of regime loyalists throughout the security forces.[41] Even at its weakest point, in the mid-1990s, the state managed to retain its monopoly on violence, with any collective use of violence by organised elements within society being quickly and forcibly punished.[42]

Even the sanctions regime, which had been designed to cripple Saddam Hussein's capability, ended up reinforcing the regime's capacity for patronage: as the formal institutions of the state shrank, a regime-controlled smuggling network grew in power and reach.[43]

Lastly, the Iraqi state developed a compelling narrative and nationalist ideology. Building upon elements of Iraqi nationalism popularised by the Ba'ath Party, Saddam Hussein utilised a nationalism that stressed Iraq's ancient and historical roots. The regime sought to create a 'hegemonic' Iraqi national identity, which institutionalised a sense of belonging to a state and nation.[44] While this claimed to be relatively inclusive of all elements within Iraqi society, it covertly developed a core affinity with the key symbols of Sunni Islam.[45]

The 2003 invasion of Iraq by the United States certainly destroyed the regime, but it also destroyed the coercive and infrastructural power of the state. The subsequent reconstruction of Iraq's political, coercive, ideological and economic structures has been an arduous and ultimately unsuccessful process.

## State power under Maliki

The causes of the rapid collapse of the Iraqi army in June 2014 lie at the heart of the problems presently facing the entire Iraqi state. The 2003 disbandment of the Iraqi army by the US left a space within Iraqi society for the formation of sub-state militias. These groups provided rough-and-ready order, in the process earning the loyalty of sections of society. From 2004 onwards, as Iraq descended into insurgency and then full-blown civil war, Washington set out to quickly restore the indigenous coercive capacity of the state, thereby reducing the costs of the occupation, attempting to provide sustainable security and facilitating the departure of US forces from the country.

However, the collapse of the Iraqi armed forces earlier this year stemmed from two weaknesses created by the haste with which they were rebuilt. Firstly, Iraq's military, like the rest of its institutions, have been undermined by the corruption that has infected and debilitated the whole state. Junior Iraqi officers have complained that defence officials demand bribes of $3,000 for a place at the Officer Training Academy, with the price of promotion to general as much as $30,000. Repaying these costs leads to the creation of 'ghost payrolls' comprised of fictitious soldiers, estimated to have defrauded the Ministry of Defence of 25% of its annual wage budget. Similar dynamics have led to the embezzlement of funds earmarked for soldiers' food and fuel.[46] It has been suggested that, before June 2014, soldiers in Mosul had to buy and prepare their own food.[47] Corruption this severe would have been obvious to front-line soldiers, undermining their ability to fight effectively while sapping their morale and will to defend the state.

Beyond corruption, Maliki's direct interference in Iraq's armed forces broke their coherence. Following his appointment as prime minister in 2006, he worked successfully to 'coup-proof' the army, binding its senior commanders and paramilitary units to him personally, and subverting the formal chain of command. The new Iraqi military was built with such haste that the institutionalisation of political oversight became fragile. Concerned about his political vulnerability, Maliki exploited this weakness, using the Office of the Prime Minister to strengthen his hold on the army, special forces and the intelligence services.

Maliki controlled the security forces by creating two extra-constitutional organisations. The first, the Office of the Commander in Chief, was originally envisaged by American advisers as a coordinating forum that the prime minister would chair. But Maliki quickly realised its potential importance, and increased its staff, influence and reach. He moved the organisation into the Office of the Prime Minister, appointing a close ally as its head.[48] Subsequently, the Office of the Commander in Chief began to issue orders directly to battalion leaders, which had the effect of circumventing and destroying the army's chain of command.[49] The office then directly involved itself in the appointment and promotion of senior army staff.[50]

Maliki's second extra-constitutional innovation to control the security forces centred on the proliferation of Provisional Command Centres in unstable areas across Iraq. Beginning in February 2007 with the Baghdad Security Plan, the Baghdad Operations Command was created to coordinate all Iraqi forces in the city, including the police and the army.[51] A central office under Maliki's control appointed and directed one general for each province, who had command and control of both the police and the army. This undermined the Ministry of Defence's command and control of the army, and gave Maliki the power to place his personal and political allies in positions of command in the most strategically sensitive areas of the country.

The collapse of the army's Second Division in Mosul demonstrated the negative effects of politicising the upper echelons of the armed forces. Two senior army officers who benefited from a very close relationship with Maliki – Lieutenant-General Ali Ghaidan, commander of Iraqi ground forces, and Lieutenant-General Abboud Qanbar, commander of joint operations – flew into Mosul on 7 June 2014 to personally oversee the fight against ISIS.[52] Yet as the group advanced on the main army base in the city, both quickly fled the city before it fell. The morale of their subordinates was damaged by the incident, particularly after it was reported that the generals had made their escape disguised as civilians.

The fall of Mosul therefore highlighted the weakness of the Iraqi army. But the other two pillars of the Iraqi state had also been undermined for at least six years. A state's infrastructural power, the delivery of services and governance to its population, is a crucial aspect of the legitimacy that ties it to the population. The institutions of the Iraqi state have been undermined by profound corruption.

In Transparency International's Corruption Perceptions Index, Iraq placed 175th out of 182 countries in 2011; 169th out of 174 in 2012; and 171st out of 177 in 2013.[53] Iraq's anti-corruption institutions scored just five out of 100 points.[54] This level of corruption directly hinders the state's ability to deliver services and direct reconstruction efforts. The government's contracting process has been described as 'the father of all corruption issues in Iraq' by Judge Rahim al-Ugaili, the most senior government figure responsible for rooting out corruption during 2008–11.[55] Contracts are frequently awarded to firms affiliated with senior Iraqi politicians.

These companies are often given large cash payments before work has started, and are able to ignore complaints of substandard work due to their political connections.

Iraq is an oil-rich state and, as such, should have little problem in providing government services. But the entrenchment of corrupt practices throughout the Iraqi government has resulted in abysmal services and infrastructure. According to a 2011 estimate by the United Nations, just 26% of the population was covered by the public sewage network. That meant that 83% of the country's wastewater was untreated. Two-thirds of Iraqi households directly rely on the public supply for drinking water, but in 2012 surveys suggested that up to 25% of them received only two hours of water per day.[56] According to surveys by the Iraq Knowledge Network, only 38% of households rated the availability of drinking water as 'good'.[57] The UN estimates that 7.6m Iraqis, or 25% of the population, lack access to safe drinking water.[58]

Electricity has become the population's main touchstone for judging the capacity of their state and its cause. In August 2011, as temperatures reached 50°C, Minister of Electricity Ra'ad Shalal al-Ani resigned after it became known that he had signed $1.7bn in contracts for developing Iraq's electricity industry with two dubious foreign companies.[59] That same year, the Iraqi Knowledge Network found that Iraqi households received on average just 7.6 hours of electricity from the national grid each day, with 79% of those surveyed describing electricity delivery as 'bad' or 'very bad'.[60] Approximately one-third of Iraq's electrical supply was being lost before it reached users.[61] In June 2013, the Ministry of Electricity reported that 22% of the national grid's power-generation capacity was not being utilised, due to a lack of fuel or water, or other inefficiencies.[62]

The combination of inadequate infrastructural power and pervasive corruption means that the state has a very low institutional presence within Iraqi society. This has created deep alienation from the state and the widespread perception that it is being governed only to the benefit of a small kleptocracy. As a national problem, the grievances caused by the lack of basic services are not necessarily sectarian in nature. Yet the government's failure to provide these services can be co-opted in the sectarian rhetoric used by key members of the ruling elite, laying the groundwork for greater sectarian tension over the distribution of resources.

As a security and institutional vacuum developed, the population began to seek other security guarantors and social-service providers. This enabled religious and political groups – such as the Badr Brigade, the Sadrist movement and the latter's Mahdi Army – to step in where the state had failed.[63] These entrepreneurial groups justified their actions in sectarian terms, and gained public support by exploiting the population's needs, providing political, coercive and economic leadership.

The destruction of the final pillar of state strength, ideological power and legitimacy, is probably the most difficult to rebuild. Opinion polls taken in the years immediately following regime change showed that the Iraqi population had a strong commitment to a unified state and was bound to it by a vibrant nationalism. In February and May 2004, they found support for a strong centralised state with Baghdad as its capital. The Iraqi Centre for Research and Strategic Studies reported that 64.7% favoured a politically centralised, unitary state as opposed to a federation, while 67% said that they wanted both fiscal and administrative centralisation. Polls taken in 2008 found that 66% of respondents favoured a central government, compared to the 23% that preferred a regional government and the 9% that wanted separate states.[64] Oxford Research International polls from February, March and June 2004 found broadly similar views. In response to the question 'which structure should Iraq have in the future?', 79% of respondents answered 'one unified Iraq with a central government in Baghdad'. Although the figures differed according to the ethnic and regional background of those questioned, only 12% of Kurds, and 3.8% of all those surveyed, called for Iraq to be broken up into separate states.[65]

However, since the formation of the Iraqi Governing Council in 2003, Iraqi politics has been organised around the *muhasasa* system. This involves the apportionment of cabinet seats among those who claim to represent Iraq's different religious and ethnic communities.[66] Cabinet posts, along with the positions of prime minister and president, are allocated in line with a sectarian formula that also takes into account the number of seats each party wins in the elections. This logic of sectarian representation was first used in 1992 by the Iraqi opposition in exile, when it formed the Iraqi National Congress (INC) to oppose Ba'athist rule. The INC's executive bodies and council were staffed 'according to sectarian, ethnic and ideological affinities'.[67] The US and the UN readily adopted this method to form the Iraqi Governing Council, a body that was meant to act as a receptacle for Iraqi sovereignty while the country was under US occupation.[68] But, in reality, the system has led the ministries' payrolls and budgets to become the private fiefdoms of the parties to which they are awarded; personal and political corruption has been left to run rampant, as has incoherent governance.

The *muhasasa* system was certainly imported into Iraqi politics by the US occupying forces and their allies, the formerly exiled politicians. However, as electoral politics got under way, the system combined with the use of overtly sectarian rhetoric to dominate electioneering and government formation. This process was driven by the formation of the United Iraqi Alliance (UIA), an electoral coalition designed to maximise the Shia vote. Ali Allawi argues that Grand Ayatollah Ali al-Sistani, the most senior and revered Shia religious figure in Iraq, urged the establishment of the UIA in September 2004, giving it his blessing during the first national elections after regime change.[69] In the aftermath of that decision, most political parties sought to solidify and maximise votes from their constituencies by using religious and ethnic rhetoric. Although the elections of 2005, 2006 and 2010 were followed by slow government formation that involved a series of negotiations between and within electoral coalitions, in each case the *muhasasa* system was ultimately used to form a government of national unity. The logic of this system also shaped negotiations after the national elections of April 2014, leading to the formation of a new government and the appointment of Haider al-Abadi as Iraq's prime minister.

The formation of the UIA had the predictable side effect of alienating citizens who could not share in a Shia-majoritarian vision. They included those whose identity had primarily been secular and nationalist. But, as Iraq's political discourse increasingly featured references to religious and ethnic groupings, the ranks of the disaffected came to be dominated by Iraqis who had come to see themselves as part of a specifically Sunni demographic. During the insurgency and the civil war, sectarian rhetoric was used to justify rising civilian casualties, population transfers and mass-casualty attacks.[70] By 2006, the conflict was presented in an aggressively divisive, sectarian way. The majority of Iraq's ruling elite still uses this language, albeit to varying degrees.

The *muhasasa* system and the accompanying sectarian political rhetoric has been used to divide Iraq's population into groups based on ethnic and religious affiliations, a tactic that has maximised political mobilisation for the majority of political parties. Yet it has also driven rising alienation from the state among Iraq's Sunnis. In a 2014 poll, 66% of Sunni respondents viewed the decisions of the Iraqi government as illegitimate, in comparison to 31% of Shia respondents; 83% of Sunnis believe that Iraq is headed in the wrong direction.[71]

The Sunni estrangement from the state started with the de-Ba'athification campaign, which was begun by the US in 2003 but has since been used by senior members of Iraq's ruling elite as a weapon to discredit their rivals.[72] The Sunni community, with justification, perceived de-Ba'athification as a vehicle for linking them to the crimes of Saddam Hussein and his regime. The process was once again used as a political tool in the run-up to the 2010 national elections. The Accountability and Justice Commission, the government body charged with implementing de-Ba'athification, issued edicts that sought to ban 511 individual candidates and 14 party lists from the elections. The exclusions were intended to damage those coalitions seeking to mobilise the electorate on the basis of secular and nationalist manifestos.

However, the alienation of the Sunni community from the state reached its peak shortly after 20 December 2012, when there was a raid on the house of Rafi al-Issawi, then the finance minister, and his bodyguards were taken into custody. This replicated an event that had occurred one year earlier: the arrest of Vice-President Tariq al-Hashemi and his bodyguards. Hashemi was allowed to flee into exile, but his bodyguards confessed to terrorism offences and he was sentenced to death in absentia. Hashemi was not a particularly effective or popular politician. As a result, his arrest resulted in little popular protest. Issawi, on the other hand, has had a strong political constituency in his home province of Anbar, and won international respect for his effective and non-partisan management of the Ministry of Finance.

The raid on Issawi's house, and his subsequent resignation in March 2013, triggered mass protests across the Sunni-dominated northwest of Iraq. The move mobilised Iraqi Sunnis because they had felt increasingly excluded from national politics since the 2010 elections, cut off from the benefits of oil wealth and discriminated against by the Iraqi security forces. From December 2012 to April 2013, tens of thousands of people demonstrated in Anbar's two biggest cities, Fallujah and Ramadi. The protests quickly spread into the neighbouring provinces of Diyala and Nineva.

The government brought in the Iraqi army to break up the demonstrations, causing the deaths of nine people at the end of January 2013 and a further 40 the following April. Accordingly, in a May 2014 poll, 86% of Sunni respondents expressed negative views of the Iraqi security forces.[73] The use of state-sponsored violence to break up popular protests left a legacy of resentment and alienation among Iraq's Sunni population, increasing hostility towards the Maliki government and, in turn, the Iraqi state. The steady rise in politically motivated violence during 2013 can be seen as a direct result of both the suppression of the protest movement and the underlying grievances that triggered the demonstrations.

The profound sense of alienation felt by Iraqi Sunnis is the major driver of the ISIS revolt. It is unsurprising that the group has found it easiest to gain control of the areas in which the protests of 2013 and the harsh government-backed crackdown occurred. In the aftermath of the 2010 elections, a contest in which there was a high Sunni turnout, those who voted saw their key political representatives driven from government on trumped-up charges of terrorism.

Since the regime change of 2003, Iraqis have been politically mobilised, their governments chosen and the civil war justified in ideological terms that deliberately undermine unitary nationalism, in favour of accentuating divisive sub-state identities. This is not a return to the supposedly dominant religious identities some would argue have always animated Iraqi politics. Instead, it is the deliberate fostering or reinvention of sectarian identities by the ruling elite, which judged this the best way to rally an electorate deeply alienated from the state by corruption and deficient institutions. The Iraqi state was greatly weakened by Maliki's attempts to monopolise power; failure to combat endemic corruption or deliver the most basic of social services to the population; exclusionary policies; and cultivation of sectarian identities.

Against this background, the seizure of Mosul by ISIS and its swift advance across a wide swathe of Iraqi territory was the direct result of a set of structural weaknesses built into the political system established after regime change. Without significant changes to the Iraqi state's coercive, infrastructural and ideological functions, the group will continue to whittle away at the vestiges of state power.

## Can the Iraqi state be rebuilt?

The first step in dealing with ISIS will be to defeat it militarily. However, the challenge posed by the group cannot be met solely through military means. The successful long-term stabilisation of Iraq will require recognition of the political problems that created the space in which it has thrived. The group's forerunner, al-Qaeda in Iraq, was beaten militarily by the application of US-led counter-insurgency tactics from 2007 onwards. However, because the 'surge' did not tackle the underlying political dynamics of the Iraqi civil war, ISIS managed to rebuild from the remnants of al-Qaeda in Iraq, expand its area of operations and go on to become more powerful than its predecessor. A broad-based political process will therefore be essential to the group's total defeat and the future stability of Iraq.

Abadi's appointment has the potential to be a positive step in the much-needed reform of the Iraqi state. But the redemptive capacity of the new government should not be overestimated. To be successful, Abadi will have to do much more than he did on 8 September, when he formed yet another government of national unity that included a token number of Sunni politicians. In fact, only 26% of ministries went to Sunni cabinet members, a 4% decrease from Maliki's last government.[74] Abadi will need to transform the way in which Iraq has been run since 2005, if not earlier. Firstly, he will have to undo the damage caused by Maliki. This will certainly involve removing Maliki's powerful set of close advisers and the *Malikiyoun*, his followers who have been placed in influential positions throughout state institutions.[75] A commitment to the decentralisation of power would be a promising step for Abadi's government.

Yet the rise of ISIS cannot be blamed only on mistakes made during Maliki's tenure, as this severely underestimates the size of the problem Iraq faces. The corruption that has undermined the Iraqi state from within is an integral part of the *muhasasa* system. The system has, in effect, privatised the Iraqi state, allowing politicians to appropriate national assets, both for personal gain and to fund their parties. It has allowed a violent and divisive sectarian language to become the dominant currency of Iraqi politics. The pervasive sectarianism and corruption that have undermined the Iraqi state are the responsibility of the elite who came to power in the wake of regime change. If the threat from ISIS is to be neutralised and Iraq is to be stabilised, Abadi will not only have to reform the state but persuade the elite to work towards unifying a society it played a central role in dividing. He will need to convince Iraq's leaders to change the way they rule, moving from a corrupt, secretive approach towards honesty, accountability and transparency. Being a central member of that elite, there is little doubt that Abadi realises the size of the task he has taken on, and the great obstacles in his way.

He will also need to reform the Iraqi security services. The army will have to be rebuilt with new command-and-control mechanisms. The redistribution of power would help remove some vestiges of Maliki's consolidation of military control within his office. Corrupt practices, such as payment for promotion and the maintenance of ghost pay rolls, should also be eradicated. By doing so, trust within the rank and file could slowly return, restoring an element essential to the army's capacity to fight ISIS. In this, there is promise in the recently promoted US plan for allowing local units of the Iraqi National Guard to police their own provinces.[76] This could better integrate the Sunni population into the local security forces, thereby making them more inclusive. It would also redistribute power from Baghdad to provincial governments. Local units will be better placed to maintain and even strengthen security, especially in areas where ISIS has attempted to build local support. But this plan also has significant potential to intensify separatism in Iraq. This federalist-style initiative must be carefully implemented to avoid exacerbating sectarianism.

ISIS has continued to move through Iraqi territory largely unopposed. In certain areas, governance has been so bad that the group has been welcomed by local communities as a better option than the leadership in Baghdad. This is damning evidence of the government's failure to provide basic services, security or the rule of law to the population. Through extortion, smuggling and the illegal sale of oil, ISIS generates nearly $12m per month, a portion of which is used to provide services for the population under its control.[77] In Raqqa, the hub of the group's Syrian operations, it has provided electricity and food subsidies, repaired infrastructure, and established schools and courts.[78] The social services ISIS provides are intended to bind the local population to its rule. As such, the Iraqi government, in a process of competitive state-building, needs to strengthen its delivery of basic services such as electricity and clean drinking water, if it is to stand any chance of countering the group. The Iraqi population must be able to rely on the state for essential services.

Abadi's last, and perhaps his most daunting, task is to develop a new ideology focused on a unified Iraqi national identity. Without an ideology to tie the population to the state, his government will lack the legitimacy needed to carry out reforms and retain power. The population must begin to identify with the state as Iraqis, rather than be forced to interact with its institutions along religious or ethnic lines. This is a significant undertaking, and it will take years to reverse the sectarian rhetoric and identification stoked by exclusionary policies under Saddam Hussein and Maliki.

## Notes

1   Dan Kedmey, 'Iraq is "Run by al-Qaeda": Appalling Carnage Shows Terror Group's Resurgence', *Time*, 14 October 2013, http://world.time.com/2013/10/14/this-is-qaeda-country-blasts-and-prison-breaks-erode-iraqi-sovereignty/. In February 2014, the US government estimated that ISIS had 2,000 fighters in Iraq. Brett McGurk, 'Threat Posed by the Islamic State of Iraq and the Levant (ISIL)', testimony before the House Foreign Affairs Committee Hearing: Iraq, 5 February 2014, http://docs.house.gov/meetings/FA/FA00/20140205/101716/HHRG-113-FA00-Wstate-McGurkB-20140205.pdf. Sam Jones, 'Iraq Crisis: Sophisticated Tactics Key to Isis Strength', *Financial Times*, 26 June 2014, http://www.ft.com/cms/s/0/6436f754-fd18-11e3-bc93-00144feab7de.html?siteedition=uk#axzz366j8iglq.

2   I. William Zartman, 'Introduction: Posing the Problem of State Collapse', in I. William Zartman (ed.), *Collapsed States: The Disintegration and Restoration of Legitimate Authority* (Boulder, CO: Lynne Reiner, 1995), p. 1.

3   Antonio Gramsci, *Selections from the Prison Notebooks* (London: Lawrence and Wishart, 1998), p. 145.

4   Max Weber, 'Politics as Vocation', in H.H. Gerth and C. Wright Mills (eds and trans), *From Max Weber: Essays in Sociology* (New York: Oxford University Press, 1948), http://www.sscnet.ucla.edu/polisci/ethos/Weber-vocation.pdf.

5   Zartman, 'Introduction', p. 5.

6   Michael Mann, 'The Autonomous Power of the State: Its Origins, Mechanisms and Results', in Michael Mann (ed.), *States, War and Capitalism: Studies in Political Sociology* (Oxford: Blackwell, 1992), p. 111.

7   *Ibid.*, p. 124.

8   Nelson Kasfir, 'Domestic Anarchy, Security Dilemmas, and Violent Predation: Causes of Failure', in Robert I. Rotberg (ed.), *When States Fail: Causes and Consequences* (Princeton, NJ: Princeton University Press, 2004), p. 55.

9   Mann, 'The Autonomous Power of the State', pp. 113–14.

10  Joel S. Migdal, *Strong Societies and Weak States: State–Society Relations and State Capabilities in the Third World* (Princeton, NJ: Princeton University Press, 1988), p. 27.

11  Jennifer Milliken and Keith Krause, 'State Failure, State Collapse, and State Reconstruction: Concepts, Lessons and Strategies', *Development and Change*, vol. 33, no. 5, November 2002, p. 761.

12  Mann, 'The Autonomous Power of the State', p. 115.

13  Kasfir, 'Domestic Anarchy, Security Dilemmas, and Violent Predation', p. 55.

14  Andrea Kathryn Talentino, 'The Two Faces of Nation-building: Developing Function and Identity', *Cambridge Review of International Affairs*, vol. 17, no. 3, October 2004, p. 569.

15  James D. Fearon and David D. Laitin, 'Ethnicity, Insurgency and Civil War', *American Political Science Review*, vol. 97, no. 1, February 2003, p. 81.

16  *Ibid*. pp. 75–6.

17  Talentino, 'The Two Faces of Nation-building', p. 557.

18  Michael Billig, 'Reflecting on a Critical Engagement with Banal Nationalism – Reply to Skey', *Sociological Review*, vol. 57, no. 2, May 2009, p. 349; Christopher Phillips, *Everyday Arab Identity: The Daily Reproduction of the Arab World* (Abingdon: Routledge, 2013), p. 4.

19  Eric Davis, *Memories of State: Politics, History and Collective Identity in Modern Iraq* (Berkeley, CA: University of California Press, 2005), p. 2.

20  Mann, 'The Autonomous Power of the State', p. 129.

21  Talentino, 'The Two Faces of Nation-building', p. 564.

22  *Ibid*, p. 571.

23  Zartman, 'Introduction', p. 6.

24  See Toby Dodge, 'Can Iraq Be Saved?', *Survival*, vol. 56, no. 5, October–November 2014, pp. 7–20.

25  Leslie H. Gelb, 'The Three-State Solution', *New York Times*, 25 November 2003, http://www.nytimes.com/2003/11/25/opinion/the-three-state-solution.html.

26  Gökhan Cetinsaya, *Ottoman Administration of Iraq, 1890–1908* (Abingdon: Routledge, 2011).

27  Reidar Visser, 'Historical Myths of a Divided Iraq', *Survival*, vol. 50, no. 2, April–May 2008, pp. 95–106.

28  Reidar Visser, 'Centralism and Unitary State Logic in Iraq from Midhat Pasha to Jawad al-Maliki: A Continuous Trend?', *Historiae*, 22 April 2006, http://historiae.org/maliki.asp.

29  Mohammad A. Tarbush, *The Role of the Military in Politics: A Case Study of Iraq to 1941* (London: Kegan Paul International, 1982), p. 17.

30  *Ibid*.

31  Peter Sluglett, *Britain in Iraq, 1914–1932* (Oxford: Ithaca Press for the Middle East Centre, 1976), pp. 268–9.

32  Tarbush, *The Role of the Military in Politics*, p. 15.

33  Toby Dodge, *Inventing Iraq: The Failure of Nation Building and a History Denied* (New York: Columbia University Press, 2003); Malik Mufti, *Sovereign Creations: Pan-Arabism and Political Order in Syria and Iraq* (New York: Cornell University Press, 1996), p. 25.

34  Davis, *Memories of State*, pp. 14, 46, 48, 53.

35  Dodge, *Inventing Iraq*.

36  Mufti, *Sovereign Creations*, pp. 183–5.

37  *Ibid*., p. 200.

38  Toby Dodge, 'US Intervention and Possible Iraqi Futures', *Survival*, vol. 45, no. 3, Autumn 2003, pp. 106–7.

39  Charles Tripp, 'After Saddam', *Survival*, vol. 44, no. 4, Winter 2002–03, p. 26; Dodge, 'US Intervention and Possible Iraqi Futures', p. 107.

40  Dodge, 'US Intervention and Possible Iraqi Futures', p. 107.

41  Faleh A. Jabar, 'The Iraqi Army and Anti-Army: Some Reflections on the Role of the Military', in Toby Dodge and Steven Simon (eds), *Iraq at the Crossroads: State and Society in the Shadow of Regime Change* (Oxford: Oxford University Press for the IISS, 2003), p. 116.

42  Toby Dodge, *Iraq: From War to a New Authoritarianism*, Adelphi 435–5 (Abingdon: Routledge for the IISS, 2013), p. 32.

43  Toby Dodge, 'The Sardinian, the Texan and the Tikriti: Gramsci,

the Comparative Autonomy of the Middle Eastern State and Regime Change in Iraq', *International Politics*, vol. 43, no. 4, September 2006.

44   Davis, *Memories of State*, pp. 276–7.

45   Fanar Haddad, *Sectarianism in Iraq: Antagonistic Visions of Unity* (London: C. Hurst & Co., 2011), p. 33.

46   Alexandra Zavis, 'Iraq Troops Not Ready to Go It Alone', *Los Angeles Times*, 1 September 2008, http://www.latimes.com/news/ nationworld/iraq/complete/la-fg-army1-2008sep01,0,7199960.story; Ernesto Londono, 'Lower Oil Prices Lead Iraqi Security Forces to Cut Payrolls, Halt Key Purchases', *Washington Post*, 20 May 2009, http://www.washingtonpost.com/ wp-dyn/content/article/2009/05/19/ AR2009051903259.html; Nir Rosen, 'Iraq's Fragile Peace Rests on Its Own Forces', *National*, 9 September 2010, http://thenational.ae/apps/ pbcs.dll/article?AID=/20100910/ REVIEW/709099998/1008.

47   Yasir Abbas and Dan Trombly, 'Inside the Collapse of the Iraqi Army's 2nd Division', *War on the Rocks*, 1 July 2014, http:// warontherocks.com/2014/07/ inside-the-collapse-of-the-iraqi-armys-2nd-division/.

48   Barak A. Salmoni, 'Responsible Partnership: The Iraqi National Security Sector after 2011', Washington Institute for Near East Policy, May 2011, p. 14.

49   Linda Robinson, *Tell Me How This Ends: General David Petraeus and the Search for a Way out of Iraq* (New York: PublicAffairs, 2008), p. 157.

50   Anthony H. Cordesman, Adam Mausner and Lena Derby, *Iraq and the United States: Creating a Strategic Partnership* (Washington DC: Center for Strategic & International Studies, 2010), p. 268.

51   International Crisis Group, 'Loose Ends: Iraq's Security Forces Between U.S. Drawdown and Withdrawal', 26 October 2010, p. 7, http://www. crisisgroup.org/~/media/Files/ Middle%20East%20North%20 Africa/Iraq%20Syria%20Lebanon/ Iraq/99%20Loose%20Ends%20-%20 Iraqs%20Security%20Forces%20 between%20US%20Drawdown%20 and%20Withdrawal.pdf.

52   'Ali Ghaidan and Abboud Qanbar arrive to Nineveh', Shafaq, 7 June 2014, http:// english.shafaaq.com/index.php/ security/10061-ali-ghaidan-and-abboud-qanbar-arrive-to-nineveh.

53   See Transparency International, 'Corruption Perceptions Index', http://cpi.transparency.org/.

54   Special Inspector General for Iraq Reconstruction, 'Quarterly Report and Semiannual Report to the United States Congress', 30 January 2012, p. 9, http:// psm.du.edu/media/documents/ us_research_and_oversight/sigir/ quarterly_reports_eng/us_sigir__ report_to_congress_january_2012. pdf.

55   Special Inspector General for Iraq Reconstruction, 'Quarterly Report and Semiannual Report to the United States Congress', 30 July 2011, p. 8, http://www.globalsecu-rity.org/jhtml/jframe.html#http:// www.globalsecurity.org/military/ library/report/sigir/sigir-2011-07_ report.pdf | | | SIGIR%20July%20 30,%202011%20Quarterly%20

and%20Semiannual%20Report%20 to%20Congress.

56  Special Inspector General for Iraq Reconstruction, 'Quarterly Report and Semiannual Report to the United States Congress', 30 January 2011, p. 98; 30 April 2011, p. 119; and 30 January 2012, p. 76, http:// www.globalsecurity.org/military/ library/report/sigir/; and http:// psm.du.edu/media/documents/ us_research_and_oversight/sigir/ quarterly_reports_eng/us_sigir__ report_to_congress_january_2012. pdf.

57  Iraq Knowledge Network, 'Essential Services Fact Sheet', 1 December 2011, http:// reliefweb.int/report/iraq/ iraq-knowledge-network-essential-services-factsheet-december-2011.

58  Special Inspector General for Iraq Reconstruction, 'Quarterly Report and Semiannual Report to the United States Congress', 30 January 2011, p. 98; 30 April, p. 119; and 30 January 2012, p. 76.

59  Ben Lando et al., 'Power Deals Could Lead to Minister's Ouster', Iraq Oil Report, 7 August 2011, http:// www.iraqoilreport.com/energy/ electricity/power-deals-could-lead-to-ministers-ouster-6047/.

60  Iraq Knowledge Network, 'Essential Services Fact Sheet'.

61  Special Inspector General for Iraq Reconstruction, 'Quarterly Report and Semiannual Report to the United States Congress', 30 October 2012, http://cybercemetery.unt. edu/archive/sigir/20131001093031/ http://www.sigir.mil/files/ quarterlyreports/October2012/ Report_-_October_2012. pdf#view=fit.

62  Special Inspector General for Iraq Reconstruction, 'Final Report to Congress', 30 September 2013, http://cybercemetery.unt.edu/ archive/sigir/20131001094237/ http://www.sigir.mil/publications/ quarterlyreports/September2013. html.

63  Alissa J. Rubin, 'Cleric Switches Tactics to Meet Changes in Iraq', New York Times, 19 July 2007, http:// www.nytimes.com/2007/07/19/ world/middleeast/19sadr.html.

64  Pros and Cons, 'Opinion Polls/Surveys: Jan. 2003 – Jan. 16, 2009', http://usiraq. procon.org/view.resource. php?resourceID=000673#II.A.

65  See Toby Dodge, Iraq's Future: The Aftermath of Regime Change, Adelphi 372 (Abingdon: Routledge for the IISS, 2005), p. 55.

66  See Adeed Dawisha, 'Iraq: A Vote Against Sectarianism', Journal of Democracy, vol. 21, no. 3, July 2010, p. 37.

67  Ali A. Allawi, The Occupation of Iraq: Winning the War, Losing the Peace (New Haven, CT: Yale University Press, 2007), p. 53.

68  Samantha Power, Chasing the Flame; Sergio Vieira de Mello and the Fight to Save the World (London: Penguin, 2008), p. 417; James Dobbins et al., Occupying Iraq; A History of the Coalition Provisional Authority (Santa Monica, CA: RAND Corporation, 2009), p. 45; Allawi, The Occupation of Iraq, p. 164.

69  Allawi, The Occupation of Iraq, pp. 341, 343, 390.

70  Nir Rosen, 'Anatomy of a Civil War', Boston Review, 8 November 2006, http://bostonreview.net/BR31.6/ rosen.php.

[71] D3 Systems, 'Crisis in Iraq: A View from the Ground', 18 June 2014, http://www.d3systems.com/news-events/crisis-in-iraq-a-view-from-the-ground/.

[72] On the effects of de-Ba'athification on Iraqi politics, see Toby Dodge, 'Enemy Images, Coercive Socio-engineering and Civil War in Iraq', *International Peacekeeping*, vol. 19, no. 4, August 2012, pp. 461–77.

[73] D3 Systems, 'Crisis in Iraq'.

[74] Joel Wing, 'Iraqi Premier Abadi's Cabinet Sworn in Amongst Political Disputes', Musings on Iraq, 10 September 2014, http://musingsoniraq.blogspot.com/2014/09/iraq-premier-abadis-cabinet-sworn-in.html.

[75] For an excellent explanation of this, see Joel Rayburn, *Iraq after America: Strongmen, Sectarians, Resistance* (Stanford, CA: Stanford University Press, 2014), pp. 49–58.

[76] Brett McGurk, 'Iraq at a Crossroads: Options for U.S. Policy', statement before the Senate Foreign Relations Committee, 24 July 2014, http://www.foreign.senate.gov/download/mcgurk-testimony-07-24-14.

[77] *Ibid.*

[78] Aaron Zelin, 'The Islamic State of Iraq and Syria Has a Consumer Protection Office', *Atlantic*, 13 June 2014, http://www.theatlantic.com/international/archive/2014/06/the-isis-guide-to-building-an-islamic-state/372769/.

# CHAPTER TWO

# Iran, the Gulf States and the Syrian Civil War

Emile Hokayem

An essential driver of the Syrian civil war has been the involvement of Iran, Saudi Arabia, Qatar and, to a lesser extent, the United Arab Emirates in every aspect of the struggle. Their role has influenced the calculations, positioning, behaviour and fortunes of the principal Syrian players. Irrespective of whether the effect was intended, this regional competition has revealed and deepened the many fault lines that cross Syrian politics and society. It has also exacerbated the polarisation of the Middle East.

In the case of Iran and the major Gulf states, 'spill-in' – an effect in which a growing security vacuum attracts external interference – is a more apt description of the dynamics at play than 'spill-over'. As none of these countries border Syria, they have so far largely escaped the direct consequences of the war that have overwhelmed its immediate neighbours, such as refugee flows and threats to security. While they had not yet occurred at the time of writing, it was likely that Iran and the major Gulf states would at some point experience spillover effects in the form of jihadist activity or regional security aftershocks.

Viewing the struggle over Syria as central to a rapidly changing Middle East order, each of these countries has invested massively to secure an outcome aligned with its political and security interests. Unsurprisingly, each has approached its involvement in Syria as part of larger regional ambitions, leading to friction, rhetorical escalation and brinkmanship. However, this investment has proven costly and inconclusive for all concerned: the complex Syrian terrain and intricate regional politics have frustrated their quixotic hopes of a quick, clean victory.

The multifaceted assistance provided by Iran to President Bashar al-Assad's embattled regime, and by the Gulf states to the fragmented rebellion, have been key to their political survival and military operations. Without either Iran or the Gulf states' support, it is unlikely that their corresponding allies would have survived until now, at least in their current form.

Iran has proven considerably more committed, competent and coherent than its Gulf rivals; the expertise, experience and strategic patience it deployed in support of the Syrian regime to a great extent facilitated Assad's recovery from serious setbacks in 2012. In contrast, the war in Syria has exposed not only the political and operational limitations of the Gulf states, but also the rivalries among them.

In particular, the contest between Iran and Saudi Arabia has shaped the conflict in profound, lasting and unintended ways. Their competition, which plays out on several battlefields across the Middle East, has enduring strategic, ideological, sectarian and political dimensions that preceded, have affected and have been amplified by the struggle over Syria. Indeed, it is there that these two dominant regional powers have pursued their most overtly confrontational policies.

Grasping the nature of the Iranian–Saudi struggle is therefore central to understanding the Syrian conflict. Often portrayed as either a purely sectarian feud, pitting Sunnis against Shi'ites, or a traditional competition for regional hegemony, the contest in reality fuses elements of identity politics and geopolitics. Both countries are authoritarian theocracies that claim leadership of the region and the Islamic world, and have nurtured ideological and operational networks across the Middle East. While both have at times pursued non-sectarian strategies, they have found their sectarian partners to be the most reliable and effective tools for projecting power. Their decade-long deployment of sectarianism as an instrument of power and mobilisation is having a perverse effect, one that increasingly transcends and constrains geopolitical considerations.

Profound divergences between the key Gulf states, particularly Saudi Arabia and Qatar, have had an equally significant impact on the performance of the Syrian political and armed opposition. The latter's calculations and behaviour have been moulded by expectations from, and rifts among, the Gulf monarchies. Involving both overt and covert action, and amplified by the Turkish role, the Saudi–Qatari contest has proven especially damaging for the Syrian opposition, and for the overall effort to unseat Assad.

The crisis in Syria is often described as primarily a proxy war between Iran and Saudi Arabia. To be sure, regional spill-in exacerbates an already tortuous situation. This prism, while understandably convenient, is analytically problematic. There is considerable evidence of Iranian involvement in Syria – at the request of the Syrian government – that qualifies as direct intervention.

Moreover, the emphasis on the proxy nature of the conflict obscures the fact that local and transnational dynamics remain its prime drivers. The growth of actors with local and transnational agendas and resources has fragmented both the regime and the rebellion; they have lost coherence in the process, making a settlement with widespread regional support even more difficult to reach and implement. Although outside powers attempt to manipulate the militias involved in the conflict, none of them have direct control over a decisive number of fighters. The transnational jihadist organisation known as the Islamic State of Iraq and al-Sham (ISIS), for instance, has positioned itself against all such outsiders, and has an independent project.

Therefore, while the reduction or resolution of Saudi–Iranian tensions could lower levels of violence and perhaps open the way for a political process, this would not be enough in itself to pave the way for an inclusive and viable transition to peace.

## The early stages

When the Syrian uprising ignited in March 2011, Iran and the Gulf states appeared surprised and unsure of the course to adopt. Observers assumed that, thanks to an adequate mixture of personal popularity, co-optation and repression, the Assad regime was immune to the kind of public pressure that had unseated auto-crats in North Africa. The Syrian leader had proven resilient prior to the rebellion, surviving years of isolation for his management of Lebanese affairs, opposition to the US occupation of Iraq and close relationship with Iran, Hizbullah and Hamas. Having been forced to withdraw from Lebanon in 2005, he was able to return to the regional scene from 2006, due to help from Turkey and Qatar, US setbacks in the Middle East, and Hizbullah's victory in its 2006 war with Israel. In 2010 even Saudi Arabia, whose king Assad had derided as a 'half man' only a few years earlier, agreed to a détente with Syria.[1]

The context in which the Syrian revolution started was trou-bling for the conservative Gulf monarchies. They were prompted to counter the revolutionary tide by the forced resignation of long-time ally Hosni Mubarak in Egypt, the rise of the Muslim Brotherhood across North Africa and dissatisfaction with US policy, as well as fears that popular dissent could spread further. This meant that even challenges to the disliked Assad regime were unwelcome. Unlike his Iranian ally, Assad refrained from condemning the Gulf states' intervention in Bahrain in March 2011, temporarily earning him their goodwill.

They saw the uprising as an opportunity to subtly alter Assad's strategic orientation. As a result, in the first months of the Syrian insurrection, the official Gulf position remained on balance favourable to the Assad regime. The Gulf states calculated that the political cover, religious legitimacy and much-needed capital they could extend in exchange for limited political concessions would sway Assad. Such a shift would have amounted to a remarkable diplomatic victory and could have gradually distanced Syria from Iran, an enduring objective of Saudi Arabia and the UAE.

The most substantive effort in this regard came from Qatar, then Assad's most important Gulf ally, and Turkey, whose Islamist prime minister Recep Tayyip Erdogan had struck up a personal and political friendship with the Syrian president. Both countries encouraged Assad to adopt political reforms and broaden his government to include mainstream Islamists without fundamentally changing the nature of the system. Doha and Ankara hoped that such a course would benefit their Brotherhood allies, who were then on the rise throughout the region.

Arguably, the Qatari and Turkish approach to Assad was flawed, and exposed a misunderstanding of his mindset and calculations. He proved unwilling to allow even cosmetic Islamist participation in his government or to part ways with Iran; more fundamentally, he shared an ingrained conviction with his inner circle that any tangible concession amounted to suicidal weakness.

The Qatari strategy also assumed that the Brotherhood had lasting influence in Syrian society, despite a three-decade absence and widespread resentment of the movement, and that popular discontent would recede as a result of such a limited arrangement. Finally, it rested on the Gulf states' limited understanding of Syrian society, which resulted from years in which their outreach had focused on Syria's ruling clique and business elite, at the expense of the disenfranchised rural and suburban classes that formed the body of the popular movement.

By late summer 2011, Gulf preferences had been altered by the escalation of violence in Syria, growing media coverage of the revolution and the subsequent popular outrage across the Arab world, as well as Saudi, Qatari and Turkish frustration with Assad. In August, the Saudi monarch warned that

> what is happening in Syria is not acceptable for Saudi Arabia ... Syria should think wisely before it's too late and issue and enact reforms that are not merely promises but actual reforms. Either it chooses wisdom on its own or it will be pulled down into the depths of turmoil and loss.[2]

This announcement indicated a radical shift in Gulf policy in favour of regime change. Seeking to broaden management of the crisis, the Gulf states aimed to mobilise the Arab League and apply gradual pressure to Assad through regional and international condemnation, sanctions and political isolation. This move reflected the Sunni monarchies' greater activism in the Middle East, best illustrated by their backing of the NATO intervention in Libya. The recourse to the Arab League was made possible by their temporary domination of the regional body due to the paralysis of member states traditionally averse to foreign intervention, such as Yemen, Algeria and Iraq.

The new activism was also reflected in the Gulf-based media coverage of the Syrian revolution, with more airtime and column inches devoted to the uprising, particularly denunciations of the Assad regime that often had a sectarian tone. In parallel, Gulf governments allowed an unprecedented public mobilisation in favour of the rebellion, permitting the large Syrian diaspora to raise funds from Syria, as well as from domestic sources. A variety of networks – including those centred on religious and humanitarian organisations – became crucial providers of non-state funding and assistance to the Syrian rebels. As the revolution became militarised, many of these networks turned into ideological structures supporting the increasingly radical groups fighting in Syria, often benefiting from the nonchalance of authorities in the Gulf.

## The Gulf states back Assad's ouster

By late 2011, the existential threat to Assad had become clear to all external actors, as popular mobilisation continued in the face of the Syrian regime's escalating brutality. Attempts to organise and strengthen the opposition at home and abroad gained momentum under local and international pressure. A strategic rationale in favour of rapidly ousting Assad began to crystallise in the key Gulf capitals of Riyadh, Doha and Abu Dhabi. Riyadh in particular sought to correct recent changes in the regional balance of power that had benefited Iran. With competition in the Gulf constrained by the military dominance of the United States and a shared aversion for direct escalation, the weak states of the Levant appeared to be the main battleground for regional supremacy.

Importantly, victory in Syria would reverse the loss of Iraq. The regional balance had been upset by the rise of Iraqi Shia parties following the fall of Saddam Hussein and the growing influence of Iran in Baghdad, profoundly unnerving the Gulf states. Lacking the capacity to offset those changes and frustrated with the failure of US policy, the Sunni monarchies opted to ostracise the new political elite in Baghdad, and treated it as inimical to their interests.

While the Gulf states had previously tried to counter Iranian and Syrian power in Lebanon and Palestine – a frustrating and costly game, given the complex demographics and politics there – they calculated that a victory in Syria could decisively shift dynamics in both countries. And the Assad regime had a long history of interference in Lebanese and Palestinian affairs, to the detriment of Riyadh and its allies. A new dispensation of power in Damascus would also decisively limit Iran's reach in the Levant by severing the link to Hizbullah, its principal ally.

This rationale was based on the underlying assumption that the make-up of Syrian society worked to the advantage of the Gulf states. Accounting for more than 70% of the population, Syria's Sunni community was thought to overwhelmingly oppose the Alawite regime of Assad. The Sunni monarchies also believed that they had a considerable understanding of, and influence over, the inner workings of the regime and Syrian society as a whole. This was due to the Gulf states' links with Syria, which included tribal affiliations; the large numbers of Syrian expatriates who resided in Saudi Arabia, Kuwait and the UAE; shared religious networks and business interests; and relations between the ruling elites.

## Navigating and managing the Syrian rebellion

The shortcomings of the Gulf states were rapidly exposed in their attempts to form and empower a representative Syrian opposition leadership, and to organise and equip a military force able to effectively challenge Assad. A combination of faulty assumptions, political disunion and operational failure considerably hampered what would have in any case been a difficult task.

Saudi Arabia and Qatar oversaw separate and frequently contradictory efforts to oust Assad. Both deployed money, political capital and media capabilities to that purpose. They cooperated to mobilise the UN and their Western allies in the cause, and later joined the international contact group known as the Friends of Syria. Both countries encouraged defections from the regime's political and military elite, and provided refuge and other support to an increasing number of oppositionists. Estimates of Qatari aid to the Syrian rebellion range from $1 billion to $3bn in its first two years, according to the *Financial Times*.[3]

Riyadh and Doha differed on two crucial matters: their preferred allies inside the Syrian opposition and rebellion, and their regional partners. Saudi Arabia's broad range of contacts in Syria comprised liberals, bureaucrats, businessmen and tribal chiefs with traditional ties in the Arabian Peninsula, as well as Muslim clerics of various persuasions, including Salafists. The kingdom's broad strategic orientation and antipathy towards the Brotherhood secured the support of the UAE (although the latter proved cautious in dealing with Syria). The Jordanian monarchy, politically aligned with Riyadh and dependent on Gulf financial assistance, became their prime partner in the region. Jordan's proximity to Syria, competent intelligence and security services, and transnational tribal links made it a useful platform for providing support to Syrian allies.

Qatar's list of contacts was shorter, comprising secularists, businessmen and, most importantly, the Syrian Muslim Brotherhood and its associates. Doha's pan-regional support for the Brotherhood derived from a conviction that the Arab revolutions of 2011 would inevitably bring populist Islamists to power. Qatar has been home to prominent clerics aligned with the Brotherhood, including TV preacher Yusuf al-Qaradawi, and Doha expected that the movement's transnational networks would shore up its Syrian branch. Qatar found an ally in Turkey, which shares a long border with Syria and whose ruling party has travelled in the Brotherhood's orbit. Ankara made similar calculations about political change in the Arab world, finding validation for its approach in the group's initial successes in Tunisia, Libya and Egypt. Erdogan and Emir Hamad bin Khalifa Al Thani both regarded Assad's rejection of their efforts early in the uprising as a humiliating personal and political affront.

As the Gulf monarchies set the ouster of Assad as their objective, they sought to organise a political opposition that could credibly represent the revolutionary movement and acquire international legitimacy. There were no candidates with the requisite means and political experience, however, as authoritarian rule in Syria had left few well-established oppositionists inside the country, and exiled dissidents were unknown to most Syrians.

Crucially, revolutionary activists and movements emerging inside the country were largely unknown abroad, and were rarely swayed by either the traditional opposition or the Gulf states.

Saudi–Qatari rivalry quickly complicated the difficult task of organising the Syrian opposition. Politically, the struggle centred on the leadership of the various umbrella organisations purporting to represent the Syrian revolution. As the opposition's best-organised group, the Syrian Muslim Brotherhood seemed positioned to dominate the political opposition, despite lacking the appeal and power of its North African counterparts. The Syrian National Council (SNC) was the first entity; although nominally headed by secularists, the Brotherhood and its allies were able to control its internal functioning. In late 2012, Western frustration, and Saudi and Emirati displeasure with the SNC, coincided with a Syrian initiative to revamp and broaden the opposition. The new entity, called the National Coalition for Syrian Revolutionary and Opposition Forces (NC), subsumed the SNC and thus diluted the influence of the Brotherhood. Saudi Arabia and the UAE appeared to be intent on preventing the domination of the Syrian opposition by the movement, and as a result sponsored nationalists, secularists and tribal chiefs.

This competition encroached on the operations of the opposition. Ahmad al-Jarba, a Saudi-supported candidate, became president of the NC in 2013, following a heated contest with Mustafa Sabbagh. The latter, a Qatari favourite, subsequently quit and then rejoined the NC. A similar dynamic unfolded when the NC established in 2014 an interim government: Jarba deposed Ahmad Tohme, its prime minister and a Brotherhood sympathiser, and tried to impose a Saudi-leaning candidate.

The rivalry also affected diplomacy over Syria. Doha gave Syria's seat at the 2013 Arab League summit to the political opposition, and allowed it to open an embassy in Qatar, while other Gulf states remained more cautious. Such divisions and theatrics eroded the credibility of the opposition, not only on the international stage but also in the eyes of many Syrians, who increasingly saw its leaders as mere pawns.

On the military front, Saudi Arabia and Qatar competed over the leadership and strategy of the Free Syrian Army (FSA) – the nominal rebel franchise – and the multitude of other rebel groups, including Islamist ones. Early on, the process of supplying weapons to the largely disorganised rebels proceeded in haphazard, opportunistic ways, exacerbating inefficiency and competition. In spring 2012, military operations centres in Jordan and Turkey staffed by Western, Arab and Turkish operatives were tasked with receiving, assessing and processing requests for military assistance. To the frustration of Western governments, however, Saudi Arabia and Qatar developed parallel channels to expedite the funding and arming of favoured recipients.

This direct assistance to the rebel brigades reflected the mistrust between the two Gulf powers, and created new qualms for Western states. Working through myriad middlemen, Saudi and Qatari intelligence identified, cultivated and funded Syrian militias. Qatar naturally privileged the Brotherhood's Shields of the Revolution Council, as well as groups with ties to the movement, such as the al-Tawheed and Ahfad al-Rasul brigades primarily operating in the north. Saudi Arabia supported many FSA battalions formed of defectors in the south, but also groups with a Salafist orientation. Later, the Supreme Military Council was ostensibly set up as the main interlocutor and conduit for the Syrian rebels, under Western supervision and guidance. However, the Gulf states' perception of US retrenchment made them less disposed to use such mechanisms. They had expected that Washington would gradually take on a greater coordinating and operational role; by resisting this, the Obama administration unwittingly widened divisions between them.

Ultimately, the uncoordinated, competitive character of the initiative to arm the rebels contributed to the progressive fragmentation of the rebellion, and influenced the positioning of Syrian armed groups eager to obtain support. Injections of weaponry into the battlefield at times translated into military advances, but were not regular enough to overcome Assad's military superiority. Just as important was the fact that neither Saudi Arabia nor Qatar provided a significant amount of direct military training or organisational and operational guidance to the rebels, lacking as they did both the will to do so and experience in these areas.

Moreover, Gulf states faced the reality that financial support did not necessarily lead to control on the ground. Rebel groups behaved opportunistically, seeking support from any quarter and changing loyalties when needed. Ideological proximity was not always sufficient leverage. The Salafist militia Ahrar al-Sham received considerable funding from Gulf individuals but little from Riyadh, as its leaders had ties to al-Qaeda. Jaysh al-Islam, a large Salafist group operating primarily around Damascus, has obtained Saudi support thanks to religious ties with clerics from the Sahwa movement, which blends Wahhabi theology with Brotherhood-style activism.

The limitations of financial support were made clear by the disconnect between many rebel groups and the political opposition, both of which were funded by Saudi Arabia and Qatar. At crucial junctures, some rebel groups refused or denounced political initiatives by the SNC and the NC, including the latter's participation in UN-mediated talks with the Assad regime. Other groups, such as the Syrian Revolutionaries Front, endorsed such talks partly in the hope they would obtain Saudi or Qatari support as a reward.

As radicals began to dominate the rebellion, there arose the risk that Saudi–Qatari competition and the Saudi–Iranian contest would assist in the rise of extreme Salafist groups. There have been many reasons for the Gulf states' complacency towards individuals funding radical groups and the recruitment of young people by these movements. In the first three years of the uprising, Gulf leaders saw jihadists as an unwanted, if unavoidable, by-product of the conflict, whom it was better to co-opt and manage in the short term (although Emirati leaders have remained a notable exception, as they oppose all forms of political Islamism). The risks of this approach seemed acceptable due to the expectation that Assad would quickly fall, allowing Gulf-aligned groups to come to power. Kuwait's open political environment and banking system, and its established network of religious charities, allowed it to serve as the main Gulf hub for jihadist propaganda, funding and recruitment.

But the assumptions made by the Gulf monarchies were shaken by the rise of al-Qaeda affiliate Jabhat al-Nusra in 2012, and by the revival of ISIS the following year. Both organisations were clearly antagonistic towards the Gulf states, who as a result were compelled to address the jihadist threat (and were encouraged to do so by the US). Blamed by their allies and foes for having been at the very least negligent in preventing the growth of jihadism, the monarchies suffered damage to their credibility and leverage, to Iran's benefit. Concern about regional spillover and the threat posed by ISIS, which increased rapidly following the group's advances in summer 2014, meant that the ouster of Assad was no longer the highest priority for Western powers.

The Gulf states also had contradictory positions on Iran, which were further separated by intra-Gulf Cooperation Council disputes. Saudi Arabia clearly saw itself as Iran's ideological and strategic rival in a region-wide confrontation. It sought to rally other Arab states to counter Iranian influence, and lobbied against Western concessions to Tehran on regional-security and nuclear matters. Riyadh hoped that it could outspend an overstretched and financially weakened Iranian government on the Syrian battlefield.

Doha avoided direct confrontation with Tehran and sought to separate its Syria policy from wider relations with the Iranians. This was in part motivated by the need to maintain a regional balance against Riyadh, which it perceived as the greater threat. Turkey supported Qatar's approach, and maintained cordial relations with Iran despite clear policy differences in Iraq and Syria.

Finally, as the conflict grew more complicated and it became clear that the Gulf states had underestimated Assad's resilience, various Syrian players began to express mixed feelings about Saudi–Qatari competition, and to blame the rivalry for tainting their revolutionary cause and fuelling extremism. This view reflected a sense that, rather than posing a unified challenge to Iran, the key Gulf states had allowed their differences to undermine their ultimate objectives, thereby hindering their Syrian allies.

## Iran comes to Assad's rescue

The uprising also posed an unprecedented challenge to Tehran. In many ways, the nature of the alliance between Syria and Iran was reflected in the latter's failure to forecast – and, after the conflict started, to recognise – the legitimacy, potency and wide popular base of the revolution.

What began in the 1980s as a tactical relationship between broadly different political systems with a common enemy (namely, Saddam Hussein's Iraq) had by the time of the Syrian conflict evolved into a strategic and ideological alliance against the US-backed Middle East order. Hizbullah grew from a proxy into the third pillar of this axis thanks to its political and military victories. Having experienced regional and international pressure during the 2000s, Assad sought and obtained legitimacy by associating himself with Iran and Hizbullah. The alliance rested on a narrow base, however, as it involved only a few powerful actors in the upper echelons of the Iranian, Syrian and Lebanese political and security structures. This prevented the development of a genuine understanding of Syrian society in Tehran. Indeed, mutual perceptions were shaped not by societal exchanges but by interactions among senior personnel.

For Iran, the fall of the Assad regime would have amounted to a strategic setback and a limitation of its Levantine reach. Despite occasional disagreements, the alliance had withstood Western and Arab attempts to woo Assad. Syria had proved a reliable ally, and a vital logistical conduit to rejectionist Lebanese and Palestinian factions. Assad's membership of the resistance camp and the ostensible support of many Syrians provided Iran with a much-needed Arab cover and precious cross-confessional appeal. This partnership was seen as a resilient force multiplier in an otherwise hostile regional environment. Tehran stood to lose more than any other party from the fall of Assad and the severing of the connection to Hizbullah, Iran's primary instrument of deterrence and retaliation against Israel and the US, and its ultimate Arab champion.

As the uprising gathered momentum, Iran sought to differentiate Syria's upheaval from that elsewhere in the Arab world, which Supreme Leader Ayatollah Ali Khamenei had welcomed as an 'Islamist awakening'. Adopting Assad's rhetoric, Tehran portrayed the Syrian revolution as the work of violent local actors who had been manipulated by foreign powers (namely, the West, the Gulf states and Israel) and were eager to weaken the rejectionist alliance. By doing so, it alienated a wide range of Islamist actors. These included not only predictably hostile groups, such as the Salafist movements that saw Shi'ites and Alawites as heretics, but also the Muslim Brotherhood and moderate Islamist movements with an affinity for Iran's style of governance.

Early in the uprising, Iranian officials counselled relative moderation in the use of force to avoid alienating greater numbers of Syrians. The clique around Assad dismissed such advice, opting for an overwhelming security response intended to deter further dissent. Iranian security personnel, fresh from crushing the 2009

Green Revolution, were by mid-2011 providing covert technical and operational advice on containing the protests and dismantling the networks of activists. After admitting that the very Islamist forces it had praised in Egypt and Tunisia were organic elements of the Syrian uprising, Tehran attempted in late 2011 to reach out to these factions and reach an agreement with them that would be favourable to Assad, putting forward proposals for limited Islamist participation in government. However, the fact that both Assad and the Brotherhood's representatives in Syria were opposed to such a settlement showed Iran's naivety, and its failure to understand the fundamental dynamics of the struggle.

By late 2011, Iranian decision-makers understood that the uprising posed an existential threat to the Syrian regime. The fundamental issue for Iran was whether there was an alternative power dispensation that excluded Assad but would still secure its strategic interests. Iranian diplomats became occupied with the search for a 'Syrian Karzai', as Tehran put it, an initiative that was seen abroad as an attempt to softly depose Assad. Regardless of how sincerely they approached this task, the reality was that, to all intents and purposes, Assad was the regime. The organisation of the Syrian state, based on *assabiyyah*, or kinship, made it impossible to remove him and his top lieutenants while keeping the system in place. Most importantly, powerful constituencies in Tehran saw Assad as an indispensable ally, and equated Syria's security with Iran's security.[4] For them, the cost of securing Assad's survival, however high, was ideologically and strategically justified.

This effort seemed daunting at first, given Assad's rapid decline. Starting in 2011, Hizbullah leaders provided their Iranian allies with dire assessments of Assad's prospects, following defections in his military and a progressive loss of control. A senior Iranian lawmaker reported a conversation between Khamenei and Hizbullah leader Hassan Nasrallah that took place eight months into the revolution:

> Nasrallah told me, 'We went to the Sayyed [Khamenei] and we reported to him that it seems that Bashar Assad and his government in Syria is finished. But the Sayyed said, "No it's not true. We must just do our duties. If we do our duties, Assad and Syria will be stable."'[5]

In January 2012, a visit to Damascus by General Qassem Suleimani – commander of the Quds Force, an elite group within the Iran Revolutionary Guard Corps (IRGC) – appeared to have sealed the Iranian commitment to Assad. A comprehensive strategy to shore up the regime was subsequently put in place. The first official acknowledgement of Iranian operations alongside Assad's forces came in May 2012, when General Ismail Gha'ani, deputy commander of the Quds Force, declared, 'if the Islamic Republic was not present in Syria, the massacre of people would have happened on a much larger scale'.[6]

Iranian assistance gradually increased, both in magnitude and visibility. Tehran helped Syria circumvent Western and Arab sanctions, and extended credit lines and other payment facilities to the country's ministries and central bank. It also mobilised allies in the region, convincing Iraqi Prime Minister Nuri al-Maliki, once at odds with Assad, to assist in the movement of goods and weapons through Iraqi territory, and to facilitate Syrian trade and finance through Iraqi banks.

Iran proved essential to Assad's military adaptation and resilience. Its greatest contribution was its mentoring and development of the National Defence Forces, a collection of regime militias that supplemented and at times replaced the shrinking conventional force. The IRGC deployed the experience in counter-insurgency that it had acquired in operations across the region, particularly those in Balochestan. Modelled on the Iranian Basij, the National Defence Forces are composed of fighters primarily recruited from Alawite communities and minorities loyal to Assad, who are tasked with controlling territory rather than projecting force. Iranian officials have claimed credit for establishing this force, with a former IRGC commander bragging that 'Iran has formed a second Hezbollah in Syria'.[7] While such comments seem to exaggerate the force's overall performance, they capture the centrality of Iran's role in helping Assad adapt to the rebel challenge.

Tehran also provided an uninterrupted flow of weaponry to his forces, through the main civilian and military airports of Damascus, and helped reorganise Syria's battered conventional military for urban warfare.[8] The capture in August 2012 of 48 IRGC soldiers by Syrian rebels confirmed the scale of Iranian involvement. (The men, who had just landed in Syria as part of a much larger group, were later released in a swap deal.) Since 2012, several senior Quds Force commanders operating in Syria, including General Hassan Shateri and General Abdullah Eskandari, have been killed during clashes or assassinated. The IRGC's area of operations includes the key central corridor between Damascus and Aleppo. While they often served in an advisory capacity, some Iranian units also took part in the fighting, as evidenced by footage that surfaced in 2012 and 2013.[9]

Iran rallied a variety of sectarian militias. Its personnel facilitated Hizbullah's foray into Syria, mentored Iraqi Shia militias deployed mainly in Damascus, and even recruited Shia fighters from Afghanistan and other countries.[10] Thousands of Shia recruits went through military training at a camp near Tehran before being deployed in Syria.[11]

To be sure, securing Assad's survival has been costly. Already facing serious economic difficulties, Tehran is estimated to have spent $15–19bn on direct support to Assad between 2011 and 2014, according to Western intelligence.[12] Sanctions and political isolation, as well as domestic discontent, complicated the public case for an expensive commitment abroad in support of an ally towards whom many Iranians were indifferent at best. There were also signs of division among the Iranian elite, with moderate factions questioning the merits of supporting Assad at the cost of increasing regional and sectarian tension, as well as hindering détente with the West. Yet the decisive outcome of Iran's domestic debate over Syria, rather than its presumed intensity, demonstrated the overriding power of hardline elements within the country.

Publicly, Tehran framed its support of Assad as loyalty towards a reliable ally, resistance to foreign schemes to weaken the alliance, and denial of a violent challenge to what it portrayed as a legitimate and popular regime. Hossein Amir Abdollahian, the Iranian diplomat in charge of Middle East affairs, explained that 'we aren't seeking to have Assad remain president for life. But we do not subscribe to the idea of using extremist forces and terrorism to topple Assad and the Syrian government.'[13] In parallel, Iran declared an apparent interest in promoting reconciliation among select Syrian factions, and in joining regional diplomacy to end the conflict.

Iran's involvement in, and justification of, Assad's brutality has further alienated many Sunnis and Arabs. Its hard-won image as a champion of Arab and Muslim causes will be tainted for some time to come.[14] Although Tehran insists that it does not have a sectarian regional policy, it has resorted to sectarian strategies of mobilisation and empowered sectarian actors, as have they proved to be the most capable defenders of the Syrian regime. Tensions with Hamas, its most significant Sunni ally and an affiliate of the Palestinian Muslim Brotherhood, have since 2012 contributed to a greater vilification of Iran as a Shia power. In an Arab world dominated by Sunnis, such a reversal of perception has benefited its main rival, Saudi Arabia.

By 2014, it seemed that the Iranian investment had paid off: Assad would survive in the medium term and Tehran's regional position would be reinforced. Iran's centrality to the political resolution of the war featured in every discussion on Syria, potentially providing a significant diplomatic return on its investment. And its regional ambitions were boosted by ideas such as the proposal, first floated in 2012, of a settlement negotiated alongside Saudi Arabia, Turkey and Egypt, to the exclusion of Western powers. Similarly, the failure of diplomatic talks from which the Iranians were excluded (such as those in Geneva) only reinforced Tehran's sense of importance. It was also able to claim that the effort to unseat Assad had generated the gravest threat to Middle East security: takfiri jihadism.

The investment has resulted in Assad's financial and military reliance on Iran. Defectors describe the relationship as one of total Iranian control over the Syrian leader, although it is likely that they exaggerate in order to portray Assad as a mere pawn who relinquished Syrian sovereignty and sullied Arab honour.

Nonetheless, Assad's high degree of dependence is problematic for Iran. Is he so important to Tehran that he believes that he can count on perpetual, unconditional support? Or is he so weak that he is only sustained by Iran, which cannot find a suitable alternative? Mutual perceptions are difficult to gauge. Some Syrian officials view Tehran's support as evidence that Assad is essential to its regional schemes, and that he can therefore take the alliance for granted. Others speculate that Assad has become a card to be played in negotiations. On the Iranian side, there is great frustration at both the cost incurred and Assad's inflexibility, including his refusal to make even cosmetic concessions to loyal oppositionists. In September 2013, Minister of Foreign Affairs Javad Zarif told an Iranian newspaper that 'we believe that the government in Syria has made grave mistakes that have, unfortunately, paved the way for the situation in the country to be abused'.[15]

The Syrian regime's reliance on militias also poses challenges. While Tehran has indeed nurtured competent and loyal allies inside Syria, advisers from the Iranian government and Hizbullah have complained that Assad's forces are unethical, incompetent and lacking in commitment.

The sustainability of Iran's role has increasingly been called into question following the ISIS advance in Iraq. If Tehran could not foresee and prevent the rise of a Sunni jihadist foe in a Shia-dominated country where it is the foremost external actor, how could it hope to sustain the minority-centred Assad regime? Many believe Iran has inherited two failed states that make demands on Iranian personnel and resources.

Ironically, the radicalisation of the Syrian opposition has led to fewer expressions of dissent in Iran. In the country's media and official statements, Syria has been portrayed as the front line in a war on Tehran and Iranian society alike.

## The key asymmetries in regional competition over Syria

Regional competition is only one dimension of the complex Syrian conflict. However, it is analytically interesting to compare the two sets of regional actors in isolation.

Iran has so far been able to secure its short- and medium-term objectives. The balance of the fundamental operational, political and strategic asymmetries remains in its favour. Barring a radical (and unlikely) shift in Iranian or Gulf policy, these imbalances will continue to shape the conflict, but will result in neither total victory nor total defeat.

Iran came to the rescue of a weakening but known partner with which it had 30 years of close security and political ties. Helping to defend an embattled ally and establish an acceptable military equilibrium was easier and less costly than its competitors' efforts to engineer an appealing political alternative and build a credible military threat to the Syrian regime.

Iran's paramount objective – the preservation of Hizbullah as a strategic actor in the Levant – prioritised the protection of key urban centres, infrastructure and supply routes into

Lebanon over the territorial integrity of Syria. Losing control over regions in eastern and northern Syria was unsatisfactory, but temporarily justifiable.

For the Gulf states, however, victory could only be achieved through the capture of Damascus and the ascent to power of actors aligned with their interests. These unprecedented goals demanded an ambitious strategy of territorial and political conquest. Yet the monarchies struggled to adapt to a complex political opposition and armed rebellion with often unrealistic aims and weak organisational structures. Even if Assad were to be ousted, this would not settle the Gulf monarchies' disagreements on crucial matters, such as the future shape, composition and orientation of a new Syrian government.

Iran's portrayal of the uprising as manipulated by foreigners and driven by sectarianism was in line with its existing ideological, political and religious orientation. As the Syrian opposition fractured, radicalised and sought foreign assistance, the lie became truth to some extent. The narrative was gradually accepted in the West, where it became the lens through which many viewed the conflict.

By contrast, the Gulf states embraced the narrative that a peaceful, democratic revolution was sweeping Syria. Yet this clashed with the general aversion to political change in Riyadh and Abu Dhabi, leading to considerable scepticism about their position among many Arabs and Westerners.

An additional complication for the Gulf states was that few in the West believed their portrayal of the Sunnis as victims of discrimination. Many Westerners saw Sunni extremism rather than Shia radicalism as the greatest threat, in light of the persecution of minorities in Sunni-dominated countries and the events that followed the 2003 US invasion of Iraq.

Once Iranian leaders decided to support the Syrian regime, they demonstrated unity of purpose and effort by giving responsibility for decision-making to the IRGC and harmonising their assistance to Assad. Resources were allocated to ensure the political, economic and military viability of their ally. Although there was occasional tension between Iranian advisers and Syrian forces, it did not damage the relationship.

The Gulf states increasingly disagreed about how best to unseat the Syrian president. Disputes over recipients of aid, political objectives and military matters eroded their professed unity of purpose. The lack of centralised decision-making led to inefficient, even counterproductive, efforts to provide assistance. Frustration with the lack of progress caused Riyadh to change strategies, replacing the overseer of its early efforts, then-intelligence chief Prince Bandar bin Sultan.

Iran worked through existing state bodies with bureaucratic and disbursement capabilities, and was therefore well placed to apportion resources in a relatively short time. This made for comparatively smooth assistance to the beleaguered Syrian regime.

The Gulf states lacked experience in distributing wartime aid, and had to channel financial and humanitarian support through newly formed groups that did not have the know-how, coordination or mechanisms to distribute resources in a timely and efficient manner. Riyadh and its allies have also had to coordinate with other states to identify or establish agencies capable of distributing humanitarian and military aid, with the result that their responses to the urgent demands of the rebels have often been slow or otherwise ineffective.

There is no evidence that Tehran has withheld arms deliveries to Assad as the result of disagreements. Despite the opacity of Iran–Syria relations, it appears unlikely that Assad's political management, battlefield comportment or war crimes have limited Iranian support. This was shown in 2013, when aid from Tehran continued unabated despite a string of chemical-weapons attacks that were reportedly condemned by Iranian politicians.[16]

Mindful of the concerns of their Western partners, the Gulf states have often had to exercise caution and restraint. Western intelligence and military representatives supervised much of the assistance to the Syrian rebels channelled through operations rooms in Turkey and Jordan. Groups' suitability to receive arms was determined by criteria such as ideological and religious orientation; battlefield behaviour; relations with the political opposition, civilians and radical actors; managerial competence; and accountability. There were limitations on the type and quantity of weapons delivered, particularly anti-aircraft missiles. In many instances, arms were not supplied to rebel groups that opposed both the regime and ISIS but were considered too radical or unreliable, such as those fighting in Deir ez-Zor during summer 2014.

In articulating and implementing its policies in Syria, Iran has had few external constraints. Moscow, Assad's other key ally, was largely aligned with Tehran in terms of objectives and tactics, and was equally unwilling to attach conditions to the assistance it provided. While Iran and Russia had different interlocutors in Damascus, they largely worked in parallel with one another. Moscow accepted any Iranian ally in Syria, no matter how brutal, sectarian or unknown they might have been.

The alliance was markedly different to the Gulf states' complex and often tense relationship with the US, the United Kingdom and France. The overriding Western fear that jihadists would benefit from military assistance (directly or indirectly) contributed to the restrictions on arms supplies. Many of the Sunni monarchies' partners in the Syrian rebellion were either unfamiliar or unacceptable to Washington, and the Gulf states' strategic dependency on Western powers meant that they had to consider how disagreements over Syria could affect the wider relationship. Divisions between the monarchies, and their tolerance of sectarian actors, alienated Western powers seeking to empower moderate elements of the opposition.

Riyadh and Doha anticipated that the US would eventually head and coordinate the effort to oust Assad, both politically and operationally. However, the Obama administration's minimalist approach to Middle East crises and unwillingness to get entangled in Syria precluded a more active American role. For the Gulf states, US policy was frustrating because Washington refused to take its traditional leading role yet constrained their behaviour. Several of the Gulf monarchies saw dithering in Washington as indicative of a reduced commitment to their security and a reluctance to decisively counter Iran. As a result, Saudi Arabia and Qatar pursued increasingly risky policies in Syria throughout 2012 and 2013, until their limited success forced a rethink.

Tehran's operations in Syria benefited from alliances with local groups. The country's small Shia community, fearful for its survival and for the safety of its holy sites, turned to Iran for military assistance and political guidance, becoming a major source of fighters for pro-regime militias. Iran has also provided support to members of the Alawite community (which is nominally associated with Shi'ism). Tehran's message resonated with minorities such as the Christians, as its form of political Islam was seen as less extreme than that practised by Riyadh. Despite their misgivings, many minority groups remained loyal to the Assad regime due to concerns about their security and standing. Some of these pro-regime minority groups were conveniently located in areas of utmost importance to the Syrian and Iranian governments (such as the Sayeda Zeynab suburb of Damascus), while the rebels were strongest in peripheral territories.

The Gulf states had to deal with a complex Sunni community. Saudi Arabia and Qatar initially calculated that their tribal and religious allies could mobilise coherent and reliable fighting units across Syria, but they were soon proven wrong. Supplies of weapons and funding did not guarantee loyalty and leverage. The political, religious and social diversity of the Sunni community proved difficult to understand, let alone manage. Large segments of the elite and the middle class backed Assad, while many preferred to wait for a clear victor to emerge before taking sides. This made achieving victory in the major cities considerably more costly and difficult. As a result, the bulk of the rebel fighting force was composed of the alienated rural and suburban poor, some of whom were organised along tribal or regional lines, and were prone to revenge and radicalisation. The Gulf states' natural allies in Syria had convoluted loyalties and little recent fighting experience.

Once the rebellion had been militarised, Iran was able to call upon a variety of sectarian militias that looked to the Quds Force for ideological and organisational guidance. Most prominent among these battle-hardened groups were Lebanon's Hizbullah and Iraq's Asaib Ahl al-Haq and Kataib Hizbullah. These organisations benefited from recent fighting experience under Iranian guidance, organisational readiness and, in the Lebanese Hizbullah's case, proximity to Syria's main battlefields. Their mobilisation was facilitated by closer alignment between Tehran, Damascus and Baghdad, and by Hizbullah's control of Lebanese security.

Saudi Arabia and Qatar lacked proxy militias, and usually preferred to enter into transactional relationships with existing political groups, or to work through intermediaries. While some of these partners had access to weaponry, none displayed the same level of operational and logistical preparedness as Iran's allies.

Iran's doctrine of asymmetric defence and long history of involvement in countries undergoing civil strife provided it with tactics and instruments that it could quickly deploy in the service of Assad. Since the 1980s, the IRGC has mastered the art of developing and training allied forces in Lebanon, Afghanistan and Iraq, and has been able to rely on the Quds Force, which is dedicated to operations abroad. Iranian advisers have been able to provide a wide variety of assistance, ranging from communications monitoring and intelligence gathering to battlefield mentoring and the organisation of fighting units. Simply put, Iran had the institutional and bureaucratic capabilities to conduct a long, multi-dimensional engagement in another country.

Saudi Arabia and Qatar had little experience of power projection, and fewer diplomatic and intelligence resources. Riyadh's recent operations were confined to an inconclusive 2009 intervention against Houthi rebels in Yemen, while Doha's were limited to a NATO-backed mission to train and support Libyan fighters in the rebellion against Muammar Gadhafi two years later. Saudi Arabia's much-vaunted involvement in Afghanistan during the 1980s had in fact consisted of funding and facilitating interactions between Afghan rebels and US and Pakistani intelligence, rather than direct training or battlefield engagement.

Furthermore, the Gulf states' limited military and intelligence capabilities created a dependence on Lebanese, Turkish, Jordanian and Iraqi middlemen who were eager to turn a profit, even if it meant exaggerating their competence, access and results. While these competing actors lacked a geographical bridge into Syria, Iran benefited from established logistical access to the country through air routes, and overland through Iraq.

Riyadh and Doha recognised that using Lebanon as a base would have threatened the country's fragile stability, and would have been complicated by Hizbullah's dominance there. While ostensibly a Saudi client-state, Jordan made complex calculations about whether and how to facilitate support for the rebellion. The Hashemite monarchy's decisions were shaped by the preferences of its other allies, particularly the US and Israel. Amman also factored in spillover effects relating to refugees, cross-border incidents, the jihadist menace and potential acts of revenge by Assad. It therefore had an ambivalent attitude towards the Syrian rebels, offering tightly controlled refuge and training to small numbers of fighters, but opposing more ambitious programmes. For its part, the powerful and independent-minded Turkey sought to set the terms of Syria policy, regardless of whether it clashed with Washington or the Sunni monarchies. Accordingly, Ankara restricted Gulf aid travelling through Turkish territory.

But Iran's greatest advantage was perhaps that it approached the struggle over Syria as part of a long game that was being played out across the region and required strategic patience, or the ability and willingness to accept seemingly high immediate costs to secure future gains.

While shoring up the Assad regime was expensive, there was only a limited risk that this would translate into widespread discontent in Iran. In their approach to the Syrian conflict, hardliners in Tehran were aligned with Shia radicals at home and across the region. The latter sought state guidance and sponsorship to defend the Assad regime, and to counter what they perceived as a growing Sunni threat to their survival. Dissenters, in comparison, came primarily from small and powerless segments of the Iranian opposition.

Over time, the Iranian media's lack of coverage of the Syrian war, alongside rising Sunni extremism in Syria and Iraq, reduced criticism of Tehran even more. The Iranian government's support for Assad came to be accepted as the necessary cost of countering the jihadists before they reached home soil.

Riyadh in particular faced the risk that its ideological foes, who posed an existential threat, would benefit from Saudi support for the rebellion. State-backed Salafist ideology, governmental complacency and private funding facilitated the growth of extremist groups that opposed the Saudi government, such as ISIS and Jabhat al-Nusra. This profound dilemma and the risk of blowback were at the heart of Saudi deliberations over the appropriate strategy in Syria. One faction in the Saudi government argued that the jihadist groups were a by-product of the war better countered after Assad had been ousted, and advocated greater involvement in Syria, even if it meant the distasteful, momentary accommodation of extremist groups. This reasoning was also prevalent in Qatar. A more cautious faction in Riyadh argued that such a strategy was too dangerous, and that the resulting mobilisation of Saudi youth and establishment of a jihadist statelet nearby would significantly exacerbate the extremist challenge.

## ISIS and regional competition

The ascendance of ISIS has profoundly affected competition in the Middle East, and has exposed the contradictory positions of each regional power. The group's 2013–14 advance in Iraq and Syria, which culminated in the fall of Mosul and the conquest of northern Syria, has led many Middle East states to change policy. It has also forced the return of the US as a military actor, albeit in a manner that has satisfied no one.

It is unlikely that the rise of ISIS will reduce regional tensions. Despite overhyped meetings between Iranian and Saudi officials this year, the positions of Riyadh and Tehran have not significantly changed. Saudi Arabia has continued to prioritise the ouster of Assad, seeing this as a necessary condition of the fight against the jihadist group, while Iran has claimed that defeating ISIS requires the acceptance of the Assad regime and a consensus against Sunni extremism.

For the Gulf states, short-term satisfaction at the political demise of Maliki had to be balanced against the long-term threat of the jihadist movement. Blamed for accommodating and even stoking extremism to depose Assad, Saudi Arabia and Qatar have suffered damage to their credibility in Washington. In response, they have joined the US-led coalition against ISIS, seeking to improve their image, shape American strategy in Syria and prevent Washington from seeing Iran as an alternative partner.

Tehran was deeply unsettled by the ISIS advance in Iraq, which exposed its Iraqi allies as weak and unreliable, and forced further Iranian intervention in the country. Yet on the international stage, Iran has used ISIS gains to criticise the recklessness of Western and Arab patronage of the Syrian rebellion, and to pose as a responsible actor.

The fight against the group has also created complications for US policy that are directly relevant to the contest between the Gulf states and Iran. To the dismay of the Sunni monarchies, US and Iranian interests overlapped on the matter of combating Sunni extremism. In Iraq, Iran appeared as an indispensable, if problematic, partner in removing Maliki, shoring up the new government and supporting local resistance to ISIS. Although direct military coordination was unthinkable, Washington and Tehran engaged in complementary efforts, with Iraqi and Kurdish forces receiving both support from US airpower and Iranian military advice on the ground.

In Syria, US coordination with Iran would only spur Sunni radicalisation and antagonise the Gulf states. President Barack Obama acknowledged as much when he stressed that any viable anti-ISIS strategy would require the active involvement of the Gulf countries, Syria's Sunni community and the rebels who oppose Assad.

An additional layer of complexity has been added by the nuclear diplomacy between Tehran and the P5+1 powers. The Sunni monarchies fear that America will agree to a nuclear deal with Iran to obtain cooperation on regional security issues. Such a linkage would reinforce exaggerated, if legitimate, Gulf concerns about a US strategic realignment towards Iran. Tehran's centrality to every Middle East crisis in which Washington is involved, however, only highlights the limitations of the Gulf states.

## Acknowledgements

The author wishes to thank Andrew Kelly and Islam El Tayeb for their research assistance.

# Notes

1  Robert F. Worth, 'Arab Leaders, Angry at Syrian President, Threaten Boycott of Summit Meeting', *New York Times*, 8 March 2008, http://www.nytimes.com/2008/03/08/world/middleeast/08syria.html.

2  'Saudi Arabia Calls for Syrian Reforms', Al-Jazeera, 8 August 2011, http://www.aljazeera.com/news/middleast/2011/08/201187213922184761.html.

3  'How Qatar Seized Control of the Syrian Revolution', *Financial Times*, 17 May 2013, http://www.ft.com/intl/cms/s/2/f2d9bbc8-bdbc-11e2-890a-00144feab7de.html.

4  Roula Khalaf and Abigail Fielding-Smith, 'Assad Vows Syria Will Defeat "Foreign Conspiracy"', Press TV, 26 August 2012, http://www.presstv.com/detail/2012/08/26/258291/syria-will-defeat-foreign-conspiracy/.

5  'Iranian MP: Nasrallah Believed Assad Would Fall', *Daily Star*, 28 November 2013, http://www.dailystar.com.lb/News/Middle-East/2013/Nov-28/239187-iranian-mp-nasrallah-believed-assad-would-fall.ashx#ixzz2lwurLSAf.

6  James Reynolds, 'Iran and Syria: Alliance of Shared Enemies and Goals', BBC, 8 June 2012, http://www.bbc.co.uk/news/world-middle-east-18369380.

7  Arash Karami, 'Former IRGC Commander's Comments on Syria Censored', Al-Monitor, 6 May 2014, http://www.al-monitor.com/pulse/originals/2014/05/former-irgc-commander-syria-comments-censored.html.

8  Phil Sands, 'Iran's Secret Night Flights to Arm Syria's Assad Revealed', *National*, 27 October 2013, http://www.thenational.ae/world/middle-east/irans-secret-night-flights-to-arm-syrias-assad-revealed.

9  'Footage Claims to Show Iranians in Syria', BBC, 15 September 2013, http://www.bbc.com/news/world-middle-east-24103801.

10  Farnaz Fassihi, 'Iran Pays Afghans to Fight for Assad', *Wall Street Journal*, 22 May 2014, http://online.wsj.com/news/articles/SB10001424052702304908304579564161508613846.

11  Farnaz Fassihi, Jay Solomon and Sam Dagher, 'Iranians Dial Up Presence in Syria', *Wall Street Journal*, 16 September 2013, http://online.wsj.com/news/articles/SB10001424127887323864604579067382861808984.

12  Interviews with Western intelligence officials, 2013 and 2014.

13  Michelle Moghtader, 'Iran Says Does Not Seek Indefinite Power for Assad', Reuters, 2 April 2014, http://www.reuters.com/article/2014/04/02/us-iran-syria-idUSBREA311X220140402.

14  'Iran's Global Image Largely Negative', Pew Research Center, 18 June 2014, http://www.pewglobal.org/2014/06/18/irans-global-image-largely-negative/.

15  Alireza Nader, 'What to Do Now? Iran Torn on Syria', United States Institute of Peace, 11 September 2013, http://iranprimer.usip.org/blog/2013/sep/11/what-do-now-iran-torn-syria.

16  Juan Cole, 'Former Iranian

President Slams Syria for Gassing Own People: Sign of Deep Divisions in Tehran', 3 September 2013, http://www.juancole.com/2013/09/president-gassing-divisions.html.

This essay was first published in the December 2014–January 2015 issue of *Survival*.

# CHAPTER THREE

# Assessing Syria's Jihad

## Charles Lister

The conflict in Syria has changed significantly since the first signs of an armed insurgency began to emerge in late May 2011. While the largely nationalist-minded Free Syrian Army (FSA) gradually devolved into an amorphous gathering of locally focused militia units with minimal command links to a leadership in Turkey, the capabilities and influence of Salafist and Sunni jihadist groups expanded considerably.

The Syrian insurgency has had an overt Sunni jihadist component since 23 January 2012, when Jabhat al-Nusra announced its emergence and claimed responsibility for its first attack – a suicide bombing in Damascus on 23 December 2011, which killed 40 people.[1] However, Jabhat al-Nusra had in fact been covertly active on a minimal scale in Syria from at least August 2011, thanks to the release of Islamist detainees from Syrian prisons under a series of presidential amnesties in May–June 2011; to the presence of a number of existing al-Qaeda-linked jihadist cells; and to the arrival of then senior ISIS commander Abu Mohammed al-Jawlani from his base in Mosul, Iraq.

Therefore, by early 2012, a quickly expanding Syrian insurgency already contained a core Sunni jihadist component, as well as a number of fast-growing conservative Salafist groups, such as Ahrar al-Sham, Liwa al-Islam and Suqor al-Sham, all of which were established by detainees released from Sednaya Prison in 2011.

The few FSA groups that did evolve into genuine insurgent organisations with a broad geographical reach, such as Kataib al-Farouq, soon fell victim to government siege and a divided, external opposition-support structure, headed by Gulf states whose individual interests meant their actions too often proved contradictory and divisive, rather than mutually productive. The rapid proliferation of armed factions meant that by mid-2013, the Syrian insurgency contained at least 1,000 operationally independent insurgent units, some of which were entirely dependent upon external support, while others remained limited to extremely localised theatres.[2]

Despite a number of grand initiatives launched by Syria's exiled opposition in Turkey in coordination with the Friends of Syria Group, a genuinely effective, centralised command-and-control structure for Syria's armed opposition has continually failed to emerge. Amid such an intensely chaotic environment, not to mention the horrific brutality of this protracted conflict, the prospects for a growth of jihadism have been consistently strong.

As such, the Syrian jihad has become a truly international phenomenon, with at least 15,000 foreign nationals from at least 90 countries having engaged in combat in the country since 2011.[3] This represents a rate of foreign-fighter influx into a civil conflict that is unprecedented in modern history.[4]

The two principal jihadist actors in Syria are the al-Qaeda affiliate Jabhat al-Nusra and the now notorious Islamic State of Iraq and al-Sham (ISIS). While ISIS grew exponentially in Syria and Iraq in 2013–14 and has established something close to a proto-state across vast swathes of both countries, Jabhat al-Nusra remains an integral part of the transnational al-Qaeda movement, whose modus operandi has consistently incorporated a clearly defined focus upon posing an international threat.

Thus, Syria is now home to a broad range of extremely capable jihadist organisations whose existence poses a very real immediate and long-term threat to regional and international security. With ever-increasing attention being paid to the need to find a solution to the conflict in Syria and to countering the existence of ISIS, Jabhat al-Nusra and other jihadist groups, it is vital to understand their structures and internal dynamics; their specific driving ideology and objectives; their tactics and strategy; their sources of finance; and their regional and international links.

## ISIS: a counter-state movement

ISIS has existed in a number of guises for at least the past 15 years. In 1999, under the leadership of Ahmad Fadil al-Nazal al-Khalayleh (better known as Abu Musab al-Zarqawi), a small group primarily manned by Jordanians operated covertly in Jordan and overtly in Kandahar and Herat, Afghanistan. Starting as Jund al-Sham and quickly renaming itself Jamaat al-Tawhid wal-Jihad, Zarqawi's group established connections with the senior leaderships of both al-Qaeda and the Taliban, with the former providing start-up funds for a training camp and the latter designating a plot of land in western Herat for that purpose.[5]

Since then, what is now known as ISIS (the group has begun to refer to itself simply as 'Islamic State' since proclaiming a caliphate on 29 June 2014) has become a genuinely formidable insurgent organisation in command of approximately 25,000 full-time fighters across Syria and Iraq.[6] Capable of acting as a three-headed force, comprising units devoted to terrorist, insurgent and light-infantry roles, ISIS has conquered territory stretching from Akhtarin in Syria's Aleppo governorate to as far as Sulaiman Bek, 680km away in Iraq's Salah ad Din province. Having failed in its first venture into governance and the establishment of an Islamic state between 2006 and 2008, ISIS, under the leadership of Ibrahim Awwad Ibrahim Ali al-Badri al-Samarrai (better known as Abu

Bakr al-Baghdadi) is making a determined and considerably more successful second attempt.

Much of this success is a result of a qualitative evolution within ISIS's internal structure and strategy, not to mention the benefits the organisation has reaped from exploiting the catastrophic decline in stability in Syria. While the principal objective has long been the establishment of a viable Islamic state, realising this aspiration has been dependent upon a centrally managed enhancement of the strategic model first designed by Zarqawi.

Since suffering considerable losses during the US-funded and tribally led *Sahwa* (or Awakening) in Iraq in the late 2000s, ISIS has executed a methodical strategy of recovery, and today has largely eclipsed al-Qaeda. Organisationally, ISIS is structurally independent and financially self-sufficient, which has provided an invaluable element of strategic self-determination and a near-total insulation from typical counter-terrorist financing measures. However, this independence also provides opportunities for ISIS adversaries to exploit, thereby turning core strengths into potentially existential weaknesses.

Despite the intense international focus on ISIS's offensive operations in Iraq since June 2014, the organisation retains its capital city in Syria (Raqqa) and appears to treat its Syrian territory as the most valuable and sustainable. Since being forced to withdraw from Syria's western governorates of Latakia and Idlib, as well as western parts of Aleppo, during a moderate rebel offensive in early 2014, ISIS has since consolidated its most strategically valuable territory and launched a concerted counter-offensive.

After crushing a rebellion by the al-Sheitaat tribe in mid-August and taking near-total control of Syria's eastern Deir ez-Zor governorate, and then capturing the government's last remaining position at al-Tabqa air base, ISIS took full control of Raqqa governorate in late August. Meanwhile, ISIS forces have sustained offensive operations in the predominantly Kurdish northeastern governorate of al-Hasakah and across parts of northern Aleppo. Combined with its territorial control and influence in Iraq, ISIS has had the capacity to earn as much as $2 million per day through the sale of oil and agricultural produce, not to mention additional income derived from its still-extensive extortion networks, internal taxation systems, and activities on the regional black market.[7]

## Organisational structure

Almost immediately upon succeeding to power as ISIS leader in April 2010, Abu Bakr al-Baghdadi set about taking a firm grip over the organisation's senior command. His newly appointed right-hand man, a former colonel in the Saddam-era Iraqi Army, Samir Abd Mohammed al-Khleifawi (or Hajji Bakr – killed in January 2014[8]), reportedly took charge of an Iraq-wide assassination campaign targeting ISIS commanders suspected of potential disloyalty.[9] One consequence of this apparent campaign – whether intentional or not – was that the organisation's senior leadership, particularly its military command, has become almost entirely Iraqi[10] and staffed by individuals with professional military experience. However, responsibility for other aspects of ISIS administration, such as media, law enforcement, recruitment and religious guidance, were typically left open to non-Iraqis, particularly Europeans, Saudis and Tunisians.

From a broader perspective, Baghdadi's personal shaping of his senior-leadership command structure also induced an intense level of personal loyalty to him as the self-styled *emir al-mu'minin* (commander of the faithful). Structurally, this helped reinforce the pre-existing state-like structure first formed in the organisation's early days in Iraq in late 2006, whereby its leadership structure took a pyramidal form, with Baghdadi at the top, followed by two deputies, a Shura Council and a cabinet of ministers, and then a council of provincial governors and their individual military commands. Across this structure lies ISIS's War Council, which features prominently in terms of its effect upon the organisation's day-to-day operations and future prospects. The respective commanders for operations in Iraq and Syria retain positions on a par with the Shura Council and are likely to be prominent members of this inner circle.

Within the broad context of ISIS's total leadership structure, Baghdadi appears to represent the definitive source of apparent religious legitimacy. Although far from being a graduate of an esteemed Islamic institution such as al-Azhar in Egypt, Baghdadi does hold a PhD in Islamic studies from the Islamic University of Baghdad and has been an imam and a preacher at his hometown mosque in Samarra.[11] Intriguingly, this is a greater level of official Islamic education and experience than was ever held by Osama bin Laden or al-Qaeda's current leader, Ayman al-Zawahiri. Within ISIS's wider international support base, this distinction is extremely important. Nonetheless, while Baghdadi does appear to provide some degree of perceived religious legitimacy as leader, it is almost certainly his immediate deputies who have been responsible for designing and implementing the years-long strategy of rebuilding and expanding since the late 2000s.

In addition to shaping ISIS into a tightly controlled, fiercely loyal and surprisingly professional organisation, Baghdadi also reinforced an almost bureaucratic management style within the national, provincial and local levels of administration. Militarily, ISIS maintained a clear reporting structure from a local level, through the provincial command, and up to the War Council. The level of internal reporting in this regard, and the level of detail involved, has been demonstrated during each of the previous two years in highly detailed annual military reports made up of close to 200 pages of statistics and analysis.

The ISIS Ministry of Finance managed a similarly complex mechanism for both the gathering of money and its controlled distribution to areas or specific cells particularly in need. For example, while ISIS was thought to have been earning between $70–200m per year in late 2006 through a combination of kidnapping for ransom, extortion and oil smuggling,[12] by June 2014 the organisation was earning in excess of $12m per month from activities in Mosul alone;[13] and by September 2014, it was earning approximately $2m per day through its control and sale of oil in Syria and Iraq.[14] The management of such an expanded financial operation, particularly when operating as a sub-state organisation during conflict, requires a very capable financial-management structure.

Having established such a tight-knit and relatively professional command structure, Baghdadi has helped develop an extremely proficient insurgent organisation capable of attaining its stated goals on the military, political and religious fronts. Crucially, it also seems quite likely that the death of one individual, including potentially even Baghdadi himself, may not necessarily pose an existential challenge to ISIS's durability.

### Tactics and strategy

In the three-year lead-up to ISIS's capture of Mosul and its declaration of a caliphate in June 2014, the group conducted an intricately planned and methodically implemented military strategy aimed at reinforcing and consolidating sectarian dynamics in Iraq and, from 2013, sowing divisions in Syria.

With regards to Iraq, ISIS used 2011 to begin an acceleration of its operational recovery, involving renewed recruitment, expanding operations in both scale and scope, and exploiting an increasingly perceptible sectarian mindset feeding off the revolution in Syria. Then followed two twelve-month campaign plans. From July 2012–July 2013, *Operation Breaking the Walls* sought to release imprisoned members, particularly senior commanders, and to expand the geographical reach of ISIS attacks. Following on from this operation's grand finale – the breaking out of approximately 500 prisoners from Abu Ghraib prison on 21 July 2013[15]

– ISIS announced and began *Operation Soldiers' Harvest*, which explicitly sought to undermine the confidence and capabilities of Iraqi security forces and to exploit continuing sectarian tensions resulting from the perceived repression of Iraq's Sunni minority by its Shia-led government under Prime Minister Nuri al-Maliki.

In Syria, ISIS has consistently sought to exploit its tactical strengths, particularly an ability to deploy small units on multiple fronts, all using rapid mobility to ensure an element of surprise and overwhelming aggression. The frequent use of suicide bombers at the initiation of offensive manoeuvres has also repeatedly proven a key advantage in penetrating otherwise tough enemy defences. Since ISIS's dramatic gains in Iraq post-June 2014, significant quantities of weaponry, including US-made armoured Humvees, M16 and M4 rifles, and M198 howitzers, have been transferred into the Syrian theatre and have been used to considerable advantage in battles against both the government and opposition.[16]

ISIS also relies upon presenting itself as a brutal fighting force willing to carry out horrific acts of violence. Such demonstrative violence, in the form of mass executions and the violent displacement of minorities, for example, is, in and of itself, a tactic intended to intimidate enemies and weaken their resolve in the face of advancing ISIS forces. The fact that the group appears to invest considerable resources into presenting its brutality at a near-professional level on multiple social-media platforms and in several languages serves to enhance this intimidation factor and also to encourage further recruitment.

On a more strategic level, ISIS represents a military force that is heavily dependent upon sustaining momentum but that is also centrally concerned with consolidating key strategic territory. This results in what could be termed a cyclical ink-spot strategy, whereby operational intensity tends to switch from one key zone of control to another, each time gradually expanding that specific area of operations. By continually shifting its most intensive front lines, ISIS places its opponents on the back foot while managing to maintain sufficient momentum to appear the actor with the advantage. Except where faced with an enhanced counter-strategy, as occurred in areas of northern Iraq following the initiation of US air-strikes on 8 August, this strategy continues to destabilise areas on the periphery of ISIS's effective boundaries of control, thereby making them vulnerable to future conquest.

Territorial control is a fundamental facet of ISIS's overarching strategy, as this allows it to expand its Islamic rule and acquire more income-earning capacity. The latter is of critical importance for sustaining the former, which ISIS must necessarily maintain in order to justify its very existence. In addition to enforcing its rule through a system of civil and religious law-enforcement structures, incorporating the introduction of traditional *hudud* (fixed) and *qisas* (discretionary) punishments, ISIS also spends considerable financial resources on the provision of social services to civilian populations under its control. It is common, for example, for ISIS to finance the subsidising of staple-food costs and to help fund the supply of food and money to the poor and elderly; to cap rent prices and provide free bus transport, children's education, healthcare and vaccinations; and to undertake the general maintenance of local infrastructure. Amid a wider context of spiralling violence and instability, such services are a key facet of ISIS's attempt to present itself as offering a sustainable and workable alternative to the existing state-based system offered by the Syrian and Iraqi governments.

Since the initiation of coalition air- and cruise-missile strikes in Syria, the targeting of ISIS-controlled, makeshift oil refineries in the east will have significantly eroded the scale of the organisation's income-earning capacity. However, while in isolation this will reduce ISIS's ability to fund the provision of services to civilians under its control, the targeting of oil resources at the source may provide ISIS with an opportunity to push the blame onto the international community. Instead, it would have been wiser to target the group's capacity to transport oil as a product, which it does throughout northern and eastern Syria within an effective, internal oil market. In fact, since July 2014, the scale of ISIS oil exports to foreign buyers has steadily reduced in favour of the creation of an independent, internal market, thus affording a more tightly controlled income source.

### Foreign fighters and recruitment

A majority of the approximately 15,000 foreign fighters who are thought to have travelled to Syria and Iraq are likely to have joined ISIS, although it is reasonable to surmise that a notable portion of these will have died in combat or returned home. Although the vast majority of ISIS's leadership structure is Iraqi, the group relies heavily upon maintaining a visible foreign-fighter component, both for the way this shores up its core image of being a transnational Islamic force building an Islamic state for the entirety of the *ummah* (community of believers) and for the role these fighters play as willing suicide bombers.

The majority of ISIS's recruitment efforts take place through its skilful exploitation of varied social-media platforms and the production of slick, near-professional video and photographic content. In early 2014, what was then already a proficient social-media apparatus began producing content in multiple languages besides Arabic, thus signalling a clear effort to present to a wider audience and convey a global image. Following the initiation of US air-strikes in northern Iraq, the sheer scale and effectiveness of ISIS's media effort appeared to attract a significant (and probably government-prompted) disabling of official social-media accounts. For three consecutive days in August (11–13), for example, Twitter deleted all ISIS provincial accounts, only for new ones to be re-established hours later.[17] After the third day, ISIS failed to re-establish an official presence on Twitter, and following a brief foray onto a privacy-focused, independent platform known as Diaspora, it established a complete series of accounts on the Russian VKontakte platform.

While foreign passports may potentially provide future opportunities for ISIS to attempt attacks in the Western world, European and American fighters are of more immediate value. Firstly, their visible presence in ISIS's sizeable media operation plays a key role in encouraging further recruitment, not only from the West but also from the wider world. With regards to Western foreign fighters in particular, a monitoring of the online pro-jihadist community within European countries tends to suggest that individuals are susceptible to being influenced by groupthink, which is further reinforced by micro communities of British, French and German jihadists online. The additional recruitment of Western nationals into ISIS and their subsequent appearance as fighters on social media or in official ISIS media releases serves to stimulate this cycle of recruitment.

ISIS also benefits from inciting foreign states to develop more restrictive internal security policies aimed at countering extremism and preventing individuals from travelling to carry out jihad. While domestically these policies may appear to hinder attempts by potential jihadists to join the cause abroad, they can also potentially harden the perceptions of those who may have already begun to question the value of remaining at home.

Finally, ISIS can also benefit from individual skill sets provided by foreign recruits. A case in point is ISIS's alleged chief of media operations, a Syrian–American national named Ahmad Abousamra.[18] Born in France and privately educated in a Catholic school in Massachusetts, Abousamra gained a college degree in computer science and went on to work at a telecommunications company – qualifications which, in addition to his fluency in Arabic and English, may have made him in an invaluable cog in ISIS's media operations.[19]

## Regional expansion and interests

ISIS's immediate strategic priority is to consolidate the key underpinnings of what it calls its *dawla* (state). This will involve defeating any potential opponents within the boundaries of its *wilayat* (states), to integrate means of transport and communication between them, and to enhance the level of Islamic rule in key municipalities. Doing so will require considerable kinetic activity, particularly considering the increasing international military attention on definitively combating ISIS militancy. In Syria, the group will also seek to undermine the capabilities of the armed opposition in the north, particularly by continuing its offensive in northern Aleppo, exploiting tensions between Turkey and the Kurdistan Workers' Party (PKK), and seeking to gain control of or block opposition access to the two key northern border crossings of Bab al-Hawa and Bab al-Salameh. These tasks will be made considerably more challenging amid a concerted international effort to counter ISIS in Iraq and Syria.

As such, there is unlikely to be any immediate ISIS strategy to expand its official operations beyond the immediate Syria–Iraq sphere. However, ISIS appears at least minimally operationally active in Lebanon following on from its escapade into the border town of Arsal in early August. The group's subsequent beheading of captive Lebanese soldiers appears to be gradually engendering the tense socio-political conditions it is so reliant upon for establishing a genuine operational base.

Meanwhile, ISIS also retains a growing base of support and activism in Saudi Arabia and Jordan.[20] In the short to medium term, it is quite possible that ISIS will seek to further enhance the conditions – insecurity, sectarian hostilities and political tensions – necessary for the group's expansion into these new areas, but this is unlikely to mean it will carry out attacks.

That said, should a regional or international coalition emerge that involves itself in an all-encompassing campaign against the group, the likelihood of ISIS-directed or -influenced attacks in Turkey, Jordan, Saudi Arabia or Lebanon would certainly increase. Increased rates of arrest in Saudi Arabia and Jordan, and continuing instability in areas of Lebanon and southern Turkey, suggest that conditions in these areas are conducive to a one-off attack.

As for attacks in Europe or the United States, it is unlikely that ISIS will have the necessary spare resources in the coming months to launch an officially directed operation that far afield. However, should US air-strikes continue, and should additional Western states choose to augment such military action against ISIS, the chance that returning ISIS fighters – or indeed, individuals already in Europe or the US with no direct jihadi experience – could attempt to carry out independent attacks at home will undoubtedly rise. ISIS has explicitly called on Muslims around the world to target Westerners, with the cases of terror suspects Mehdi Nemmouche and Ibrahim Boudina in France and Abdul Numan Haider, Adam Dahman and Omarjan Azari in Australia, along with spiralling rates of arrest in the UK throughout 2014, suggesting that this is already happening.[21]

## Jabhat al-Nusra: a transnational movement

Having been established by a prominent ISIS commander in 2011, Jabhat al-Nusra has since emerged as an independent al-Qaeda affiliate based in Syria and currently commanding approximately 6,000 fighters. Since its public emergence in January 2012, the group has evolved considerably. While its first six months of operations in Syria saw it act as a stereotypical terrorist organisation, killing dozens of civilians in spectacular urban bomb attacks and raiding largely civilian targets deemed supportive of the government, by August 2012 it had transformed into a professional insurgent group coordinating with nationalist FSA units.

The effects of this strategic evolution and political pragmatism meant that when the US designated it as an alias of al-Qaeda in

Iraq (AQI) in December 2012, opposition civilians marched the following Friday to the theme of 'We are all Jabhat al-Nusra'.[22] The failure throughout 2013 of the moderate opposition to practically unite its armed factions under an efficient and representative structure meant that Salafist and jihadist factions, including Jabhat al-Nusra, grew significantly in size and influence.

However, the emergence of several Western-backed, moderate rebel coalitions since late 2013 in Syria has encouraged a further evolution within Jabhat al-Nusra. These moderate coalitions – such as Harakat Hazm, the Syrian Revolutionaries Front and the Southern Front – were initially established to combat the spread of ISIS, but their continued and increasingly prominent existence since the expulsion of ISIS fighters from areas of northern Syria has meant that Jabhat al-Nusra now perceives their role as a potential threat. This development, combined with ISIS's overshadowing successes, has prompted Jabhat al-Nusra to begin adopting a far more self-assertive and unilateral approach to its operations, particularly in the northern governorate of Idlib and in Daraa in the south.[23]

While ISIS has proven itself to be working against the Westphalian nation-state system, Jabhat al-Nusra has so far operated in accordance with and in recognition of state boundaries. While it has explicitly stated an intention to establish an Islamic emirate in Syria, it perceives itself as operating within a wider network of al-Qaeda affiliates around the world, and therefore ultimately loyal to the al-Qaeda leadership in Afghanistan–Pakistan and to their *emir al-mu'minin*, the Taliban leader Mullah Mohammed Omar.[24]

### Organisational structure, foreign fighters and recruitment

Like ISIS, Jabhat al-Nusra is a tightly controlled organisation with intense levels of secrecy surrounding its senior leadership. Structurally, Jabhat al-Nusra operates a pyramidal leadership command, with Jawlani at the top, followed by a Shura Council and then by councils specifically for war and sharia.[25] Jabhat al-Nusra operates individual provincial commands in seven specified regions: Aleppo, Hama, Idlib, Homs, Qalamoun, Damascus and Daraa, with the latter also encompassing Quneitra.

Until its split with ISIS in April–May 2013, Jabhat al-Nusra was financially reliant on funds received from the leadership of its then-parent group in Iraq, from internally earned income in Syria, and from al-Qaeda-linked and private donations from the wider Middle East and Gulf region. Since its split with ISIS, the group appears to have suffered a gradual decline, partly due to the loss of manpower to ISIS but also because of apparent financial constraints. It did control oil fields in al-Shadadi in al-Hasakah and the al-Omar and Conoco fields in Deir ez-Zor in late 2013 and early 2014, but has since lost control of these. Meanwhile, several of its most prominent sources of private funding have been sanctioned by the US and UN, forcing the group to become increasingly reliant on funding from al-Qaeda's senior leadership – with whom contact appears to be extremely slow or possibly obstructed[26] – and on kidnap and ransom operations, which appear to have increased notably in recent months.

Having consistently presented itself as a Syrian organisation fighting for the Syrian people, Jabhat al-Nusra's senior leadership – several of whom are Syrian, including Jawlani, the group's chief spokesman, Abu Firas al-Suri, and senior military leaders Abu Hammam al-Suri and Abu Hafs al-Binnishi – has throughout 2014 begun assuming a more foreign image, bolstered by the arrival of individuals with extensive experience within al-Qaeda. Immediately below Jawlani, Jabhat al-Nusra's senior leaders include Sami al-Oraydi (Jordanian), Maysar Ali Musa Abdallah al-Juburi (Iraqi), Abdul Mohsen Abdullah Ibrahim al-Sharikh (Saudi), Said Arif (French–Algerian), Abul Layth al-Tabuki (Jordanian), Abu Hassan al-Kuwaiti (Kuwaiti) and Abu Sulayman al-Muhajir (Australian). Moreover, in addition to Mohsen al-Fadhli (Kuwaiti), Abu Yusuf al-Turki (Turkish) and David Drugeon (French) – all of whom were targeted in a US cruise-missile strike in Aleppo in September 2014, with Turki reported killed and Fadhli and Drugeon reportedly surviving[27] – British and American intelligence officials are apparently aware of other as-yet unidentified individuals, known as the Khorasan Group, who have travelled from Afghanistan–Pakistan to bolster the core al-Qaeda presence within Jabhat al-Nusra's senior leadership.[28]

Although the number of Syrians within the senior leadership is relatively small, the group is nonetheless still primarily reliant on Syrian foot soldiers for its military operations. This Syrian compo-nent has proven an extremely valuable asset for Jabhat al-Nusra since 2012, but it may prove to be a weakness in the coming months if ISIS maintains its pre-eminence, the Syrian opposition contin-ues to struggle, and Jabhat al-Nusra's financial woes endure.

As of September 2014, Jabhat al-Nusra does not operate a specific recruitment strategy via social media or other chan-nels. Instead, it has primarily relied on enlisting Syrians who are ideologically appropriate for its cause or simply eager to fight for what has long been perceived as an extremely capable insurgent organisation. Jabhat al-Nusra does recruit foreign fighters, but many of these join out of ideological or associational allegiance to its al-Qaeda membership, rather than in reaction to an overt and public recruitment campaign. Crucially, this signifies a continued determination by some Westerners to join Jabhat al-Nusra, and thus al-Qaeda, despite that specific faction having taken a far less prominent public role in recent months. The al-Qaeda name remains a valuable instrument of legitimacy for Jabhat al-Nusra, particularly when co-opting members of existing al-Qaeda affiliates and other jihadist organisations with informal allegiance to al-Qaeda, such as the North Caucasus-based Imarat Kavkaz (IK), which has, to all intents and purposes, co-opted the largely Russian-speaking Jaish al-Muhajireen wal Ansar as its Syrian wing.

## Tactics and strategy

Due to its relatively small size and dispersed geographical presence across much of Syria, Jabhat al-Nusra often operates much like a special-operations force, with its fighters playing a front-line role in offensive operations carried out in coordination with other localised groups. A majority of its military resources are devoted to insurgent-type operations, and the frequency of terror-istic-type urban bombings is generally low, except for when the group is forced into major strategic retreats, as in the case of Homs in late April and early May 2014, when it claimed responsibility for several car bombings in pro-government districts of the city.

Like ISIS, Jabhat al-Nusra also relies upon its particular strengths: it is relatively well armed and possesses rapid-mobility capabilities; and the large majority of its fighters are highly moti-vated by their extremist ideology. Using one or multiple suicide bombers at the start of offensive manoeuvres in order to penetrate enemy defences is a valuable tactic that other, more moderate Syrian rebel groups have benefited from when coordinating oper-ations with Jabhat al-Nusra.

Strategically, the group appears to be in a state of flux. While it has previously sought to establish an operational presence across as broad a swathe of Syria's conflict as possible, by way of cooper-ating with other armed factions and opposition civilian bodies, it is now focusing its operational intensity on two principal fronts – in Idlib in the north and in Daraa and Quneitra in the south. Both of these regions have long been key Jabhat al-Nusra strongholds.

Since early 2014, the group has been covertly enforcing its influ-ence in the south, particularly by taking advantage of heightening frustration within the moderate camp at what has been perceived as insufficient assistance from the US-led operations room in

Amman, Jordan. While it has not openly fought any rival moderate groups in the south, it has kidnapped several senior Western-backed commanders, including the leader of Liwa Maghaweer al-Hauran, Abu Fuad al-Husseini, in March 2014, and the chief of the Daraa Military Council, Ahmed Nehmeh, in May 2014.[29]

Of potentially more significance is Jabhat al-Nusra's shifting posture in Idlib, where it has been attempting to outmanoeuvre core moderate factions, even fighting them on several occasions using the premise of fighting corruption and criminality, in order to take control of strategically valuable villages and towns near the Turkish border. Upon capturing these areas (such as Harem, Sarmada, Darkoush, Salqin and Binnish, captured in July 2014), it has sought to impose elements of sharia law – something it had previously not attempted to do unilaterally. That much of this activity has centred around territory near the Turkish border, and particularly on key roads leading to the major crossing at Bab al-Hawa, makes it highly likely that Jabhat al-Nusra is seeking to cut off the moderate opposition from its key source of support in Hatay. This, plus ISIS's gradual advance towards the other critical northern crossing at Bab al-Salameh in northern Aleppo, poses a potentially existential threat to Syria's moderate opposition.

Considering the less favourable circumstances under which Jabhat al-Nusra has found itself operating in 2014, it seems likely this strategic shift will continue. The fact that Abu Firas al-Suri explained in an 8 August video statement that Jabhat al-Nusra *does* intend to establish Islamic emirates in Syria, but only 'by consulting those who have an Islamist affiliation' and through the group's 'Sharia Arbitration Charter',[30] suggests its principal aim will be to establish the conditions necessary for such a goal to be achieved. Ridding key stronghold regions of Western-backed and potentially anti-jihadist, moderate rebels would seem an obvious first step in that direction.

However, in order to have any realistic hope of establishing an emirate (or emirates) in Syria, Jabhat al-Nusra will require far superior levels of financing. This is likely to be the group's most significant challenge in the months to come. In the immediate term, an increase in kidnappings appears to point towards an attempt to earn money through ransoms, but it is unlikely this will be either sufficient or sustainable in the long term.

### Ideology, objectives and possible regional expansion

Jabhat al-Nusra is a hyper-localised al-Qaeda affiliate that has, since late 2012, sought to operationalise aspects of the strategic thinking originally espoused by the veteran al-Qaeda ideologue Mustafa Setmariam Nasar (Abu Musab al-Suri) and subsequently in 2012–13 by the emir of al-Qaeda in the Islamic Maghreb (AQIM), Abu Musab Abdul Wadud (Abdelmalek Droukdel), emphasising the implementation of a patient, long-term strategy focused on integrating into local dynamics, shaping alliances, avoiding enemies and abstaining from an overly swift imposition of Islamic law. In 2012–13, Droukdel wrote a letter to his forces in Mali in which he compared AQIM to a parent and Mali to a child, stating:

> The current baby is in its first days, crawling on its knees, and has not yet stood on its two legs … If we really want it to stand on its own two feet in this world full of enemies waiting to pounce, we must ease its burden, take it by the hand, help it and support it until it stands … One of the wrong policies that we think you carried out is the extreme speed with which you applied Sharia … Our previous experience proved that applying Sharia this way… will lead to people rejecting the religion and engender hatred towards the mujahideen.[31]

Similarly, Jabhat al-Nusra's Jawlani released a statement in late 2012 telling his fighters that, 'day after day, you are getting closer to the people after you have conquered their hearts and become trusted by them' and warning against 'being hard on them': 'begin with the priorities and fundamentals of Islam and be flexible on the minor parts of the religion'.[32]

Considering Jabhat al-Nusra's shifting behaviour in Idlib and the south, it seems possible that it now feels that it has made enough progress socialising parts of Syria as to begin a more unilateral enforcement of sharia norms, although the dramatic progress and victories of ISIS are sure to have accelerated the making of this decision.

Looking towards Syria's neighbours, Jabhat al-Nusra has a well-established operational presence and support base in Lebanon, having been militarily active in that country since claiming a suicide bombing in southern Beirut on 2 January 2014.[33] This presence is strongly linked to Jabhat al-Nusra's close relationship with the al-Qaeda-affiliated Kataib Abdullah Azzam, with the two organisations having carried out several joint attacks on Lebanon from inside the country and from neighbouring Syria in 2014. This relationship, along with Jabhat al-Nusra's operational activity in Lebanon, will continue for the foreseeable future, potentially expanding in scale should the Lebanese Army intensify its operations against Syrian militants in the Arsal area.

Although Jabhat al-Nusra has a potently capable presence in Quneitra along the border with the Israeli-controlled Golan Heights, where it kidnapped 45 United Nations Disengagement Observer Force (UNDOF) personnel, it is unlikely the group will seek to attack Israel in the near future. However, with ISIS seeking to establish a sustainable support base in Jordan, where al-Qaeda and Jabhat al-Nusra have long been the favoured forces amongst the country's Salafist community, it is possible that Jabhat al-Nusra could seek to carry out an attack on Jordanian territory, potentially akin to the plot foiled by Jordanian authorities in October 2012.[34] Meanwhile, the group is still thought to be reliant upon logistical networks in Turkey, so it is extremely unlikely it would seek to compromise those by attacking Turkish targets.

The potential implications for international security of Jabhat al-Nusra's status as an al-Qaeda affiliate must always be borne in mind. Considering the steady arrival of senior al-Qaeda veterans and individuals from Afghanistan–Pakistan, it would appear that Syria will likely become a key centre of al-Qaeda operations and a potential launching pad for attacks against the Western world. It is far from surprising, therefore, that US intelligence operatives suspect that sophisticated bomb-making expertise may have been transferred from al-Qaeda in the Arabian Peninsula (AQAP) in Yemen to Jabhat al-Nusra in Syria for potential use in airline attacks.[35]

## Syria's wider jihadist community

In addition to ISIS and al-Qaeda, several pre-existing jihadist organisations with principal bases of operation outside Syria have established active wings inside Syrian territory, including the North Caucasus-based IK; the China- and Pakistan-based, Uighur-dominated East Turkestan Islamic Movement (ETIM); and the Lebanon-based Jund al-Sham. For these organisations, Syria provides an invaluable base, a source of training, and an opportunity to present a more international face to their organisation. Already, Russia and China in particular have expressed concern over the active role of IK and ETIM in Syria and the potential that, should the conflict there end, the consequences will be felt at home.

Syria is also now home to at least eight other jihadist groups that are likely to remain active in the countries from which the majority of their members derive, including Harakat Sham al-Islam (led and dominated by Moroccans), al-Katibat al-Khadraa and Katibat Suqor al-Izz (Saudis), Usud al-Khilafah (Egyptians), Katibat al-Battar al-Libya (Libyans), Junud al-Sham (Russians and North Caucasians), Katibat Imam al-Bukhari (Uzbekistanis), and Jamaat Ahadun Ahad (Turks). Several of these organisations are led by individuals with extensive, decades-long experience fighting international jihad with historically renowned jihadist leaders, including former Guantanamo Bay inmates, and have expressed their interest in transferring some of their experience back to their countries of origin.[36]

The majority of these groups' areas of operation remain in Syria's northwest, encompassing the governorates of Latakia, Idlib, Aleppo and Hama, with a small additional presence in Homs and the Qalamoun Mountains bordering Lebanon. During the outbreak of inter-factional conflict in northern Syria in late 2013, which gained intensity in January 2014, the majority of these groups (except Usud al-Khilafah) remained either independent or tacitly loyal to Jabhat al-Nusra. They have therefore remained largely intact, although al-Katibat al-Khadraa, Jaish al-Muhajireen wal Ansar and Harakat Sham al-Islam merged with a Syrian Islamist faction, Harakat Fajr al-Sham, on 25 July 2014 to establish Jabhat Ansar al-Din – a sizeable militant front likely commanding approximately 2,500 fighters.[37]

Should ISIS continue its gradual advance westwards towards these areas, it is possible that some of these groups will pledge allegiance to ISIS and Abu Bakr al-Baghdadi, more out of necessity than ideological fealty. This remains a significant short-term advantage for ISIS – its ability to rapidly impose military dominance and to financially co-opt potentially rival factions tends to induce pragmatic surrenders and pledges of allegiance. These are entirely reversible, however, should dynamics on the ground shift.

## Long-term implications

Increased international attention to the threat posed by ISIS has resulted in a level of urgency that makes an expansion of external military intervention in Iraq and Syria increasingly likely. Should a well-developed, multifaceted and multinational strategy against ISIS and other jihadists gain traction in Syria and Iraq, it is likely that territory will be recovered, and jihadist groups may be forced to retreat. However, this will prove deeply dependent on the provision of enhanced support and training for indigenous anti-jihadist forces and the coordination of coalition actions with them – airpower alone will not 'roll back', let alone defeat, these groups.

ISIS presents more of a target in this regard, but one that is capable of melting into predominantly civilian areas in which even precision-guided air-strikes risk causing counterproductive civilian casualties. Jabhat al-Nusra and other jihadist groups active in Syria, meanwhile, represent even more challenging targets. It is for this reason that local actors – in Syria, the armed opposition and tribes, and in Iraq, the Kurdish Peshmerga, willing Sunni tribes and the Iraqi military – must be provided with the means to play the necessary front-line role in combating the threat on the ground.

In and of itself, international intervention tends to provide an opportunity for transnationally minded jihadists to boost their image by presenting themselves as fighting their traditional 'Crusader' enemy. A cursory monitoring of pro-jihadist activities on social media in the days and weeks following the initiation of US air-strikes in northern Iraq proved the unifying effect that such intervention can have. However, should this intervention be comprehensively backed by and coordinated with local actors, militants could be faced with the more significant prospect of being forced out by their own potential constituents.

Even when military actions form a single component within a more multifaceted strategy, it is extraordinarily difficult to *totally* militarily defeat an armed insurgent or terrorist organisation such that it ceases to exist. Such organisations tend to withdraw back into society in order to fight another day. ISIS exemplifies this lesson, as it survived the might of a 150,000-strong American force in Iraq during the surge and the *Sahwa* in 2007–08 to emerge in its current state in Iraq and Syria in 2014.

Therefore, no matter the extent to which a coalition of outside powers chooses to intervene militarily in Syria and Iraq in the coming months, it is extremely unlikely that ISIS and other jihadist organisations will disappear altogether. In the long term, what seems most likely is that ISIS will lose a significant proportion of its Syrian members, be forced to retreat territorially, and return to acting as a typical terrorist-insurgent organisation, operating covertly from within populations. Similarly, Jabhat al-Nusra will likely become considerably smaller and complete its apparent ideological evolution into a more typical al-Qaeda faction. Meanwhile, those remaining, smaller jihadist factions in Syria that retain international interests will likely begin to splinter, with some portion of their fighters joining other, pre-existing groups in Syria and Iraq and others returning to their countries of origin or alternative active jihadist zones.

In short, Iraq and especially Syria will continue to represent relative safe havens for jihadist militants for many years to come, although the freedom of operation they currently enjoy will be considerably reduced. Therefore, the likelihood that such organisations will be able to sustain or establish sufficient territorial control as to claim the existence of their own emirate or caliphate will be considerably minimised. This will subsequently heighten the chance that such organisations will choose to strategically shift toward adding attacks against international targets to their objectives.

A less secure operating environment may potentially serve to intensify the rivalry between al-Qaeda and ISIS, with the latter having the most to lose. As a decentralised movement consisting of multiple semi-independent affiliates dispersed across the globe, al-Qaeda has many years of experience operating within unfavourable circumstances. Since its presence is focused on Syria (where severe instability is more likely to endure, when compared to Iraq), it is plausible that Jabhat al-Nusra may prove the more durable of the two organisations.

# Notes

[1] 'Declaration of the Support Front (Jabhat al-Nusra): For the People of Syria from the Mujahideen of Syria in the Fields of Jihad', Al-Manarah al-Bayda Foundation for Media Production, 23 January 2012, http://jihadology.net/2012/01/24/al-manarah-al-bayḍa-foundation--for-media-production-presents-for-the-people-of-syria-from-the-mujahidin-of-syria-in-the-fields-of-jihad-jabhah-al-nuṣrah-the-front-of-victory; 'Forty Killed, 100 Wounded in Damascus Blasts – TV', Reuters, 23 December 2011, http://www.trust.org/item/?map=forty-killed-100-wounded-in-damascus-blasts--tv/.

[2] Charles Lister, 'Syria's Insurgency: Beyond Good Guys and Bad Guys', *Foreign Policy*, 9 September 2013, http://mideastafrica.foreign-policy.com/posts/2013/09/09/syrias_insurgency_beyond_good_guys_and_bad_guys.

[3] These figures are based on the author's own research, in addition to the findings of previous studies: Aaron Zelin, 'Up to 11,000 Foreign Fighters in Syria; Steep Rise among Western Europeans', ICSR, 17 December 2013, http://icsr.info/2013/12/icsr-insight-11000-for-eign-fighters-syria-steep-rise-among-western-europeans/.

[4] Thomas Hegghammer, 'The Rise of Muslim Foreign Fighters: Islam and the Globalization of Jihad', *International Security*, vol. 35, no. 3, Winter 2010–11, pp. 53–94.

[5] 'Tracking Al Qaeda in Iraq's Zarqawi Interview with Ex-CIA Analyst Nada Bakos', Musings on Iraq, 30 June 2014, http://musings-oniraq.blogspot.com/2014/06/tracking-al-qaeda-in-iraqs-zarqawi.html; Bruce Riedel, *The Search for Al Qaeda: Its Leadership, Ideology, and Future* (Washington DC: Brookings Institution Press, 2010), p. 94.

[6] This figure is based on the author's own research. The CIA has estimated ISIS strength at 31,000, although that likely includes unofficial, tribally aligned fighters temporarily co-opted by ISIS during its advances in Iraq in 2014. See 'CIA: As Many As 31,000 Islamic State Fighters in Iraq, Syria', Voice of America, 11 September 2014, http://www.voanews.com/content/kerry-secures-arab-backing-for-push-against-islamic-state/2446934.html.

[7] Indira A.R. Lakshmanan, 'Islamic State Now Resembles the Taliban with Oil Fields', Bloomberg, 25 August 2014, http://www.bloomberg.com/news/2014-08-25/islamic-state-now-resembles-the-taliban-with-oil-fields.html.

[8] Anthony Loyd, 'Deadly Revenge of Saddam's Henchmen', *Times*, 14 June 2014, http://www.thetimes.co.uk/tto/news/world/middleeast/iraq/article4118901.ece.

[9] As claimed in an apparent leak from ISIS via the Twitter account @Wikibaghdady, collated here: http://justpaste.it/e9oq.

[10] One notable exception to this is Tarkhan Batirashvili (Omar al-Shishani), a former sergeant in the Georgian military who now commands ISIS military operations in Syria.

11  See the biography of Abu Bakr al-Baghdadi by Turki al-Binali, a senior ISIS sharia official, published online on 15 July 2013 at http://justpaste.it/33nl.

12  Matthew Levitt, 'Declaring an Islamic State, Running a Criminal Enterprise', *The Hill*, 7 July 2014, http://thehill.com/blogs/punditsblog/211298-declaring-an-islamicstate-running-a-criminal-enterprise.

13  Amanda Macias and Jeremy Bender, 'Here's How The World's Richest Terrorist Group Makes Millions Every Day', *Business Insider*, 27 August 2014, http://www.businessinsider.com/isis-worldsrichest-terrorist-group-2014-8.

14  Indira A.R. Lakshmanan and Anthony DiPaola, 'Islamic State: Oil Magnates of Terror', *Businessweek*, 4 September 2014, http://www.businessweek.com/articles/2014-09-04/oil-smuggling-vital-to-islamicstates-expansion.

15  Kareem Raheem and Ziad al-Sinjary, 'Al Qaeda Militants Flee Iraq Jail in Violent Mass Break-out', Reuters, 22 July 2013, http://www.reuters.com/article/2013/07/22/us-iraq-violenceidUSBRE96L0RM20130722.

16  This observation is based on the author's own research and monitoring of ISIS operations in Aleppo, Raqqa, Hasakah and Deir ez-Zor since June 2014.

17  Dan Friedman, 'Twitter Stepping up Suspensions of ISIS-affiliated Accounts: Experts', *New York Daily News*, 17 August 2014, http://www.nydailynews.com/news/world/twitter-stepping-suspensions-isisaffiliated-accounts-experts-article-1.1906193.

18  Ahmad Abousamra is wanted by the US Federal Bureau of Investigation (FBI) for his alleged involvement in jihadist activities, as detailed on the FBI website: http://www.fbi.gov/wanted/wanted_terrorists/ahmad-abousamra/view.

19  Michele McPhee and Brian Ross, 'Official: American May Be Key in ISIS Social Media Blitz', ABC News, 3 September 2014, http://abcnews.go.com/blogs/headlines/2014/09/official-american-may-be-key-inisis-social-media-blitz.

20  On Saudi Arabia see, for example, 'Pro-ISIL Graffiti Found in Saudi Schools', *Gulf News*, 2 September 2014, http://gulfnews.com/news/gulf/saudi-arabia/pro-isil-graffiti-found-in-saudi-schools-1.1379728; and Ian Black, 'Saudi Arabia Intensifies Crackdown on Extremist Groups', *Guardian*, 2 September 2014, http://www.theguardian.com/world/2014/sep/02/saudi-arabia-isis-jihadis-iraq-syria-extremists-crackdown. On Jordan see, for example, William Booth and Taylor Luck, 'Jordan Fears Homegrown ISIS More Than Invasion From Iraq', *Washington Post*, 27 June 2014, http://www.washingtonpost.com/world/middle_east/jordan-fears-homegrown-isis-more-than-invasion-from-iraq/2014/06/27/1534a4ee-f48a-492a-99b3-b6cd3f-fe9e41_story.html; and John Reed, 'ISIS Support Grows in Restive Jordanian Town', *Financial Times*, 29 June 2014, http://www.ft.com/intl/cms/s/0/7077c86c-fe18-11e3-b4f1-00144feab7de.html.

21  Yara Bayoumy, 'Isis Urges More Attacks on Western "Disbelievers"', *Independent*, 22 September 2014, http://www.independent.

co.uk/news/world/middle-east/
isis-urges-more-attacks-on-west-
ern-disbelievers-9749512.html;
Umberto Bacchi, 'France: "ISIS
Jihadist" Mehdi Nemmouche to be
Extradited Over Brussels Jewish
Museum Attack', *International
Business Times*, 26 June 2014, http://
www.ibtimes.co.uk/france-isis-
jihadist-mehdi-nemmouche-be-
extradited-over-brussels-jewish-
museum-attack-1454356; Paul
Cruickshank, 'Raid on ISIS Suspect
in the French Riviera', CNN, 28
August 2014, http://edition.cnn.
com/2014/08/28/world/europe/
france-suspected-isis-link/; 'Abdul
Numan Haider Was "Stabbing
Police Officer" When He Was
Shot Dead', *Guardian*, 3 October
2014, http://www.theguard-
ian.com/australia-news/2014/
oct/03/abdul-numan-haider-stab-
bing-policeman-when-he-was-
shot-dead-court-hears; Shane
Green, 'The Young Faces of
Terror', *Sydney Morning Herald*,
27 September 2014, http://www.
smh.com.au/national/the-young-
faces-of-terror-20140926-10mf9v.
html; '"Hundreds" of UK Terror
Arrests This Year', Sky News, 17
October 2014, http://news.sky.com/
story/1354762/hundreds-of-uk-
terror-arrests-this-year.

22  'Syrians March in Support of
Jabhat al-Nusra Militants',
France 24, 16 December 2012,
http://www.france24.com/
en/20121216-syria-march-support-
jabhat-nusra-militants-us-terrorist/.

23  Charles Lister, 'The "Real" Jabhat
al-Nusra Appears to be Emerging',
*Huffington Post*, 7 August 2014,
http://www.huffingtonpost.com/

charles-lister/the-real-jabhat-al-
nusra_b_5658039.html.

24  Jason Burke, 'Al-Qaida Leader
Announces Formation of Indian
Branch', *Guardian*, 4 September
2014, http://www.theguard-
ian.com/world/2014/sep/04/
al-qaida-leader-announces-forma-
tion-indian-branch.

25  This passage is based on the
author's own research.

26  'Zawahiri Falls Off the Map, Is
Rebuked by Top Al Nusra Figure',
Intelwire, 18 August 2014, http://
news.intelwire.com/2014/08/zawa-
hiri-falls-off-map-gets-rebuked-by.
html.

27  Thomas Joscelyn, 'US Airstrikes
Target Al Nusrah Front, Islamic
State in Syria', *Long War Journal*, 23
September 2014, http://www.long-
warjournal.org/archives/2014/09/
jihadists_claim_al_n.php; Barbara
Starr and Pamela Brown, 'U.S.
Airstrikes Probably Didn't Take
Out Terror Targets in Syria, Officials
Say', CNN, 30 October 2014, http://
edition.cnn.com/2014/10/29/world/
al-qaeda-khorasan-group-syria/.

28  Peter Bergen, 'Syria: The American
Al-Qaeda Suicide Bomber',
CNN, 31 July 2014, http://edition.
cnn.com/2014/07/31/opinion/
bergen-american-al-qaeda-suicide-
bomber-syria/; Eric Schmitt, 'Qaeda
Militants Seek Syria Base, US
Officials Say', *New York Times*, 25
March 2014, http://www.nytimes.
com/2014/03/26/world/middleeast/
qaeda-militants-seek-syria-base-us-
officials-say.html?_r=0.

29  Phil Sands and Suha Maayeh,
'Syria: Al Qaeda Kidnapping
Could Open a New Battleground',
*National*, 6 May 2014, http://

www.thenational.ae/world/syria/al-qaeda-kidnapping-of-syrian-commander-could-open-new-front.

30  Thomas Joscelyn, 'Al Nusrah Front Spokesman Explains Differences with Islamic State in Video Appearance', *Long War Journal*, 13 August 2014, http://www.longwarjournal.org/archives/2014/08/al_nusrah_front_spok.php.

31  Rukmini Callimachi, 'In Timbuktu, Al-Qaida Left Behind a Manifesto', Associated Press, 14 February 2013, http://bigstory.ap.org/article/timbuktu-al-qaida-left-behind-strategic-plans.

32  Hassan Hassan, 'Jihadis Grow More Dangerous As They Conquer Hearts in Syria', *National*, 6 March 2013, http://www.thenational.ae/thenationalconversation/comment/jihadis-grow-more-dangerous-as-they-conquer-hearts-in-syria#full.

33  Mitchell Prothero, 'Syria's Nusra Front Claims New Suicide Bombing in Hezbollah's Beirut Enclave', McClatchy DC, 21 January 2014, http://www.mcclatchydc.com/2014/01/21/215250/syrias-nusra-front-claims-new.html.

34  'Jordan "al-Qaeda Plot Uncovered"',

BBC News, 21 October 2012, http://www.bbc.com/news/world-middle-east-20023830.

35  Josh Halliday and Vikram Dodd, 'Airport Security Stepped Up in Britain Over Bomb Plot Fears', *Guardian*, 3 July 2014, http://www.theguardian.com/uk-news/2014/jul/02/airport-security-stepped-up-al-qaida-bomb-plot.

36  Leaders with long experience include Junud al-Sham's leader Murad Margoshvili (or Muslim al-Shishani) and military chief Abu Bakr al-Shishani, both of whom commanded jihadist fighters in Chechnya and Dagestan alongside Ibn al-Khattab and Ruslan Gelayev in the late 1990s. Examples of former Guantanamo Bay inmates include Harakat Sham al-Islam's now-deceased founding leader, Ibrahim Bin Shakaran (Abu Ahmad al-Maghribi), a former senior leader in the Moroccan Groupe Islamique Combattant Marocain (GICM) who attended training in al-Qaeda's al-Farouq camp in 2001, before being detained in Pakistan after fleeing Afghanistan in late 2001.

37  This figure is based on the author's own research and calculations.

This essay was first published in the December 2014–January 2015 issue of *Survival*.

# CHAPTER FOUR

# Turkey's Syria Predicament

Henri J. Barkey

In the first weeks of October this year, an array of tanks waited on Turkey's southern border, their commanders watching carefully as the Islamic State of Iraq and al-Sham (ISIS) fought to capture the nearby Syrian–Kurdish town of Kobane. The Democratic Union Party (PYD), the force defending the town and an offshoot of Turkish insurgent group the Kurdistan Workers' Party (PKK), sought help from the powers allied against ISIS: the European Union, NATO, the United Nations, Turkey and, above all, the United States. But Ankara was reluctant to directly intervene in Kobane; it refused to allow help to reach the defenders and denied Washington permission to fly offensive operations out of the US Air Force base at Incirlik, in southern Turkey. Despite the threat that ISIS posed to the country further down the line, Ankara's preference appeared to be for the town to fall, thereby dealing a heavy blow to the Syrian Kurds.

The battle for Kobane began shortly after the release of 49 hostages captured by ISIS as it overran the Turkish consulate in Mosul, along with the rest of the city, on 10 June 2014. Those held included the consul general, other staff and their families, two children and a number of security personnel. The Iraqi Kurds warned

Ankara of Mosul's imminent collapse five days in advance, but the Turks took their time evacuating the consulate in the belief that ISIS would not dare to invade the building. In securing the safe release of the hostages, Turkey appeared to have struck a deal that involved the release of 50 ISIS fighters held by another jihadist group.[1] The episode proved to be not just embarrassing for Ankara, but emblematic of Turkey's fortunes in the Middle East.

## The predicament

Ankara finds itself on the horns of a dilemma. The Arab Spring, the Syrian crisis and the dramatic rise of ISIS in both Iraq and Syria have undermined years of effort in constructing a new foreign policy, upending its relations with states in the Middle East and the West, particularly America. Turkey also has to worry about how its own Kurdish population will be affected by both Kobane and the emergence of jihadist sympathisers within Turkish territory, some of whom have supplied ISIS with fighters and materiel.

Ankara and Washington were for the first two years oblivious to the regional transformation caused by the war in Syria, which has spilled over into Iraq and Lebanon. The sectarian, ethnic and political conflicts precipitated in Turkey's neighbourhood will persist for years, if not decades. The Syria–Iraq border ceased to function as a meaningful boundary soon after the Syrian insurrection began. Turkey, Qatar, Saudi Arabia and the United Arab Emirates added fuel to the fire by providing funds and other support to jihadist groups willing to take on Damascus. The Kobane crisis has added a new element, the Kurds, who have a presence in all of the countries in which the conflict is occurring, and whose nationalist aspirations have been boosted psychologically.

Syrian President Bashar al-Assad's continued hold on power is a major setback for Turkey, after three years of civil war and all the effort to oust him. Ankara put its reputation on the line by jettisoning Assad, as improved Turkey–Syria relations had been the quintessential success story of early foreign-policy initiatives by Recep Tayyip Erdogan (who was then prime minister, and is now president). Assad's resilience and America's refusal to establish no-fly zones in Syria ultimately led Erdogan to bet on jihadist opposition groups. The breakdown of this approach has cascaded into Turkey's wider foreign policy, damaging Ankara's relationships with neighbouring powers, as well as allies such as Washington. Still, Turkey's Syria predicament has been caused by more than its own mistakes, and is linked to developments such as the souring of the Arab Spring; the collapse of new Middle East regimes, such as the Muslim Brotherhood government in Egypt; continued unrest throughout the region; and the Arab Gulf regimes' minimal efforts to countenance change, fearing its ramifications for their own societies. (Turkey has received little blame for the failures of former Iraqi Prime Minster Nuri al-Maliki, whose Shia-dominated government was often criticised by the increasingly pro-Sunni Ankara.)

Frustrated with the military weakness and internal bickering of the moderate Free Syrian Army (FSA) and its political allies, the Turkish government began to surreptitiously support al-Qaeda offshoot Jabhat al-Nusra. Despite Ankara's vehement denials of involvement with the group, Turkey became a conduit for jihadists travelling to Syria from all over the world. This created problems in the relationship with Washington, as the Obama administration pressured Ankara to declare Jabhat al-Nusra a terrorist organisation and curtail its unofficial support of the group. But by the time Turkey agreed to do so, it was too late: ISIS had eclipsed Jabhat al-Nusra, renaming itself the Islamic State.[2] While the two organisations have often been at odds with one another, they are nonetheless cut from the same cloth. The main precursor of ISIS, the Islamic State of Iraq, established Jabhat al-Nusra as a subsidiary to fight the Assad regime, before the success of its creation in attracting large numbers of followers led to distrust between the groups.[3] By capturing Mosul, declaring an Islamic caliphate and allowing mercurial leader Abu Bakr al-Baghdadi to emerge from the shadows, ISIS stole a march on just about everyone. The group's ambitions are far more grandiose than those of al-Qaeda's Afghan-based central leadership, which has never publicly declared a desire to acquire and hold territory on its own. By gaining access to a wide variety of resources, the majority of which have been pillaged from captured towns and army units, ISIS has forced many jihadists to take notice and even defect to the group.

All of this complicates Turkey's immediate policy options and long-term strategy on Syria and Iraq, a fact underlined by the American and allied air-strikes on the group following its occupation of Mosul and combat successes against Iraqi and Kurdish forces. Out of concern for the fate of the Turkish hostages held by ISIS, Minister of National Defence Ismet Yilmaz went to great lengths in explaining that none of the American combat aircraft that attacked the group's positions in Iraq had embarked on the mission from the base at Incirlik.

When the Obama administration put together a coalition of Middle East powers to confront ISIS, the Turks were unwilling to join it. Ankara refused to cooperate even after aircraft from Saudi Arabia and the UAE participated in bombing runs against ISIS positions close to the border with Turkey, instead demanding that America target the Syrian regime as many times as it had the terrorist group.

The long-term consequences of the ever-expanding conflict do not augur well for Turkey. Wars of all kinds, international and civil, can cause huge social, economic and political disruption by giving rise to new and often unintended alliances, groups and environmental changes. Even if Assad is deposed soon, the effects of the war will prevent the establishment of a stable order in Syria. Ankara is already faced with a much-altered strategic geography on its borders. The Syrian Kurds may have incurred military losses in the fight against ISIS, but their efforts have bought them political power that could further their attempt to carve out a second Kurdish autonomous zone in the Middle East, an initiative that the Turkish government opposes. The defence of Kobane has not only won recognition and respect for the PYD, but led to the group actively cooperating with the US military in the fight against ISIS. The PYD's newfound popularity is also likely to force an improvement in its relations with Masoud Barzani, who as president of the Kurdistan Regional Government (KRG), the Kurdish autonomous region in Iraq, forged strong links with Ankara at the expense of his Syrian brethren.

Uncertainty is the greatest challenge facing the Turks and other parties in the conflict; there is very little either Ankara or other powers can do to produce predetermined outcomes. The war will eventually burn itself out, but in the process the region will become unrecognisable, comprising a hotchpotch of ill-defined political and military jurisdictions.

## Turkish policy on Syria and Iraq

In its approach to the Syrian conflict, Turkey appears to have suffered a self-inflicted wound. Ankara's relationship with Assad had been the high point in its 'zero problems with neighbours' policy, the signature initiative of the Erdogan administration and particularly Ahmet Davutoglu (who was then foreign minister, and is now prime minister). Erdogan and Assad had become good friends, leaving behind the tension in Turkish–Syrian relations of the 1990s, which stemmed from Syria's support for the PKK and Turkish construction on the Euphrates. Both Ankara and Damascus invested heavily in the relationship, and conducted multiple 'joint cabinet meetings'.

After the Arab Spring began, Ankara saw the swift collapse of the Tunisian, Libyan and Egyptian governments as caused by a historic tide that would also sweep away the Ba'ath regime of Syria. But before giving up on Assad, Erdogan insisted that he placate his opponents by instituting domestic reforms. Davutoglu and Hakan Fidan, head of Turkey's National Intelligence Organization (MIT), were on many occasions sent to Damascus as part of the effort. Ankara went so far as to suggest that it would support the Syrian president if he were to introduce cosmetic changes in his approach to governance. Assad would have none of it, however, and subsequently stepped up the violence against peaceful demonstrators. The Turks at this point had no choice but to call for Assad's immediate resignation, if not ouster. Erdogan and Davutoglu therefore overestimated their ability to effect change in Syria. Once the opposition took up arms against the regime, Ankara, like Washington, assumed that Assad would be gone in six months. Although he has ceded significant territory to various insurgent groups – ranging from jihadists to the 'moderates' supported by the West – Assad has held on to the crucial western parts of Syria.

The Turks were quick to help organise the opposition to Assad; they hosted conferences in Istanbul and elsewhere, and eventually assisted in the formation of its armed wing, the FSA, which established its headquarters in Turkey. Erdogan lobbied energetically for Washington to set up no-fly zones or protected areas along the Turkish–Syrian border, just as it had done in northern Iraq during the 1990s. But he was unsuccessful, as the US resisted calls for its involvement in another Middle East war.

As the conflict in Syria wore on, Ankara looked for a more effective means to fight Assad. It eventually chose the jihadists flocking there from all corners of the world, who had proven far more able to take the fight to the Syrian army. Whether out of short-term pragmatism, some greater ambition or sheer impatience, Turkey turned a blind eye to the movement of these fighters, before actively helping them to reach Syria. It also provided the jihadists with materiel. The MIT was implicated in attempts to move arms; and, most importantly, groups such as the Humanitarian Relief Foundation, or IHH, were enlisted to smuggle fighters and weapons into Syria.[4]

Turkey's developing strategy must be evaluated in the context of Ankara's goals and ambitions. The ruling Justice and Development Party (AKP) upended traditional Turkish foreign-policy calculations by abandoning decades of ambivalence towards the Middle East and an inward-looking, defensive approach in favour of a more aggressive attitude. This new assertiveness won Ankara plaudits at home and in the wider region, particularly because it was perceived as tinged with anti-Westernism.

The AKP's foreign policy aimed to build Turkish influence in the Middle East and beyond, and was built on four pillars: a vibrant economy capable of trading with everyone; strong (if unheralded) links with both Europe and the US; an increasingly dominant posture in the region, in the form of close links with Middle East regimes; and a historical and cultural affinity with neighbouring states. The party has long sought to make Turkey a global power. Although its earlier incarnations aimed to lead only the Muslim world, today's AKP is more ambitious. Initially, its strategy focused on the Middle East, primarily because proximity gave Turkey an advantage, and the area was perceived as low-hanging fruit. (Facing little competition, Ankara could penetrate and make inroads there, especially economically.) Turkey historically shunned the region in favour of European and other markets, but more recent efforts to strengthen economic ties with its southern neighbours have benefited the country in two important ways: a large rise in exports has boosted Turkish influence abroad, while fuelling growth and prosperity at home.

Nowhere was this more evident than in Syria and Iraq. In 2005 Erdogan claimed credit for convincing Assad to withdraw Syrian troops from Lebanon (much to the consternation of the French, who had orchestrated the requisite UN Security Council resolution). Ankara hoped that the change in Turkish policy on the KRG would have economic advantages (especially in the Kurdish-dominated regions bordering Iraq) and help in the push for a peace deal with Turkish Kurds.[5] Iraq subsequently became Turkey's second-largest market for exports. Erdogan understands that the domestic Kurdish problem must be resolved if Turkey is to avoid scaring away investors, which would undermine economic and political stability, and limit the country's international influence. In light of this, Ankara helped the KRG to prosper. By facilitating oil exports out of, and encouraging Turkish investment in, northern Iraq, it fostered dependence on Ankara's largesse for both energy sales and access to more distant markets.[6]

While the AKP came to power in 2002, it was not until after the 2007 elections that it consolidated its position. The contest set the party against the powerful military establishment, which initially blocked a bid for the presidency by then-Foreign Minister Abdullah Gül. But after the generals suffered a major electoral defeat and were sidelined, Gül became president. From that moment on, Erdogan's foreign policy became far more bold; he seemed to take the Americans and the Europeans for granted, correctly assuming that Turkey's importance to Western governments would prevent them from restraining his more assertive, at times counterproductive, policies. This was most evident in the failed Iranian–Brazilian–Turkish nuclear deal, which aimed to scuttle the American-led initiative for new UN Security Council sanctions on Tehran. Underlying the overall approach was an exuberant self-confidence and self-righteousness, which was exacerbated by the early successes of the Arab Spring, and by Erdogan's ability to win election after election, establishing himself as the uncontested leader of Turkey. Yet for all the increase in influence, this self-importance led Erdogan to use needlessly harsh rhetoric against leaders and countries that provoked his ire. (Paradoxically, Iran was spared such criticism, despite serious disagreements between Ankara and Tehran over policy on Syria.[7]) On issues ranging from the initial plans for Western intervention in Libya and the overthrow of the Muslim Brotherhood government in Egypt to supposed US interference in domestic Turkish politics and, of course, his pet peeve, Israel, Erdogan's inflammatory discourse often restricted his room for manoeuvre.

In Iraq, the Turks were taken aback by Maliki's overtly sectarian policies, which alienated the country's Sunni and Kurdish minorities. Erdogan initially tried to adopt a non-sectarian posture on Iraq, visiting important Shia shrines in the country. But he veered away from this neutral approach in response to Maliki's more divisive actions, which included the hounding of Vice-President Tariq al-Hashimi and, later, former Finance Minister Rafi al-Issawi, as well as support for Assad. Despite sharing many of Washington's concerns about Maliki, and having been an active and influential participant in Iraqi politics, Turkey was by 2013 isolated and largely inconsequential.[8]

## The unintended effects of war in Syria and Iraq

The conflict in Syria and Iraq has direct consequences for Turkey, on many different levels and with varying degrees of complexity. The most obvious of these is the influx of refugees. Like Lebanon and Jordan, Turkey is overflowing with Syrians who have fled the war: it is estimated that one million people have escaped to Turkey, among whom 747,000 were registered as of June 2014.[9] Ankara has done well in responding to this crisis, providing refugee camps that have received the approval of the international aid community. Many of the facilities it has provided have been of a high quality, and hence expensive to set up. They are mostly full, and the majority of refugees have preferred to settle all around Turkey. Some Syrians have successfully integrated with Turkish communities, opening their own businesses, while others have eked out a marginal existence by working as low-paid day labourers or even begging. As the International Crisis Group reports, Turks have also done well in distributing aid in Syria.[10]

The refugees pose four distinct sets of problems for Ankara. The first is the sheer cost of hosting them. Turkey has expended $4 billion so far, and claims to have received $250m in contributions from various countries and UN agencies.[11] Secondly, tensions between refugees and long-time residents have increased, leading to demonstrations against the displaced Syrians and, occasionally, their eviction from homes and businesses. The influx of refugees also appears to have fostered a rise in anti-Arab sentiment, which is problematic due to the fact that some Turkish provinces bordering Syria and Iraq are home to large numbers of citizens who speak Arabic.[12] This is politically challenging for the government, as opposition to allowing more refugees in and caring for those that have arrived crosses party lines. At the beginning of the crisis, Davutoglu suggested that Ankara would be willing to accommodate no more than 100,000 refugees within Turkey's borders.[13]

Thirdly, many refugees are unlikely to go home even if there is a political settlement in Syria. Those that remain in Turkey will include both successful individuals, such as business owners and professionals, and people for whom a devastated Syria offers few options. In any event, a settlement would not imply the rapid return of refugees, and the majority of them are there to stay. Assad is well served by the displacement of part of Syria's population: if he survives the conflict, many of those who fled will never be accepted back. Fourthly, the refugees pose a security threat because they might unwittingly provide cover for the movements of ISIS fighters or agents of the Syrian government, acting as a fifth column within Turkey.

The fighting in Syria, and to a lesser extent in Iraq, has damaged Turkish trade routes, as commercial trucks can no longer traverse Syria on their way to the Gulf. While overland exports to Iraq continued, several Turkish truck drivers were kidnapped at the time of the consulate takeover by ISIS, only to be released (after ransoms were paid, according to some press reports).

The heaviest reverberation of Turkish policy on the Syrian conflict has been felt in Ankara's regional and global position. Turkey finds itself aligned with Qatar against myriad states that oppose Muslim Brotherhood organisations in the Middle East (for a variety of reasons), one of which is Syria. And Ankara's support for Jabhat al-Nusra has angered the US; during a May 2013 visit to Washington, the Obama administration confronted then-Prime Minister Erdogan over his support for the group. The relative ease with which jihadists crossed into Syria from Turkey also alarmed many of the country's other allies, leading them to question the AKP's motives. Ankara allowed wounded jihadists to use its medical facilities, and many fighters who traversed Turkey to join Jabhat al-Nusra defected to ISIS, following the latter group's victory in Mosul and declaration of an Islamic caliphate. Ironically, the open-door policy on jihadists may have contributed to the weakening of the FSA and the rise of ISIS. European and American concern over Turkey's lackadaisical approach continued to increase, especially after the May 2014 murder of three people in Brussels by a jihadist who had returned from Syria.

Ankara's relations with Washington have reached a particularly low ebb, despite the fact that the sides need each other to manage these crises. Their approaches are diametrically opposed. While Turkey's foremost concern is the removal of Assad, the US prioritises the fight against ISIS because the group threatens Iraq, which has received significant American investment and is seen as far more important than Syria. As a result, Ankara has refrained from joining the anti-ISIS coalition that includes many Middle East countries, some of which have participated in airstrikes on the group. After the Americans announced that Turkey had agreed to the use of the base at Incirlik for the attacks, they were rebuked by Ankara. This issue is particularly vexing for Washington because it is far easier to launch air-strikes on ISIS from Incirlik than from the Persian Gulf or the American base in Doha. Turkey prefers that the US establish a buffer zone in Syria, as this could be used to increase military pressure on the Assad regime.[14] The dispute came to a head when, in an unguarded moment, US Vice President Joe Biden expressed frustration with Turkey's support for jihadists (aside from ISIS) and its stoking of sectarianism in the region.[15]

Baghdadi's group has come back to haunt Ankara, and it constitutes a real threat to Turkish security. Many Turkish citizens heeded the clarion call in Syria and entered the war, often by joining Jabhat al-Nusra or ISIS.[16] Some of these fighters will one day return home, becoming an armed, dangerous and battle-hardened element of Turkish society. Advanced logistical and support networks for ISIS have sprung up all over Turkey, and are beyond government control. There is always the possibility that both they and the returned fighters will move against their own government or their opponents at home.[17] Allies of ISIS and sleeper cells set up by the group are making life uncomfortable, if not dangerous, for both anti-Assad Syrian activists and members of the international aid community based in Turkey.[18]

Then there is the question of the Turkish troops stationed near Lake Assad, who guard a tomb purported to be that of Suleiman Shah, grandfather of the Ottoman dynasty's founder. The site is around 30 kilometres inside Syria and is recognised as Turkish territory; the troops there are resupplied every two weeks.[19] After ISIS threatened the lives of the soldiers and fighting around the tomb intensified, Turkish officials engaged in a heated discussion over options to secure the site. With much of the territory around the outpost having fallen to ISIS, it is likely that the troops are now behind a blockade of sorts. It is hard to see how Turkey could resupply the soldiers without discussing the matter with the group, suggesting that Ankara may face a second hostage crisis.

Another unintended effect of the conflict is that on the Turkish political scene, which has also experienced a degree of sectarian polarisation. There has been greater alienation among Turkish Alevis, who comprise as much as 15% of the population and follow a form of Islam similar to Shi'ism (although not identical, as they are often quite liberal in their religious customs and in their approach to the role of women). Alevis have historically been mistreated by the Turkish state, and Erdogan's perceived Sunni bias in domestic politics has exacerbated their distrust of the AKP. It might be expected that they would naturally side with the oppressed Sunni majority in Syria, but growing sectarianism has meant they have instead tended to put their faith in the rhetoric coming out of Damascus.

Erdogan inflamed matters first by insinuating that the Republican People's Party (CHP), the main opposition group, was pro-Assad, primarily because of its leader's Alevi background and the fact that Alevis have consistently voted for it. Then came his pronouncement, in the wake of a March 2013 terrorist bombing in the border town of Reyhanli, that '53 Sunni citizens have been martyred'.[20] There is no precedent for such an overtly sectarian statement by any political leader, let alone a sitting prime minister, in modern Turkish history. For the time being, Erdogan has not had to pay a political price for this increased polarisation – he was elected president in August 2014 with almost 52% of the vote – but future sectarian clashes in Turkey cannot be ruled out.[21]

The Syrian conflict has so far claimed the lives of 75 Turks. They include the 53 who died in Reyhanli; two pilots in a reconnaissance plane that crashed off the coast of Syria in 2012; those killed in the occasional shelling of Turkish border towns; and a soldier and a police officer slain in an attack in Nigde Province reportedly carried out by ISIS fighters from Syria.[22]

But considering the financial costs, refugee influx, hostage crisis and causalities, Erdogan has until now succeeded in managing the internal tensions and domestic political consequences of his policy reversals. Always on the offensive, with its overwhelming control of the Turkish media and speed to capitalise on the opposition's mistakes, the AKP has dominated the narrative on Syria. The fact that the CHP has been unable to articulate a clear and consistent policy on the conflict has not helped matters. The AKP's control of all the levers of state power means that, when the narrative is about to shift against it, the government can easily impose news blackouts and issue gag orders. This was the case with the Mosul hostages, as well as the leaked recordings of Davutoglu, Fidan and other Turkish leaders discussing policy on Syria.

A far more serious consequence of the war has been the rise of the Kurds in the Middle East, which undermines one of Turkey's fundamental strategic objectives. Ankara had hoped that the Syrian Kurds would not coalesce under the leadership of the PYD. Not only has it been disappointed in this, but the region has once again witnessed a burgeoning of pan-Kurdish ideas and imagination. Despite Erdogan's risky, revolutionary attempts to negotiate and reconcile with the Kurds at home, Turkey has been eager to check the formation of another autonomous Kurdish territory in the region, modelled on that in Iraq.

Ankara failed in its efforts to prevent the emergence of the PYD as the most important Syrian–Kurdish group. The PYD militia had been trained by the PKK well in advance of the Syrian civil war, and it refused to join the Barzani-inspired Syrian–Kurdish National Congress, which was formally part of the Syrian opposition. Moreover, it stated its intent to declare an autonomous region in northern Syria composed of three 'cantons', perhaps heralding the shape of things to come in a post-Assad era. Turkey's response was to accuse the PYD of collaborating with the Assad regime, and to dismiss attacks on the group by Jabhat al-Nusra. Ankara naturally sided with Barzani, who saw the PYD as a rival in the struggle for supremacy among the Kurds.[23] That contest even led the KRG to begin construction on a trench between its territory and that controlled by the PYD, despite the fact that many Syrian Kurds took refuge in the former area at the height of the jihadist attacks.

The advance of ISIS during summer 2014 radically changed the situation on the ground. After the group routed the Iraqi army in Mosul and elsewhere, it proceeded to attack the KRG forces that had been dispatched to fill the void. Unprepared, badly led and poorly equipped, the peshmerga faced defeat. In Sinjar Province and later in the town of Amerli, Yazidis and Turkmen Shi'ites were forced to flee ISIS. The group executed many Yazidis, whom it saw as devil worshippers, and sold women into slavery. As the outside world learnt the plight of these refugees, especially those on Mount Sinjar, the US engaged in limited air-strikes, but both the PYD and the PKK were instrumental in lifting the siege.

The outcome of these and other battles involving the PYD and the PKK, who worked in tandem with regular peshmerga units, has dramatically altered the strategic picture for the Kurds. Syrian and Turkish Kurds who came to fight were also joined by units from the Iranian–Kurdish forces based in the KRG, which have been inactive for most of the last decade. This moment of solidarity rekindled the Kurds' sense of unity and national purpose. Given their internecine feuding in recent decades, this rejuvenation should be viewed with caution. However, in an apparent attempt to move past such antagonism, Barzani travelled all the way to Makhmour, a town in the KRG proper at which the PYD and other Kurdish forces had repelled ISIS. He and some of his lieutenants had been critical of Erdogan's refusal to help the KRG during the onslaught by ISIS, and he used the opportunity to pointedly thank the Iranians for their help in the fight against the group.[24]

First in Sinjar and then in Kobane, the PYD received an important boost from Washington, as limited cooperation in the former battle blossomed into an alliance of sorts. Mindful of the Turkish reaction, the US initially hesitated to engage in the defence of Kobane. But it changed tack following the spirited efforts of PYD forces there, the international mobilisation to save the town and, most importantly, the emergence of an opportunity to inflict significant damage on ISIS, which in its zeal to capture Kobane concentrated many of its fighters and much materiel.[25] Cooperation between Washington and the PYD assumed a more formal dimension after the Americans began to rely on the group for targeting information as they stepped up air-strikes. In an even more dramatic move, the US carried out airdrops for the PYD, bringing it arms and materiel provided by the Iraqi–Kurdish authorities. This came about despite a strong warning from Erdogan, who stated that the PKK and the PYD were terrorist organisations, and that he could not understand why a NATO ally would supply arms to such a group.[26]

These developments have two sets of consequences for Turkey. Firstly, even if the momentum towards greater acceptance of the PYD is reversible, the fact is that both the group and its parent organisation are in a far better political position than they were at the onset of the crisis. The defence of Kobane has won the respect of many in the region and further afield, and once again raised questions about the Kurds' role in the international arena. This improves the PKK's bargaining position with the Turks. More importantly, it strengthens the PYD's claim for autonomy in a post-Assad Syria. The group will have the Iraqi Kurds on its side as well. Barzani may have little sympathy for the PYD, but he has to contend with Kurdish public opinion.

Secondly, in the aftermath of the Iraqi army's withdrawal, the Kurds took over territories that had been contested by Erbil and Baghdad since the 2005 adoption of the new Iraqi Constitution, including the oil-rich city of Kirkuk and its environs. The document called for the normalisation of these territories, which Baghdad controlled but the KRG claimed, by reversing the gerrymandering of former President Saddam Hussein (carried out to reduce Kurdish population proportions in certain areas), before holding referendums at the end of 2007. Neither of these conditions was met, but the Kurds are unlikely to withdraw from the territories anytime soon. This is another setback for Turkey, which in the past has drawn a 'red line' at Kirkuk's acquisition by the Kurds. Access to Kirkuk's hydrocarbon resources appears to have put the KRG in a far stronger position to declare independence, should it choose to do so, but relations between Ankara and the Iraqi–Kurdish government have significantly improved since Turkey declared that red line. In fact, the Turks sided with Erbil against Baghdad in the dispute over Kurdish oil revenues, drilling and exports. While independence was still an outcome far too problematic for Turkey to accept – mainly because of the demonstration effect on Turkish Kurds – Ankara's attitude towards the Iraqi Kurds had undergone a transformation. However, the events that followed the ISIS attacks this year undermined even the strong Turkey–KRG relationship.

The ISIS advance in northern Iraq and Kobane mobilised the Turkish Kurds in support of their brethren across the border. Violent demonstrations broke out in Turkey as the government and the Kurds once again exchanged fiery rhetoric. And even before this, the peace process undertaken by Ankara had moved slowly, burdened by a busy electoral calendar. The fear in Turkey is not that the Turkish Kurds will demand independence, but rather that they will seek some kind of autonomy in provinces that have a Kurdish majority. That prospect elicited an unusual warning from Necdet Ozel, chief of the armed forces' general staff, during a 30 August 2014 celebration of the victory over Allied armies in the Turkish War of Independence. Ozel invoked vague red lines, widely assumed to have been drawn at Kurdish autonomy, which if crossed would provoke some undefined response by the army.[27]

If Kobane falls, the peace process in Turkey could swiftly collapse. The siege, Turkish reluctance to help out and the violent demonstrations have deepened the divisions between the Turks and the Kurds.[28] The latter have been embittered by Ankara's acrimonious rhetoric against the PKK, which has gone so far as to equate the group with ISIS. Still, Erdogan calculates that Kurds have few options other than to work with him and his party, given that the CHP has failed to develop a strategy that attracts Kurdish support.

Finally, the Iraqi Kurds have benefited from increased international awareness of the problems they face: Germany, France and Britain have all pledged arms shipments to Erbil, to improve its position vis-à-vis ISIS.

## Damage limitation

Where does Turkey go from here? Although the Mosul hostage crisis was successfully resolved, the country's room for manoeuvre is severely restricted. The Suleiman Shah tomb remains a potential flashpoint; the new government in Baghdad could prove to be beneficial to Ankara in the medium term, but not immediately. Americans and Europeans have been alienated by Turkey's reluctance to join the coalition (of sorts) against ISIS established at the September 2014 NATO summit. This is not to say that Ankara has not helped, as it has allowed the US to conduct intelligence flights from Incirlik.[29] As the ISIS threat comes into focus, the US and its allies will increasingly pressure other states to be more proactive in the fight against the group. Irrespective of the need to collaborate in Syria and elsewhere, however, there has been a deep rupture in Turkish–American relations. As well as making it harder for jihadists to cross over into Syria, Turkey has started to respond to American pressure by disrupting smuggling that finances ISIS activities, especially that involving oil.[30]

Ankara has decided to limit the damage caused by discord with the US, stating disingenuously that Turkey advocated the American bombing of ISIS.[31] One should not underestimate the impact of the US decision to resupply PYD forces in Kobane; it is perhaps the first time that Washington has broken so dramatically with Ankara on a matter relating to Kurds. Erdogan has had a difficult time accepting US action.[32] However, following the US resupply decision, Turkey abruptly announced that it would allow the Iraqi peshmerga to cross into Syria from its own territory, in order to help break the siege. (Washington had earlier made this demand of the Turks, only to be turned down.[33])

Once a symbol of Davutoglu's 'zero problems with neighbours' policy, Syria has become a graveyard for Turkish ambitions of regional hegemony. Not only has Assad confounded the AKP by surviving, but the conflict in Syria and Iraq has deprived Ankara of an important claim: that it alone has the ability to shape and influence both the Arab Spring and developments in the wider region. Speaking before parliament in 2012, Davutoglu self-assuredly argued that Turkey would own, lead and serve the new Middle East.[34] Instead, as Turkey's coordinating governor in charge of Syrians said,

> there was once one enemy in Syria, but there are now three enemies [the Assad regime, the PYD and al-Qaeda affiliates]. Until one or two years ago, there was an oppressor regime and a people seeking their rights. Now … we no longer know where the bullet comes from.[35]

The Turkish dream of a sphere of shared prosperity is clearly not achievable in the immediate future.

In the meantime, the Syrian and Iraqi crises not only remind people of the instability and danger of Turkey's neighbourhood, but also that the prospect of violence spreading to the country is quite real. The one silver lining for the Turks is that they and the Iranians have managed to agree to disagree, despite the high stakes and their opposed interests in concluding scenarios for Syria.

How much longer can Turkey manage the twin crises on its borders? And will Ankara reach breaking point as it is squeezed by the refugee problem, pressure from allies, loss of stature and the Kurdish issue? The Turkish leadership faces the real danger that, contrary to its interests, these factors will combine with ISIS-generated violence in Turkey to draw the country into the morass across the border. For all the importance Ankara has attached to Syria, it has been unable to generate a long-term strategy that includes cooperation with the US and other Western states. Instead, it has relied on Qatar and, to a lesser extent, the KRG. In part, this has to do with their fundamentally different approaches to the issue of Islamic militancy. Ankara is seen as being too sympathetic to some of these groups, and as a result has poor relations with Egypt and Saudi Arabia.

One aspect of Turkey's problem is domestic. Erdogan's unchallenged rule has made the country less flexible because his government is deeply suspicious of its Western allies and feels betrayed by them. But for all the acrimony generated by the Syrian conflict, Turkey remains a central player. Although neither Washington nor European capitals can ignore this fact, the tension between them and Ankara is likely to continue for a long time, as the effect of the war will be felt far more deeply in Turkey than in the West, and there does not seem to be a magical bullet to rid the Middle East of Assad. Ankara has few choices but to rebuild its relationship with Washington before together seeking a region-wide consensus on the next steps, which will undoubtedly put the fight against ISIS before efforts to depose the Syrian president. For Turkey, this will be hard to swallow. Erdogan will, to paraphrase Churchill, try everything else before sitting down with the US and the rest of his allies.

# Notes

[1] Murat Yetkin, 'Türkiye'nin ISID'i VurduguGün', *Radikal*, 25 September 2014, http://www.radikal.com.tr/yazarlar/murat_yetkin/turkiyenin_isidi_vurdugu_gun-1214673. There may be more to this deal than has yet been made public.

[2] Sam Jones and Daniel Dombey, 'Western Focus Turns to Home-grown Jihadis as Terror Threat Grows', *Financial Times*, 6 June 2014, http://www.ft.com/cms/s/0/cf5b3b6a-ed84-11e3-8a1e-00144fe-abdc0.html.

[3] Cole Bunzel, 'Understanding the Islamic State (of Iraq and al-Sham)', Norwegian Peacebuilding Resource Center, 8 July 2014, http://www.peacebuilding.no/Regions/Middle-East-and-North-Africa/Publications/Understanding-the-Islamic-State-of-Iraq-and-al-Sham.

[4] Guillaume Perrier, 'Pourchassés Par les Rebelles Syriens, les Djihadistes se Réfugient en Turquie', *Le Monde*, 11 January 2014. Perrier interviewed two jihadists from Britain, whose scheduled transfer to Syria in an IHH ambulance was cancelled at the last minute. In December 2013, the Turkish gendarmerie stopped 35 trucks belonging to the organisation on their way to Syria. Although they were laden with munitions, the group claimed that the vehicles contained humanitarian aid. The Turkish press also revealed that the MIT was implicated in smuggling operations. This last charge became a focal point for domestic polemic, as the pro-Erdogan press levelled charges of treason and other crimes at the president's enemies, who included prosecutors, police officers and rival press organisations.

[5] Henri J. Barkey, 'Turkey and Iraq: The Making of a Partnership', *Turkish Studies*, vol. 12, no. 4, December 2011.

[6] 'Turkey "Urges" US to Permit KRG Oil Sales', *Hürriyet*, 14 August 2014, http://www.hurriyetdailynews.com/turkey-urges-us-to-permit-krg-oil-sales.aspx?pageID=238&nID=70438&NewsCatID=348.

[7] On Turkish–Iranian relations, see Henri J. Barkey, 'Turkish–Iranian Competition after the Arab Spring', *Survival*, vol. 54, no. 6, December 2012–January 2013. In October 2014, Erdogan lashed out at Ayatollah Ali Khamenei for arguing that Assad was the only leader standing up to Israel. 'Erdogan'ın Marmara Universitesi Konusma Metni!', *Gazetesiz*, 14 October 2014, http://www.gazetesiz.com/haber_yazdir.php?detayID=106208.

[8] Interview with Murat Ozçelik, former Turkish ambassador to Baghdad and Turkey's special Iraq representative. Cansu Camlibel, 'Murat Ozçelik: Irak'ta Seyirciyiz', *Hürriyet*, 18 August 2014.

[9] Soner Cagaptay and Bilge Menekse, 'The Impact of Syria's Refugees on Southern Turkey', Washington Institute for Near East Policy, July 2014, p. 1, http://www.washingtoninstitute.org/policy-analysis/view/the-impact-of-syrias-refugees-on-southern-turkey.

[10] International Crisis Group, 'The Rising Costs of Turkey's Syrian Quagmire', 30 April 2014, pp. 13–14, http://www.crisisgroup.org/

en/regions/europe/turkey-cyprus/
turkey/230-the-rising-costs-of-
turkey-s-syrian-quagmire.aspx.

11 Cagaptay and Menekse, 'The Impact
of Syria's Refugees on Southern
Turkey', p. 2. The Turkish interior
minister said 'we spent $4 billion,
the UN has spent $160 million on
aid [in Syria] and other countries
in total spent $244 million on aid'.
'Turkey Calls on World to Help
with Syrian Refugees', Anadolu
Agency, 29 September 2014, http://
www.aa.com.tr/en/turkey/397164-
-turkey-calls-on-world-to-help-
with-syrian-refugees.    Erdogan
claimed that Turkey received only
$250   million.   'Cumhurbaskani
Erdogan: 'Bati'nin Derdi Petrol',
Aksam, 23 October 2014. However,
the UNHCR budget for 2012–14
alone shows an expenditure of $450
million. UNHCR, 'Turkey', http://
www.unhcr.org/528a0a34a.html.

12 Pinar    Tremblay,    'Anti-Arab
Sentiment on Rise in Turkey',
Al-Monitor, 21 August 2014, http://
www.al-monitor.com/pulse/
originals/2014/08/turkey-syria-anti-
arab-sentiment-tremblay.html.

13 'AFAD:   Suriyeli   Siginmacilarin
Sayisi 100 Bini Gecti', T24, 15
October   2012,   http://t24.com.tr/
haber/afad-suriyeli-siginmacilarin-
sayisi-100-bini-gecti,215242.

14 'Basbakan Davutoglu, Türkiye'nin
Istedigi    Güvenli    Bölgenin
Sinirlarini Açikladi', Hürriyet, 16
October 2014, http://www.hurriyet.
com.tr/dunya/27394703.asp.    The
US responded that it would not
contemplate such action.

15 Tolga Tanis, 'Joe Biden: Erdogan
Bana "Siz Hakliydiniz" Dedi',
Hürriyet, 4 October 2014. Although

Biden had to apologise to Erdogan
for his comments – primarily
because he had cited the Turkish
leader admitting to this support
– the fact remains that the vice president simply stated on the record a
fact known to all.

16 There may be as many as 1,000
Turks fighting among the ranks
of ISIS. Ceylan Yeginsu, 'ISIS
Draws a Steady Stream of Recruits
from Turkey', New York Times,
15 September 2014, http://www.
nytimes.com/2014/09/16/world/
middleeast/turkey-is-a-steady-
source-of-isis-recruits.html.

17 There have already been clashes
between pro-ISIS groups and
university students in Istanbul, who
were protesting against the organisation's actions in Syria. 'Istanbul
Universitesi'nde ISID Karsiti Standa
Saldiri', CNN-Turk, 26 September
2014.

18 Liz Sly, 'Attempted Kidnapping
in Turkey Shows Reach of the
Islamic State', Washington Post, 22
October 2014, http://www.washing-
tonpost.com/world/middle_east/
kidnapping-of-abu-issa-a-syrian-
rebel-shows-islamic-states-
reach-into-turkey/2014/10/21/
aac04b3b-a0a7-4f34-a0b4-faf9c-
249ce5e_story.html.   Some   aid
organisations have sought to relo-
cate staff away from the border
towns due to ISIS surveillance.

19 The tomb's real origin has been
questioned by some historians. See
Ayse Hür, 'Süleyman Sah Türbesi
hakkinda   Yanlis   Bildiklerimiz',
Radikal, 24 August 2014, http://www.
radikal.com.tr/yazarlar/ayse_hur/
suleyman_sah_turbesi_hakkinda_
yanlis_bildiklerimiz-1208616.    The

tomb was actually moved because its prior location was flooded due to the Syrian's construction of a dam on the Euphrates. The tomb was recognised as Turkish territory by the French Mandate authorities, as part of the 1921 Ankara Agreement. It is unclear how many Turkish soldiers are now stationed there. Hür claimed 11, the International Crisis Group claimed 25 and some news sources have suggested that, while there were 15 before the onset of the civil war, the number has since been increased. See 'Caber Kalesi'nde Türk Askeri Sayisi Artirildi', *Bugün*, 20 July 2014, http://gundem.bugun.com.tr/turk-asker-inin-sayisi-artirildi-haberi/200383. In a leaked conversation at the foreign ministry, Fidan said that 22–8 soldiers were stationed at the tomb. 'Suriye'ye Savas Hazirligi Yapilan Konusmanin Tam Metni', *Karsi Gazete*, 28 March 2014.

20  'Erdogan'dan Sünni Vurgusu', *Taraf*, 15 June 2013, http://www.taraf.com.tr/haber-erdogan-dan-sunni-vurgusu-126288/.

21  Nick Tattersall and Orhan Coskun, 'Erdogan's Presidential Win Starts Race for New Turkish Government', Reuters, 10 August 2014, http://www.reuters.com/article/2014/08/10/us-turkey-election-idUSKBN0GA05X20140810.

22  Although Turkish officials claimed that the plane had been shot down, circumstances surrounding the event remain murky at best. According to a former senior Turkish official, it is quite possible that the plane came down as a result of a risky manoeuvre by the pilot.

23  Wladimir van Wilgenburg, 'Rival Kurdish Parties Battle for Power in Syria', Al-Monitor, 28 May 2014, http://www.al-monitor.com/pulse/ru/originals/2014/05/kurdistan-kdp-pyd-erbil-barzani-ocalan-syria.html#.

24  Hevidar Ahmed, 'Senior Kurdistan Official: IS Was at Erbil's Gates; Turkey Did Not Help', 16 August 2014, http://rudaw.net/english/interview/16092014; Isabel Coles, 'Iran Provided Weapons to Iraqi Kurds; Baghdad Bomb Kills 12', Reuters, 27 August 2014, http://uk.reuters.com/article/2014/08/26/uk-iraq-security-kurds-idUKK-BN0GQ0UL20140826.

25  Helene Cooper, 'U.S. Commander Reports Heavy ISIS Losses in Syrian City of Kobani', *New York Times*, 17 October 2014, http://www.nytimes.com/2014/10/18/world/middleeast/isis-isil-islamic-state-kobani-syria.html. General Lloyd Austin said that the Kurdish defenders had done 'a yeoman's work in terms of standing their ground'.

26  'Cumhurbaskani Erdogan: "PYD Bizim İçin PKK Ile Estir"', *Hürriyet*, 20 October 2014.

27  'Necdet Ozel: Kirmizi Cizgiler Asilirsa Geregini Yapariz', *Radikal*, 30 August 2014.

28  Rusen Cakir, '(IS)ID'in Türkiye'ye Ettigi ve Edebilecegi Kötülükler', *Vatan*, 8 October 2014, http://www.gazetevatan.com/rusen-cakir-684867-yazar-yazisi--is-id-in-turkiye-ye-ettigi-ve-edebi-lecegi-kotulukler/.

29  Tolga Tanis, 'Sorun Askeri Degil Ideolojik', *Hürriyet*, 19 October 2014, http://sosyal.hurriyet.com.tr/Yazar/197/Tolga-Tanis/77867/Sorun-askeri-degil-ideolojik.

Paradoxically, the US had flown such intelligence-gathering missions from Incirlik at Turkey's request, to monitor the PKK in Iraq.

30  Daniel Dombey, 'Turkey's Clampdown on Isis Bearing Fruit in Border Areas', *Financial Times*, 3 September 2014, http://www.ft.com/cms/s/0/910e190c-3363-11e4-9607-00144feabdco.html.

31  Verda Ozer, 'A Conversation with the Deputy Prime Minister', *Hürriyet*, 18 October 2014, http://www.hurriyetdailynews.com/a-conversation-with-the-deputy-prime-minister.aspx?pageID=449&nID=73135&NewsCatID=466.

32  In a presentation in Paris one week after the resupply operation, he continued to criticise Washington's decision. 'Cumhurbaskani Erdogan'dan Paris'te Onemli Aciklamalar', *Hürriyet*, 31 October 2014.

33  Tolga Tanis, '10 Soruda Kobani Silahlari', *Hürriyet*, 20 October 2014, http://sosyal.hurriyet.com.tr/Yazar/197/Tolga-Tanis/79146/10-soruda-Kobani-silahlari.

34  'Yeni Ortadogu'nun Sahibi Biziz', *Vatan*, 27 April 2012, http://www.gazetevatan.com/-yeni-ortadogu-nun-sahibi-biziz--446394-gundem/.

35  'Turkey Says ISIL Convoy Hit Necessary as "Threat Comes Near Us"', *Today's Zaman*, 2 February 2014, http://www.todayszaman.com/newsDetail_openPrintPage.action?newsId=338305.

This essay was first published in the December 2014–January 2015 issue of *Survival*.

# CHAPTER FIVE

# Jordan: Caught in the Middle Again

## Ben Fishman

Since the outbreak of civil war in Syria, Jordan has been contending with a flood of Syrian refugees, straining an already beleaguered economy. Moreover, the rapid spread of the Islamic State of Iraq and al-Sham (ISIS) across Iraq has substantially increased Jordan's vulnerability to extremist infiltration and terrorist attacks. All this while, King Abdullah has continued to champion a reform programme – at least in name – to address Jordan's most salient political and economic vulnerabilities following the Arab uprisings of 2011. So the last thing that Jordan needed this summer was a war between Hamas and Israel in Gaza.

Of all these problems, none threatened to expose more of Jordan's internal vulnerabilities than a brutal, extended battle between Hamas and Israel, with daily images of Palestinian children slain by Israeli bombs. Such conflict brings to the surface the distance between the monarchy and its supporters on the one hand and Jordanians of Palestinian descent on the other. Not all Palestinian-Jordanians support Hamas, and Jordan itself has no official ties to the group, though the king or his emissaries maintain contacts with the Hamas leadership. But certainly, when forced to confront the unpopular Israeli–Jordanian peace treaty or the monarchy's close relations with Israel's leaders, the sympathies of the Jordanian public lie strongly with the Palestinian people.

In other words, if Jordan can manage the tension between government and public views on the Israeli–Palestinian conflict, it should be able to continue handling the ongoing spillover challenges of the Syrian civil war. These include the growing security threats stemming from ISIS, as well as Jordan's overt participation in the as-yet not-fully-defined coalition against ISIS fighters in Iraq and Syria. Weathering the storm will, however, require King Abdullah's sustained leadership in two key areas: maintaining high levels of support for Jordan within the international community, particularly the United States, the Gulf Cooperation Council (GCC) and the IMF; and ensuring the continued progress of political and economic reforms when the regime's natural instinct will be to use security threats as justification for halting such reforms. As long as the Israeli–Palestinian conflict remains in relative remission, Jordan should be able to withstand the serious but manageable challenges imposed by the Syrian civil war and by economic pressures at home. The system could easily be overwhelmed, however, with the resumption of Israeli–Palestinian clashes in Gaza or Jerusalem, or an active diplomatic fight over Palestinian recognition at the UN.

## Direct spillover effects

Most people think of the Jordanian refugee problem in Syria as being confined to the massive refugee camp at Zaatari in the far north of the country. In reality, less than 20% of Syrian refugees in Jordan live in refugee camps, according to United Nations (UN) statistics. As of early October, the UN had registered 619,000 refugees in Jordan, out of an estimated 3 million total refugees from Syria in the region. Of those, around 100,000 live in Jordan's refugee camps, including approximately 80,000 in Zaatari and 14,000 in Azraq, where a camp with a planned capacity of around

130,000 was opened in late April of this year.[1] In effect, five times as many Syrian refugees live outside the camps as inside them, which places great strain on Jordan's economy – equivalent to that which would accompany a sudden population increase of 10–20%. The refugees require education and health services and increase the cost of energy and real estate, as well as the competition for jobs. This dynamic does not just play out in Jordan's northern governorates but also in Amman itself. The kingdom also believes that many more Syrian refugees (as many as 800,000) are living in Jordan without registering with the UN.

The fact that Jordan has managed this crisis so well – mostly without violence – is a testament to the Jordanian people's resolve and flexibility, as well as to the capacity and responsiveness of the central government in Amman. The government also benefits from the assistance of a wide range of humanitarian organisations and, most importantly, Jordan's allies in the international community.

Beyond the challenges posed by Syrian refugees, Jordan's primary security concern related to the civil war before the rise of ISIS had been a potential direct confrontation with Syria's armed forces. To that end, in summer 2013 the US military deployed *Patriot* air-defence missile batteries, a detachment of F-16s and a unit officially called CENTCOM Forward – Jordan to advance and integrate defence planning with Jordan's armed forces.[2] But as ISIS grew in strength and blitzed across Iraq in summer 2014, Jordan's threat prioritisation changed in light of the long border it now shared with the so-called 'Islamic caliphate'. On the same day that US and coalition forces acknowledged the first air-strikes against ISIS in Syrian territory, Jordan's official news agency announced that the Royal Jordanian Air Force 'destroyed a number of selected targets used by terrorist groups to dispatch their members for terrorist attacks in the Kingdom'.[3] The September strike was the first time that Jordan publicly acknowledged attacking ISIS fighters, though at least one earlier unacknowledged strike in April was widely suspected to have been carried out against ISIS and not the Syrian military.[4]

Aside from worries about external ISIS attacks against Jordanian territory, the threat of domestic extremism with potential links to ISIS remains a serious concern. Abu Musab al-Zarqawi, a native Jordanian, founded al-Qaeda in Iraq (the precursor to ISIS) and initiated its especially brutal tactics. Zarqawi was implicated in multiple plots against the Hashemite Kingdom before US forces killed him in a 2006 air-strike in Iraq. For Jordan, however, the priority will almost certainly be monitoring and penetrating domestic extremist groups who would be naturally inclined to ally with ISIS and would benefit from its resources and training to carry out attacks against the monarchy. Of particular concern for the government is the restive southern city of Ma'an, which has long hosted a population of anti-government activists and criminals, a minority of whom displayed the ISIS banner at small protests in June.[5] Nationwide, Jordan is attempting to launch an anti-radicalisation strategy, reportedly adopted in August. The scheme includes an effort to close several thousand unregulated mosques[6] and the release of prominent Salafi clerics who have condemned ISIS's tactics from prison.[7] In more traditional cases, terror suspects will almost certainly be arrested; as many as 60 suspects were reportedly imprisoned in September and October.[8] Finally, King Abdullah has spoken out forcefully against ISIS, saying in a September speech at the UN that the group does not represent the ideals and principles of Islam: 'The teachings of true Islam are clear: sectarian conflict and strife are utterly condemned. Islam prohibits violence against Christians and other communities that make up each country.'[9]

So far, it appears that ISIS's priority relates far less to Jordan and much more to consolidating its gains within Syria and Iraq, especially now that it has to defend against US and coalition air-strikes and somewhat revived Iraqi and Kurdish forces. But as the group's strategy evolves, ISIS may turn more towards supporting underground terrorism rather than seeking to seize and control territory. In such circumstances, Jordan would be high on the list of potential targets.

## Mitigating spillover through allies

At their February 2014 meeting at Sunnylands estate in Palm Springs, California, US President Barack Obama hailed King Abdullah and the bilateral relationship between the United States and Jordan. It is worth noting that the White House doesn't just give away private conferences at Sunnylands; Obama last used the estate to host his first meeting with President Xi Jinping of China. The president also travelled to Jordan, the only country on the border with Syria aside from Israel that he has visited, in 2013. As the president said at Sunnylands: 'I think it's fair to say that we have very few friends, partners and allies around the world that have been as steadfast and reliable as His Majesty King Abdullah.'[10]

Practically, the president used the meeting to announce a $1 billion loan guarantee for Jordan following a $1.25bn guarantee in 2013.[11] He also announced a five-year renewal of Jordan's direct bilateral assistance package, totalling nearly $700m per year, including military and economic aid (which is often supplemented further by support for special projects).[12] It is mainly due to King Abdullah's effective relationships with both the executive branch and Congress that Jordan has positioned itself as one of the most reliable – and thus indispensable – US allies in an increasingly unpredictable region. Those bilateral relationships transcend political ties and permeate the professional contacts between the American military and the Jordanian Armed Forces as well as the US intelligence community and the General Intelligence Directorate (GID), Jordan's intelligence arm and secret police.

If Jordan's primary ally in facing the Syria crisis is the United States, the GCC is close behind, especially in the form of Saudi Arabia and the United Arab Emirates (UAE). In 2011, the GCC pledged $5bn in aid to Jordan over five years. This package is supplemented by additional assistance from Saudi Arabia and the UAE that is not publicly disclosed, but which is intended to help support the needs of the Hashemite regime in the wake of the Arab Spring. These funds can now be assumed to be at least partially directed towards Jordan's security needs. Similarly, as the Saudis and Emiratis view Jordan in the context of their regional power struggle with the Muslim Brotherhood, Jordan is certain to seek additional financial resources from its Gulf patrons in exchange for a tougher stance against the group's Jordanian branch.

This assistance, both from the US and the GCC, is intended to help offset Jordan's perennial economic challenges, which were aggravated by increased social spending following the Arab Spring. The subsequent loss of cheap Egyptian gas due to political instability and the ensuing violence in Sinai, which effectively closed the pipeline feeding Jordan, further exacerbated the country's already ballooning budget deficit.

Jordan began taking corrective measures when it realised its debt was unsustainable and could not be covered by foreign aid alone. In August 2012, it signed a $2.1bn loan agreement with the IMF, establishing the basis for an economic-reform agenda that principally targeted widely popular but unaffordable subsidies. Jordan subsequently eliminated gasoline subsidies in November 2012 despite several days of violent rioting. Reductions to electricity subsidies began in January 2014. Other intended reform measures include cutting government expenditures (including, for the first time, the military budget), reforming the income-tax system to help raise revenues and investing in energy diversification. In April 2014, the IMF gave Jordan mostly high marks in the third and fourth reviews of its country programme, which the

IMF reported was 'broadly on track'.[13] Future reviews will focus on tax reform and administration. Over the long term, Jordan's best chance for economic recovery and overcoming its reliance on imports for 95% of its energy may be a provisionally agreed 15-year deal with Israel. This arrangement would allow Jordan to purchase $15bn worth of gas from the companies operating the Leviathan field off the Israeli coast. Though Jordan is also raising funds to invest in renewable energy sources, the mammoth gas deal would go much further in providing a reliable energy source to the country's heavily indebted national electricity company. The success of this arrangement will depend, however, on whether the importation of Israeli gas can be navigated through Jordan's sensitive domestic politics.[14]

Jordan has a series of additional donors, including the European Union and the World Bank, but King Abdullah is principally dependent on the US, the GCC and the IMF to survive the crisis in Syria. So far he has managed the crisis admirably, just as King Hussein shepherded the kingdom through decades of domestic and regional turmoil.

## Balancing reform with security

The natural instinct for Jordan's leadership when facing an external crisis with the potential to destabilise the kingdom or pose security threats is to limit public freedoms, increase the authority of the GID and return to old habits of paying the regime's most ardent supporters to enforce public order. However, because of the king's stated commitment to political and economic reform, he must maintain a delicate balance between a purported desire to pursue such reforms and a conflicting impulse, reinforced by his most conservative advisers, to prioritise stability and security over reform. How the king navigates this balance will go a long way towards determining how Jordan manages the threats posed by the Syrian civil war.

In an August 2014 interview with Jordanian newspaper *Al Ghad*, King Abdullah was presented with this very question – did he intend to slow down Jordan's reform process due to regional challenges, or would he press forward? Abdullah insisted that he would remain undeterred and would move ahead with reforms:

> Every time I am faced with a similar question my answer is always and unequivocally the same: we will not allow using difficult regional challenges – be they the Israeli aggression on Gaza, the conflict in Syria, the turmoil in Iraq or the danger of extremism – as an excuse to hesitate or regress in the reform drive. This is what I believe in – in deeds and words. The media should genuinely believe in our determination to move ahead with reform and must stop promoting any excuses arguing for a halt in reforms.[15]

For Abdullah, the objectives of reform in Jordan have remained relatively consistent, at least in name. They were demonstrated most concretely in January 2013, when parliamentary elections were supervised for the first time by an independent election commission that received very high marks from international observers. The king also repeatedly stresses his commitment to working toward 'parliamentary democracy' in Jordan and notes that the monarchy he inherited will not be the same one that the crown prince will inherit from him. However, the commitment to reform seemed to wane during the course of 2013 and early 2014, especially following the lacklustre turnout for the August 2013 municipal elections, which were supervised by the interior ministry rather than the independent election commission.

The king has proven adept at specifying key reform goals, such as decentralisation to improve local government, strengthening public-administration performance, developing political parties into blocs with concrete platforms and addressing public corruption. Many of these reform targets were established by a National Integrity Commission in early 2013. The problem, however, remains a lack of confidence in the monarchy's commitment to the actual implementation process. The key for Jordan lies not in producing all of these changes at once, but in making slow but steady progress towards concrete reform goals. This will ensure that the population can detect genuine overarching advancement towards the king's 'parliamentary democracy' target. Yet evidence of backsliding on reform initiatives also persists in several areas, most recently in approved amendments to the anti-terrorism law, widely criticised by human-rights and free-speech organisations.[16] Prior press laws targeting Internet publications, difficulties in registering civil-society organisations and a recent proposal to place the appointment and oversight of the GID and military chiefs solely in the hands of the king speak to the same pattern.

For Abdullah, little incentive to lead on reform exists outside of domestic or international pressure to do so. As such, he must have been somewhat encouraged by the results of a December 2013 poll conducted by the International Republican Institute. The report found that fewer Jordanians felt the country was headed in the wrong direction than six months earlier; it also found that Jordanians credited improved security and stability as the primary reason they believed Jordan was headed in the right direction.[17] And yet the same poll showed that more Jordanians (48%) still feel the country is headed in the wrong direction than in the right direction (39%). Moreover, respondents in surveys almost always rank economic conditions as more important than political reform – although they are closely linked, particularly on questions where complaints about governance and corruption can easily overlap.

In sum, the more King Abdullah continues to overstate his political- and economic-reform goals without delivering on them, the more difficulty he will have retaining the stability upon which Jordan and its international backers rely. Closely tied to these political reforms will be ongoing progress towards the country's IMF targets. The latter will force unpopular short-term economic decisions, particularly on subsidy reform and tax administration. However, in the longer term, these changes will enable a more sustainable economic path that will reduce Jordan's dependence on external support and increase its capacity to generate jobs. Jordan can leverage its many friends to weather the storm from the Syrian civil war, but with no end in sight for that conflict, Abdullah also must retain his own stated reform priorities to maintain the country's long-term stability. The wild card will remain the Israeli–Palestinian conflict. Jordan can face threats on two fronts at a time – from Syria and from internal pressures – but the addition of a third could prove a significant challenge. An intensified Israeli–Palestinian conflict after the most recent Gaza war, the breakdown of the peace process, confrontations in Jerusalem (where Jordan maintains a historic role as custodian of the holy sites), or a Palestinian campaign to gain recognition at the UN could easily overload the circuits and defence mechanisms upon which Jordan has traditionally relied to preserve stability.

## Notes

[1] All data supplied by the UN Refugee Agency (UNHCR), 'Syria Regional Refugee Response: Inter-agency Information Sharing Portal', available at http://data.unhcr.org/syrian refugees/country.php?id=107. See also Elisa Oddone, 'Azraq Refugee Camp Officially Opened', *Jordan Times*, 30 April 2014, http://jordantimes.com/azraq-refugee-camp-officially-opened.

[2] Thom Shanker, 'With Eyes on Syria, U.S. Turns Warehouse Into Support Hub for Jordan', *New York Times*, 15 August 2013, http://www.nytimes.com/2013/08/16/world/middleeast/for-the-us-in-jordan-command-central-is-a-steel-warehouse.html.

[3] 'Jordan Air Force Launches Air Strikes Against Terrorist Organizations', Petra News Agency, 23 September 2014, http://www.petra.gov.jo/Public_News/Nws_NewsDetails.aspx?lang=2&site_

id=1&NewsID=166253&Type=P.

4   Omar Akour and Albert Aji, 'Jordanian Jets Strike Vehicles on Syrian Border', Associated Press, 16 April 2014, http://bigstory.ap.org/article/activists-syrian-air-strikes-kill-4-rebel-town.

5   William Booth and Taylor Luck, 'Jordan Fears Homegrown ISIS More Than Invasion from Iraq', Washington Post, 27 June 2014, http://www.washingtonpost.com/world/middle_east/jordan-fears-homegrown-isis-more-than-invasion-from-iraq/2014/06/27/1534a4ee-f48a-492a-99b3-b6cd3ffe9e41_story.html.

6   Maria Abi-Habib, 'Jordan Plans Crackdown on Unauthorized Mosques to Combat Radical Islam', Wall Street Journal, 19 September 2014, http://online.wsj.com/articles/jordan-plans-crackdown-on-unauthorized-mosques-to-combat-radical-islam-1411157776.

7   Ranya Kadri and Alan Cowell, 'Militant Cleric Acquitted of Terrorism Charges', New York Times, 24 September 2014, http://www.nytimes.com/2014/09/25/world/middleeast/abu-qatada-acquitted-on-2nd-terrorism-charge.html.

8   John Reed, 'Jordan Tackles Homegrown Islamists as It Joins Attack on ISIS', Financial Times, 5 October 2014, www.ft.com/intl/cms/s/0/08fc027c-4a29-11e4-bc07-00144feab7de.html#axzz3G4yR8iBA?siteedition=intl.

9   King Abdullah II, 'Remarks by His Majesty King Abdullah II at the Plenary Session of the 69th United Nations General Assembly', Royal Hashemite Court, 24 September 2014, http://www.kingabdullah.jo/index.php/en_US/speeches/view/id/546/videoDisplay/0.html.

10  See 'President Obama's Bilateral Meeting with His Majesty King Abdullah II of Jordan', Washington DC, 14 February 2014, http://www.whitehouse.gov/photos-and-video/video/2014/02/14/president-obamas-bilateral-meeting-his-majesty-king-abdullah-ii-jo#transcript.

11  'United States and Jordan Sign Second Loan Guarantee Agreement', USAID, 5 May 2014, http://www.usaid.gov/news-information/press-releases/may-5-2014-united-states-and-jordan-sign-second-loan-guarantee-agreement.

12  Sarah Wheaton and Mark Landler, 'Obama Promises New Aid to Jordan in Refugee Crisis', New York Times, 14 February 2014, http://www.nytimes.com/2014/02/15/us/politics/syria-is-expected-to-be-main-topic-as-obama-meets-with-king-of-jordan.html.

13  International Monetary Fund, 'IMF Country Report No. 14/152 – Jordan', June 2014, http://www.imf.org/external/pubs/ft/scr/2014/cr14152.pdf.

14  Kate Galbraith, 'Jordan Finds Energy Sources in Unlikely Places', New York Times, 17 September 2014, http://www.nytimes.com/2014/09/18/business/energy-environment/jordan-finds-energy-sources-in-unlikely-places.html.

15  Junama Ghneimat, 'Interview with His Majesty King Abdullah II', Al Ghad, 10 August 2014, http://kingabdullah.jo/index.php/en_US/

interviews/view/id/514/videoDisplay/0.html.

16 'King Urged to Repeal Draconian Changes to Anti-Terrorism Law', Reporters Without Borders, 16 June 2014, http://en.rsf.org/jordan-king-urged-to-repeal-draconian-16-06-2014,46423.html; Osama Al Sharif, 'Jordan's King Pushes to Expand Military, Intelligence Authority', *Al-Monitor*, 25 August 2014, http://www.al-monitor.com/

pulse/originals/2014/08/jordan-king-constitution-amendments.html#.

17 International Republican Institute, 'IRI Poll: Jordanians Encouraged by Stability; Concerned About High Prices and Refugee Numbers', 10 March 2014, http://www.iri.org/news-events-press-center/news/iri-poll-jordanians-encouraged-stability-concerned-about-high-prices-a.

This essay was first published in the December 2014–January 2015 issue of *Survival*.

# CHAPTER SIX

# The Gulf States in an Era of American Retrenchment

**Emile Hokayem and Becca Wasser**

Barack Obama's 2009 accession to the US presidency spurred a recalibration of American policy in the Middle East, especially the Gulf. Yet the United States adopted a strategy of retrenchment in the region due not only to Obama's world view and policy preferences, but to structural factors that suggest the subsequent adjustments will outlast his tenure in the White House. High among these drivers is a general sense in US policymaking circles that the Middle East requires and expects a disproportionate amount of time, attention, capital and other resources – all of which would be better used to promote American interests in the more promising and important Asia-Pacific.

The Gulf monarchies in particular will have to adapt to the new US posture. These states have grown accustomed to American security commitments and special privileges, acquired due to their centrality to energy markets, strategic position and general alignment with Washington in a region largely resistant to US policy. For them, Washington's new attitude and stated desire to 'pivot' to Asia – later relabelled a 'rebalance' – poses significant challenges and erodes their ability to influence US policy (regardless of whether the rebalance is feasible).

Understanding the impact of the rebalance on the strategy of the Gulf states requires an assessment of their perceptions of America's evolving global role and a rapidly changing Middle East. Indeed, the rebalance is just one of the many factors that shape the monarchies' approach to security and decision-making.

For the Gulf elites, the US government has not clearly explained the doctrinal and practical implications of the rebalance. From their perspective, such ambiguity at a time of uncertainty in the Middle East exacerbates pre-existing concerns about trends in American policy. Official and private Gulf reactions to the rebalance have been largely negative, due to their latent anxiety about the long-term American role in the region.

In reality, the US defence posture in the Middle East remains mostly unchanged, and America's commitment to the external security of its Gulf partners endures. However, Washington is less willing to automatically promote or acquiesce to the regional interests of the monarchies. This is the result of political and structural factors that have been brought into relief – rather than caused – by the current upheaval in the region, and which go beyond the Obama administration's seemingly minimalist approach to the Middle East.

As such, it is difficult to identify specific behavioural changes by the Gulf states that can be primarily, let alone solely, attributed to the US rebalance. Hedging by the monarchies has been motivated by their understanding of global and regional politics and economics, and preceded any talk of the US strategic shift to Asia. But the rebalance has given them further reason to devise more autonomous security strategies, which are sometimes at odds with American policy. Their greater assertiveness in the Middle East since 2011, and their increased investment in strategies to internationalise Gulf security, can be traced back to the limited US retrenchment.

## The dynamics of Gulf security

The politics and psychology of Gulf security have been an important element of global politics since the 1970s. The presence of regional powers with far-reaching ambitions, and the importance of Gulf energy to the global economy, has generated unusual levels of external involvement in the Middle East (with mixed results for its security). For better or worse, the US military commitment and its corresponding guarantees have served as the cornerstone of the Middle East's security architecture since the Carter Doctrine was announced, in 1980. The doctrine states that 'an attempt by any outside force to gain control of the Persian Gulf region will be regarded as an assault on the vital interests of the United States of America, and such an assault will be repelled by any means necessary, including military force'.[1]

The declaration of this security umbrella coincided with and contributed to the monarchies' development as modern states, facilitated by the massive oil revenues that they began to accrue in the 1970s. At the time, they lacked the human, military and institutional capability to defend themselves. To compensate, the Gulf states courted the West, especially the US, with the aim of establishing a regional balance of power that was beneficial to their interests.

As a result, American policy in the Middle East increasingly provided the guarantees that allowed the Gulf states to stand up to stronger rivals, especially Saddam Hussein's Iraq and Ayatollah Ruhollah Khomeini's Iran. America's protection had direct, tangible benefits: its military secured vital sea lanes in the Tanker War of the 1980s, repelled the Iraqi invasion of Kuwait in 1991, and pursued a dual containment policy that isolated both Iran and Iraq during the 1990s.

The landscape of the Middle East has multiple structural imbalances and other discrepancies that, taken together, threaten Gulf security interests. These disparities are particularly vivid in the minds of Gulf leaders. The region's geography is problematic for them: while Iran and Iraq have huge territories, the Gulf states – aside from Saudi Arabia – are small and lack strategic depth. Iran occupies the whole northern shore of the Gulf, a significant geographical advantage. Several Gulf states are only able to access shipping routes via the Strait of Hormuz, through which pass not only their oil and gas exports but also much of their food and other vital goods. Iran's ability to disrupt or even halt shipping in the strait, although sometimes exaggerated, is seen as a threat to their viability. Importantly, all their key population centres and infra-structure (such as cities, industrial plants, ports and desalination facilities) are located on the shores of the Gulf and are therefore vulnerable to external threats.

Since the 1980s, the Gulf monarchies have benefited from consid-erably higher levels of development than much of the Middle East, due to their small populations and energy wealth. However, they lack the indigenous capacity to fill many key personnel positions, especially those in the military. The combined native population of the six Gulf Cooperation Council (GCC) states is roughly one-third of that of Iran, while much of their workforce is composed of foreigners with little loyalty to the state. The results of their ambitious national-development policies will be felt in a few decades' time rather than in the short term. They are relatively young states with weak institutional and administrative capabil-ities, and they lack the military history and large forces of Iran and pre-1991 Iraq. Equally, while Iran prides itself on its national cohesion, the makeup of Gulf societies could emerge as a source of instability because of the monarchies' exclusionary policies: the sense that national projects will only benefit obedient nationals is pervasive in disenfranchised segments of society, such as the Shia communities in Saudi Arabia and Bahrain, and the *bidun* (state-less) populations in the United Arab Emirates and Kuwait.

The Gulf states differ in their measures of, and responses to, regional threats. Geography, history, self-image and intrinsic power all influence their security assessments. For Kuwait, Iraq is a considerably greater threat than Iran. Oman, in comparison, views the security environment as far more benign, due to its distance from Iraq, established relations with Iran and location outside the Gulf. Muscat is most concerned about Emirati and Saudi power, and the threat of state failure in Yemen.

The smaller Gulf states also worry about Saudi Arabia's hegemony or potential collapse, given the kingdom's sheer size, and its self-image as a Sunni and regional leader. They therefore seek arrangements that check both Saudi and Iranian influence. The most prominent advocate of this approach is Qatar, a tiny but wealthy emirate that has contentious relations with Saudi Arabia. The UAE, Kuwait and Oman disagree more subtly with the kingdom.

Such structural factors have impeded the development of the GCC into an alliance for collective security. For small, young states engaged in border disputes and other regional disagreements, it makes little sense to relinquish control to an alliance that would likely become a vehicle of Saudi power, and would struggle to provide adequate external security. Instead, bilateral relations with Western powers, especially the US, have given them disproportionate influence, and have offered greater benefits than such an alliance.

The West's security role has therefore become an essential element of regional balancing, one that makes up for the Gulf states' structural weaknesses. In this regard, the monarchies have since the 1980s been consumers rather than producers of security. This arrangement proved essential in countering Iraq, deterring Iran and maintaining the open sea lanes crucial to their economic success, as well as in facilitating their integration with the global economy. Defence relations between key Western countries and the Gulf states cover a wide range of commitments and exchanges, from arms sales and training to military bases and formal agreements. Beyond these interactions, Western military bases in the Gulf count as a tripwire in case of conflict.

From a Gulf perspective, the security umbrella has created the time and space needed to develop capabilities and responses for countering myriad regional threats. It has also allowed the monarchies to pursue policies of national development, which have included investment in infrastructure and the upgrade of their legal, banking and economic frameworks.

Over time, key Gulf states implemented a grand strategy of internationalising their security. By leveraging their wealth and diversifying and deepening strategic relationships, they sought to give major global and regional powers a stake in their own security, stability and survival. This meant entangling an ever-increasing number of influential countries in a web of beneficial economic relationships, with the expectation that this would translate into greater security. The driving idea was to pre-empt crises by securing the loyalty and goodwill of as many allies as possible, not only among traditional Arab partners and the long-standing members of the UN Security Council, but also among rising global powers. This would supplement traditional security relationships with Western countries.

This approach is fundamentally at odds with Iran's view of the Middle East. Tehran portrays the presence of external military powers in the region as the main source of instability and conflict. This depiction partly reflects Iran's profound displeasure at seeing smaller, younger states assert themselves, challenging its traditional role as the hegemon in the Gulf. For the revolutionary Khomeinist regime, which opposed the status quo, the Arab Gulf states were tolerating, if not facilitating, an existential threat from the West.

Tehran therefore sought to regionalise Gulf security through a combination of diplomatic persuasion and regional power plays.

This strategy rested on the assumption that, in the absence of foreign powers, Iran would regain its natural position of leadership. Nevertheless, Tehran was overmatched and outspent by the combination of US military power and Gulf wealth. This shifted the focus of regional competition to the more complex terrain of the Levant, where fractured societies, weak states and competition over Muslim and Arab causes (particularly the Palestinian question) created an arena for Iranian–Saudi rivalry. As a result, Iran invested in asymmetric capabilities and cultivated proxies in countries and territories experiencing civil strife, including Lebanon, Palestine and, later, Iraq and Syria.

Beyond Tehran's complaints, there has been much criticism of the Gulf states' dependency on Western powers, especially the US. The monarchies' approach is often derided as free-riding that discourages the development of realistic regional policies or adequate security responses to a volatile environment. It is blamed for deficient Gulf defence coordination and military integration, as states prioritise their bilateral relations with Western partners. And it is charged with creating unhealthy relationships in which the Gulf states purchase massive amounts of superfluous weaponry, making Western governments unable or unwilling to criticise their partners' human-rights records or alleged facilitation of Islamic extremism, out of fear that this would have significant economic costs.

## The 2003 Iraq War and the transformation of regional politics

The US invasion of Iraq in 2003, and the transformations that followed, had the unintended consequence of upending the Middle East order to Iran's benefit. The Iraqi civil war that erupted soon after the invasion altered the nature of regional competition, and quickly widened the latent Sunni–Shia divide. It also exacerbated the jihadist threat, with al-Qaeda and other radical groups finding a new cause in the heart of the Arab world.

Initially ambivalent about the US effort, Gulf leaders came to agree that it was detrimental to their interests as Washington's plans in Iraq floundered. In retrospect, the survival of the regime of Saddam Hussein in a weakened form had served a strategic purpose; its demise removed a precious bulwark against Iran. The new Shia political elites that came to power in Baghdad were both unknown and decidedly antagonistic towards the Gulf states. The civil war placed the burden of championing Iraq's disoriented Sunni community on Saudi Arabia, a role for which it was ill prepared. Riyadh ultimately failed in its attempts to counter both Tehran's allies and al-Qaeda in Iraq by influencing Iraqi politics and mobilising tribal and Sunni elements in the country. As a result, the Gulf states largely withdrew from Iraqi politics and sought to isolate the Shia-dominated government in Baghdad within the Arab world, unwittingly strengthening Tehran's hand. Iran filled the vacuum by backing established Shia allies and patiently nurturing new ones. Its strategy and connections allowed it to enter Iraqi politics and, over time, to become an indispensable power broker, recognised as such even by the US.

From the perspective of the Gulf states, Washington had been strategically foolish and operationally incompetent in its management of the Iraq crisis, as well as ineffective in preventing Iran's rise. Maintaining overt security relations with Washington was complicated by intense discontent with the US, particularly the George W. Bush administration, among Arabs throughout the Middle East. This hostility was amplified by the 2006 Israel–Hizbullah war in Lebanon, and America's rejection of the Hamas government in Palestine. In 2007 a senior Gulf official described the US as both 'toxic' and 'klutzy', an indispensable security ally but a political liability.[2]

These considerations compelled the Gulf states to diversify their political and security relationships, and to counter the perception that they were dependent on the US. Their strategy was informed by economic pragmatism and an awareness that the global centre of gravity was moving east. Starting in 2005, Gulf outreach to global and regional powers increased rapidly, partly aided by rising oil prices. Following his coronation that year, Saudi King Abdullah bin Abdulaziz Al Saud pointedly chose China as the destination of his first official visit.[3] Mohammed bin Zayed Al Nahyan, crown prince of Abu Dhabi, was welcomed by an honour guard in Beijing in 2009, after which the UAE spent lavishly on its pavilion at the 2010 Shanghai World Expo. The ascent of the city states of Dubai, Abu Dhabi and Qatar is due to their inclusion in South–South networks as much as their links to traditional Western partners. The Gulf monarchies have calcu-lated that these new relationships will augment their diplomatic power. For example, as China's main oil suppliers, Riyadh and other Gulf capitals hoped that Beijing would increase pressure on Tehran over the Iranian nuclear programme.

The Gulf states also injected new life into established alli-ances with Western partners. France opened a base in Abu Dhabi in 2009, and has enhanced its defence relations with the UAE.[4] Kuwait, Bahrain, Qatar and the UAE joined NATO's Istanbul Cooperation Initiative to broaden their security interactions with the West. Saudi Arabia declined to join, as it viewed the initiative as a diversion from the goal of GCC defence integration, while Oman declined to participate out of concern that its involvement would antagonise Iran.

Despite this new diplomatic activism, however, Gulf states recognised that the US 'remained the only game in town', in the words of one Gulf leader.[5] To regain the trust of the Gulf states, and in recognition of the fact that defence and security remained the bedrock of their relationship with Washington, the George W. Bush administration launched in 2006 a series of Middle East defence initiatives, including annual strategic conferences and the Gulf Security Dialogue.[6] The latter meeting was meant to break

America's pattern of dealing with the Gulf states bilaterally, by engaging with them in a multilateral setting with the aim of rationalising and harmonising defence decision-making, planning, operations and procurement. Washington also agreed to further arms sales to the Gulf states, which included missile-defence systems and other high-end capabilities. It introduced new forms of military-to-military cooperation, especially on counter-piracy and other maritime-security issues.

Throughout this tense period, US–Gulf partnerships were maintained by converging assessments of the Iranian threat as the most pressing challenge to regional stability. For all its faults, the George W. Bush administration could hardly be accused of weakness towards Tehran. Damaged relations between Washington and Gulf capitals were repaired by their shared alarm at the spread of Tehran's influence in the Middle East, illustrated most vividly by Hizbullah's increasing domination of Lebanon, by Iran's inroads in Iraq and by the progress of the Iranian nuclear programme. In the eyes of the Gulf states, Mahmoud Ahmadinejad's 2005 appointment as Iranian president and his provocative rhetoric proved that the country's Khomeinist ethos had endured, and that the pragmatic elements of the Iranian political elite remained weak. Accordingly, several of the monarchies quietly welcomed US efforts to sanction and isolate Iran, while continuing to favour ambiguity in their relations with Tehran. But the convergence of views was somewhat undermined by the 2007 US National Intelligence Estimate, which found that Iran had suspended all research relating to nuclear weapons four years earlier.[7]

## The Gulf states and US policy under Obama

Obama entered the White House at a pivotal moment in US–Gulf relations. The new president initiated a shift in rhetoric directed at the Arab world during both a speech in Cairo and his first interview with an Arabic news channel, but his declared priority was to extricate America from unnecessary and costly wars in the Middle East, especially that in Iraq (as he had promised to do during his election campaign). Obama believed that a decade of military intervention had left America with a limited capacity to carry out nation building and to shape the Middle East order. Indeed, the American political discourse was pervaded by weariness with the region, and the sense that Arab societies were ungrateful for sacrifices made by the US. The ambiguity of, and lack of details about, the rebalance has contributed to the widely held view among the monarchies that the Obama administration is seeking an exit from the Gulf.

Obama accelerated the withdrawal of US combat troops from Iraq in 2010, despite the 2011 deadline set by the Status of Forces Agreement. But, by April 2011, it had become clear that Washington wanted to renegotiate the agreement to retain a limited troop presence, rumoured to be around 10,000–20,000 personnel.[8] In order to secure the agreement, the Americans required Baghdad to provide the soldiers with immunity under Iraqi law. The Iraqi political elite, led by Prime Minister Nuri al-Maliki, refused to meet this condition, paving the way for a full US withdrawal by the end of 2011.[9]

To smooth the way out of Iraq, Obama reversed his predecessor's policy of isolating Syria, Iran's main Arab ally. Washington saw President Bashar al-Assad as a potential partner in dealing with various crises. American officials visited Damascus to discuss border security and counter-terrorism cooperation, and to jumpstart Israeli–Syrian peace talks. This high-profile rapprochement, led by then-Senator John Kerry, culminated in the restoration of full diplomatic ties in 2010.[10] The Gulf states continued to be frustrated by Assad's resistance to their overtures, and his enduring alliance with Tehran.

Testing diplomacy with Iran was an important aspect of Obama's Middle East policy. The US administration started to soften its rhetoric on Tehran, and to explore negotiations over the Iranian nuclear programme. A rapprochement with Iran was seen as having the potential to decisively improve the strategic landscape, and to facilitate Obama's regional agenda. After issuing a message of congratulations for Nowruz in 2009, the White House refrained from unconditionally supporting the Green Movement (which decried the fraudulent June 2009 re-election of Ahmadinejad), both out of fear of hurting its cause and to keep channels open with Tehran. There was a sense that the US was slowly recalibrating its Middle East posture, and aimed at a strategic realignment with Iran in the long term.

There was little change in policy on the Gulf, however. Obama did not take up a controversial proposal by Hillary Clinton, his first secretary of state, who during her presidential bid had floated the idea of extending a formal nuclear umbrella to the Gulf states, with the aim of deterring Iran from pursuing nuclear weapons and preventing a regional arms race.

In parallel with the Iraq withdrawal, and in preparation for the drawdown in Afghanistan, the US revised its force level in the Gulf. But this adjustment did not amount to a new defence posture, despite calls in Washington for the administration to consider a much lighter footprint in the Middle East, and even an 'over-the-horizon' deployment. The current US force structure in the Gulf consists of bases in Bahrain, Qatar, Kuwait and the UAE. There are more than 35,000 US military personnel in the region, including 10,000 forward-deployed soldiers; 40 ships, some of which form a carrier strike group; and advanced weaponry, such as F-22s, *Patriot* missile systems, and assets for intelligence, surveillance and reconnaissance. In a speech at the 2013 IISS Manama Dialogue, then-US Secretary of Defense Chuck Hagel noted that the US is enhancing its military capabilities in the Middle East. Washington has since 2007 approved arms sales to the Gulf worth approximately $75 billion, and has sought to strengthen Gulf cooperation by arranging weapons deals through the GCC rather than with individual countries.[11] As US defence architecture in the region requires the maintenance of existing facilities in the Gulf, it was unsurprising that Hagel renewed a deal with Qatar to retain the Al-Udeid Air Base, and that work began on expanding the base of the US Fifth Fleet, in Bahrain (despite calls to close the facility in the US, following Manama's 2011 crackdown on the opposition).

Yet the quality of the US–Gulf relationship appears to have changed. From the perspective of the Gulf states, Obama's obstinate focus on withdrawal from Iraq and diplomacy with Iran exacerbated the post-2003 shift in the regional balance of power. The monarchies have increased their private criticism of American foreign policy, emphasising the transactional nature of their relationship with Washington. Even as Obama rallied international support for tough UN sanctions on Iran, the Gulf states regarded America's distinctly more accommodating tone as reflecting a long-term preference for strategic realignment with Tehran. Accustomed to privileged status in Washington, Gulf officials and diplomats began to complain of diminished access to the White House, and their interlocutors' relative indifference to Gulf security matters. This, they contended, illustrated Obama's detachment from, and even dislike of, traditional Arab allies. It was unclear whether this concern was genuine or merely a rhetorical device designed to achieve a diplomatic end.

Several structural factors suggest that Washington's reduced interest in the Middle East could outlast the Obama presidency. The US policy and defence establishment continues to believe that Washington provides a global public good by ensuring a steady supply of energy from the Gulf states to the world economy, even if America's own imports from the Middle East have dwindled in recent years. As the US faces new budgetary constraints and other structural changes, however, there has been renewed scrutiny of this role, particularly its political and economic costs, and its unintended consequences.

American forces in the Gulf require significant funding. The US defence budget has doubled in the past decade, due to the 'war on terror' and the conflicts in Afghanistan and Iraq (a cost deemed necessary during the George W. Bush years).[12] Following the onset of the financial crisis in 2008, the Obama administration sought to cut defence spending, a policy reflected in the Pentagon's quadrennial defence reviews and subsequent budget reductions.

The Gulf states saw the reduced American military presence as the result of both strategic choices, such as the withdrawal from Iraq, and economic duress. In 2013 the US Department of Defense chose not to deploy a second aircraft carrier to the Gulf, anticipating $50bn in defence cuts.[13] More recently, the chief of naval operations stated that this decision was unlikely to be reversed.[14] While such revisions have no operational impact on Washington's ability to meet its security commitments, they have helped create the perception that the Gulf states are becoming less important to the US, and have raised questions about the sustainability of the American presence in the Middle East.

The 'shale-gas revolution' has also made disentanglement from the region seem more likely to many Americans, by bringing closer the much-discussed goal of US energy independence. In 2013 only around one-fifth of America's energy imports came from the Gulf.[15] This presaged another shift in dynamics: with Asian economies emerging as the main importers of Gulf oil, an expectation arose in the US and the Gulf states that the burden of providing security to sea lanes would be gradually shared with Asian powers. China and other Asian countries are often seen as free-riding on US military commitments in the Middle East, benefiting from the protection of maritime trade routes while avoiding direct political responsibility and financial costs. Indeed, the price of such protection in the Gulf is estimated to be between $86bn and $104bn per year.[16]

The announcement of the pivot to Asia typified Washington's recalibration of its global interests and policy focus. Publicly, US government officials emphasised the strategic rationale for the move, which included the peaceful resolution of regional disputes in Asia; the construction of cooperative regional security architecture; the enhancement of Asian allies' capabilities, with the aim of fostering self-sufficiency; and the strengthening of US defence capabilities there.[17]

Militarily, the rebalance has meant increased defence cooperation and a redistribution of military assets. The US intends to increase the military financing it provides to Asian countries by 35%, and to reinforce this by increasing military education and training by 40%, by 2016.[18] The US Department of Defense has laid out plans for new military deployments in the Asia-Pacific. These include the stationing of approximately 2,500 marines in Darwin, Australia; an additional army battalion in South Korea; two missile-defence destroyers in Japan; and three littoral combat ships in Singapore.[19] The US is deploying advanced aircraft and weaponry to the region, with a focus on early-warning capabilities, as well as systems for intelligence, surveillance and reconnaissance. The Pentagon aims to operate approximately 60% of navy and air-force units out of the Pacific by 2020.[20] It is likely that America will increase its troop deployments to the Philippines, and will enhance defence cooperation with Vietnam and Malaysia.[21]

Gulf elites usually express concern about the effects of the rebalance in private meetings, in contrast to their public criticism of US policy on Iran and Syria. A rare exception to this came in a 2013 comment by Prince Turki al-Faisal, a prominent Saudi royal and former ambassador to the US, who stated that the rebalance was further evidence of America 'ceding the role that it used to play' in the Middle East.[22] Conversely, other Gulf officials sought to link the success of the rebalance to an enduring US commitment to their security.[23]

## The Arab uprisings

To Washington's dismay, its plans for gradual, controlled retrenchment were disrupted by the political upheaval that swept the Arab world in 2011. The conservative Gulf monarchies, aside from Qatar and Oman, believed that the Arab uprisings damaged a regional order from which they benefited; heralded the rise of popular Islamist, and perhaps radical, movements that would oppose their rule; and politicised their largely quiescent populations, potentially destabilising them. The discord also exposed deep divisions among GCC states, with Doha's championing of political change incurring the fury of Riyadh and Abu Dhabi.

Washington's support for the uprisings, which it welcomed as an inevitable and necessary change, only sharpened Gulf concerns about US policy and reliability. Elites in Saudi Arabia, the UAE, Bahrain and Kuwait blamed the US (somewhat unfairly) for abandoning Hosni Mubarak, Egypt's autocratic president and a close Gulf ally, and for rapidly accepting the Muslim Brotherhood as a viable political alternative. Riyadh and Abu Dhabi saw the rise of the Brotherhood as a security and ideological challenge that needed to be checked (hence their support for the July 2013 ouster of Mohammed Morsi, Mubarak's successor, which led to the election of General Abdel Fattah el-Sisi).

The uprising in Bahrain resulted in a crisis of confidence among the US and its key Gulf allies. For Washington, it was a domestic matter best addressed through internal dialogue and political reform, a message carried to the Bahraini monarch by then-Secretary of Defense Robert Gates in March 2011. In contrast, Manama and its Saudi and Emirati allies portrayed the crisis as orchestrated by Iran, implementing a GCC provision to deploy troops in support of the royal family. They perceived Washington's policy as having endangered regime security, a crucial issue in the Gulf.

America's detached approach to the Arab world has been best illustrated by its policy on Syria. For the Gulf states, the popular challenge to Assad's rule provided an opportunity to check Iranian power and compensate for the loss of Iraq. Although Obama called for Assad's departure, the American president was eager to avoid extensive involvement in Syria that would echo the costly political and sectarian entanglements he had pledged to avoid. As the Syrian uprising became a civil war, the Gulf states compared American restraint unfavourably with Russia's unconditional support for Assad.

The Gulf monarchies were particularly dismayed by Obama's failure to uphold his 'red line' on the Syrian regime's use of chemical weapons. His dithering during August and September 2013, as he made a case for military intervention only to back off soon after, raised questions about broader US credibility. Washington's acceptance of an imperfect diplomatic deal to remove the Syrian chemical arsenal, rather than punish Assad for his use of the weapons, was seen as a reflection of Obama's professorial style and aversion to risk. By needlessly requesting a congressional vote on the use of force in Syria, Obama jeopardised a presidential prerogative that the Gulf states saw as fundamental to their relations with the US. Having deemed Congress sympathetic to Israel and hostile to their interests (particularly after 9/11), the Gulf states had focused their energy on building a strong relationship with other parts of the US government, particularly the White House and the Department of Defense.

Gulf leaders were aggravated by Obama's decision to redouble his efforts to engage with Iran just as doubt was cast on US credibility. In March 2013, Washington and Tehran opened a secret bilateral channel that would run alongside ongoing multilateral diplomacy. Hosted by Oman, the resulting talks preceded Hassan Rouhani's June 2013 election to the Iranian presidency, and remained unknown to the Gulf states until they were leaked in the media and by a concerned Israel. The negotiations led Iran and the P5+1 to sign an interim nuclear deal in November of that year, potentially paving the way for a comprehensive agreement.[24]

The secret manner in which the interim deal was reached unnerved Saudi Arabia and the UAE. Despite American assurances that the talks only covered nuclear issues, they strongly suspected that regional security had been discussed. Indeed, several Gulf leaders and analysts suspected that Obama's cancellation of the strike on Assad was partly motivated by the need to protect the diplomatic track with Iran.

Many Gulf officials saw Obama as simultaneously naive and reckless on Egypt; diffident and cynical on Syria; opportunistic and unreliable on Iran; and generally dangerous on Gulf security. They believed that a rushed, badly designed American withdrawal was creating an environment in which non-Arab actors – namely Iran, Turkey and Israel – gained influence at their expense.

Like his predecessor, Obama launched regional defence initiatives in the hope that strong military cooperation would smooth relations with his Gulf partners. Hagel's 2013 announcement that the US would sell defence equipment to the GCC as a bloc centred on integrated ballistic-missile defence to counter Iran's missile threat.[25] In June 2014, the defence ministries of the US and the GCC convened in Jeddah for their first meeting on mutual security issues, which included missile defence and cyber threats.[26] Washington regards greater Gulf defence integration as lessening America's political and financial burden in the Middle East, streamlining its planning and operations, and optimising its contribution. In the short term, such integration requires greater US involvement to harmonise defence capabilities and train Gulf militaries. To this end, in January 2014, Obama issued a directive on the sale of defence equipment and services to the GCC, intended to complement annual US–Gulf military exercises.

But Washington's aim for the Gulf states to take on greater responsibility is constrained by their unspoken preference for bilateral deals. This misalignment highlights a fundamental divergence in regional security perceptions, with the result that the US is tied down in several defence relationships that are less than ideal.

## Hedging, assertiveness and competition

The Gulf states faced long-term uncertainty over whether they had misconstrued policy disagreements with the US as its intention to leave the Middle East (in the same way that the United Kingdom had left the Gulf, in 1971); whether American retrenchment would be sustained or reversed by a future administration; and whether events in the region and their own diplomacy would compel a change in Washington's policy.

In the meantime, however, the monarchies sought to make urgent adjustments. Firstly, they focused on the strategy of internationalising Gulf security. Their theatrics, such as Saudi Prince Bandar bin Sultan's derision of the US before European officials, sought to downgrade the relationship with Washington by publicly shifting their attention to an array of other partners, cultivated through economic interaction and preferential treatment. The message to the Obama administration and local audiences was that the monarchies had developed alternative options and matured, thanks to their embrace of globalisation. This was reflected in the decisions to award the 2022 World Cup to Qatar; Dubai's organisation of the 2020 World Expo; and Abu Dhabi's successful bid to host the UN's International Renewable Energy Agency. Each success was intended to portray the monarchies as responsible members of the international community, worthy of global protection and goodwill.

The Gulf states have paid special attention to Asian powers. This approach is made particularly attractive by the fact that India, Japan, South Korea and China are major importers of Gulf oil and gas; Malaysia, Indonesia and Singapore receive significant investment from the monarchies; South Asian countries provide cheap labour; and Asian manufacturers export technology and other goods to Arab markets. An equally important consideration is that relations with certain Asian countries are unaffected by hindrances in dealing with Western entities, such as political baggage and stipulations relating to social, labour, human-rights and environmental factors. Gulf leaders are especially interested in China and India, due to their size and global ambitions. Beijing's seat on the UN Security Council, and resulting influence on key international-security and economic-governance discussions, makes it an indispensable contact. China's growing military capabilities have captured the attention of the monarchies, especially due to its naval deployments in the Arabian Sea. A historical interlocutor of the Gulf states, India is increasingly viewed as a promising partner, despite its limited power-projection capabilities and geopolitical insularity. Crucially, the monarchies' engagement with India and China is motivated by a desire to counter Iran's traditional influence in New Delhi and Beijing, which has been based on solidarity among developing nations. Saudi Arabia has also nurtured its privileged relationship with Pakistan. Riyadh uses its ties with nuclear-armed Islamabad, which are based on religious affinity and strategic expediency, as a means of keeping Iran in check, and demonstrating that it has security partnerships beyond those with the West.

At the same time, various Gulf states have continued to strengthen their security relationships with Western states other than the US, including the UK and, more importantly, France. The monarchies calculate that they can influence Washington indirectly, through Paris and London.

France aligned with Saudi Arabia and the UAE by taking an uncompromising stance in nuclear negotiations with Iran, and by advocating military action against the Assad regime. Paris's relative disinterest in human rights and political reform in the Gulf helped to make it a viable ally, as did the fact that its presidents have recently carried out military interventions without seeking parliamentary approval. Beyond its base in Abu Dhabi, French military involvement in the Middle East has included intelligence support for the Saudi military during its 2009 intervention against Houthi forces in Yemen, and assertive counter-piracy missions in the Arabian Sea and the Gulf of Aden. Security cooperation between Paris and Riyadh has extended to Lebanon, where both capitals sought to shore up the Lebanese military as a means of balancing Hizbullah.

After a long absence from the Gulf following its 1971 withdrawal, the British government sought to re-establish military relations with the monarchies, hoping that the move would be welcomed by leaders there, many of whom had been educated in the UK. London benefited from the perception that its policy on Bahrain was somewhat aligned with that of Riyadh and Abu Dhabi, despite the fact that the UK had hosted Brotherhood leaders and Gulf dissidents, and that the British Parliament had shown interest in Middle East political issues. As a consequence, the UK has agreed new weapons deals with Oman, the UAE and Saudi Arabia, and has begun to build naval facilities in Bahrain.

Simultaneously, there has been a significant increase in Gulf criticism of US policy. Washington has been publicly denounced by Saudi princes such as Mohammed bin Nawaf Al Saud, who serves as ambassador to the UK. Writing for the *New York Times* in December 2013, he warned that 'we believe that many of the West's policies on both Iran and Syria risk the stability and security of the Middle East. This is a dangerous gamble, about which we cannot remain silent, and will not stand idly by.'[27] The tightly controlled media in Saudi Arabia, the UAE, Kuwait and Bahrain repeated this argument, accusing Washington of collusion with both the Brotherhood and Iran.

American officials have acknowledged this state of affairs. In January 2014, Director of National Intelligence James Clapper cautioned that 'the unhappiness of some Arab Gulf States with US policies on Iran, Syria, and Egypt might lead these countries to reduce cooperation with the United States on regional issues and act unilaterally in ways that run counter to US interests'.[28]

The Gulf states' displeasure has taken on a more tangible form in their direct opposition to US preferences and policy. In Egypt, Riyadh and Abu Dhabi contributed to the joint popular mobilisation and military coup that unseated the Qatar-backed Morsi, as well as subsequent repression of the Brotherhood. Although they were often frustrated with Morsi, American officials viewed him as Egypt's democratically elected president, and believed that his ouster would radicalise disgruntled Islamists across the Middle East. After the Obama administration imposed limits on US arms sales to Cairo, Sisi approached Russia and obtained promises for UAE-funded purchases of weapons.

The stabilisation of post-Gadhafi Libya also put the US at loggerheads with its Gulf allies. Doha and Abu Dhabi supported opposing factions in Libya's parliament and among the country's militias, providing funding, military assistance and media coverage to their respective allies. Their involvement helped to derail the UN-supported plan for a political transition and security reforms. By summer 2014, Emirati jets had allegedly conducted air-strikes against Islamist militias besieging Tripoli International Airport, while Doha had stepped up its delivery of weapons to Libya, effectively precluding a political resolution in the country.[29]

As the US adopted economic sanctions on Russia over the Ukraine crisis, the crown prince of Bahrain visited Moscow to sign an agreement between Mumtalakat, his country's sovereign-wealth fund, and the Russian Direct Investment Fund.[30] During the 2012 Manama Dialogue, Prince Salman bin Hamad bin Isa Al Khalifa thanked London profusely for its support, but made no mention of Washington, an omission widely interpreted as a calculated snub.

Yet the greatest source of political and strategic tension between the US and its Gulf allies remained the conflict in Syria. The massive Saudi and Qatari investment in arms and funding for rebel groups clashed with America's far more cautious approach, which was shaped by concern over state collapse and regional escalation. Washington repeatedly dashed hopes that it would take the lead in supporting the Syrian rebels, raising questions about American calculations over Syria and the Middle East order.

While the US invested in the formation of a credible Syrian political opposition, and explored diplomatic paths towards a negotiated transition with Russia, the Gulf states prioritised the fight against Assad. The monarchies claimed that he would only negotiate if his regime had been weakened, and made a humanitarian argument in favour of intervention. Angered by US hesitation and Assad's resilience, Qatar and Saudi Arabia pursued increasingly risky policies, becoming complacent about jihadist funding and recruitment. This caused alarm among many in Washington, who worried that the proxy war would fuel Islamic extremism, but Riyadh and Doha argued that the extremist groups in Syria could be countered only after Assad had been defeated. In 2012, weeks after Washington designated al-Qaeda affiliate Jabhat al-Nusra a terrorist organisation, Qatari Minister of Foreign Affairs Khalid bin Mohammed Al Attiyah countered 'I am very much against excluding anyone at this stage, or bracketing them as terrorists, or bracketing them as al-Qaeda'.[31]

The Gulf states found unlikely allies in their attempts to shape American policy. Their positions on Syria and Iran converged with those of influential US senators also frustrated with the Obama administration. Despite perceived hostility to the monarchies in Congress, many senior American legislators came to believe that the White House was spurning valuable allies and unduly courting Iran. This shared concern led to unprecedented meetings between Republican senators and Saudi officials in Riyadh, just as the kingdom publicly expressed its discontent with the US. Around the time it emerged that US Secretary of State Kerry had referred to Saudi intelligence chief Bandar bin Sultan as 'the problem', the latter pointedly met with Republican lawmaker Bob Corker.[32] In early 2014, Senator John McCain effusively praised Saudi policy at a security conference in Munich, saying 'thank God for the Saudis and Prince Bandar, and for our Qatari friends'.[33] Such manoeuvres seemed intended to influence the US government by creating elite and media pressure.

The final element of the Gulf states' response was their rein-vigoration of regional integration plans. The GCC intervention in Bahrain had served as a catalyst for their ambitions. As the US seemed unreliable and, in the case of Bahrain, potentially reckless, the monarchies made plans to tighten cooperation on domestic and external security. They reasoned that greater ownership of their own security would increase their policy options and protect them against Western pressure. Defence integration was required to develop greater power-projection capabilities, and a rapid-reaction force that could respond to crises such as that in Bahrain. Following this logic, the Saudi monarch announced in late 2011 his intention to transform the GCC into a Gulf Union. This idea received enthusiastic Bahraini endorsement, but a tepid response from other members of the organisation. Nevertheless, Saudi pronouncements created momentum and public interest in the idea of stronger, more comprehensive Gulf cooperation at a time of uncertainty. A unified military command, designed to oversee 100,000 troops across the region and to replace the Peninsula Shield Force, was announced in 2013.[34]

In parallel, there was a significant improvement in rela-tions between Saudi Arabia and the UAE, which had previously clashed over several bilateral and foreign-policy issues. This was facilitated by their shared perception of a Brotherhood threat, concerns about Iran and Syria, discontent with Qatar's maverick behaviour in the region, and misgivings about US policy. Accordingly, Riyadh and Abu Dhabi experienced a remarkable policy and operational convergence, best reflected in their joint support of the Sisi regime in Egypt. Comprising the two largest military and economic powers in the Gulf, this alliance appeared to have formidable clout. The rapprochement has resulted in joint military exercises, an increase in state visits and laudatory coverage in each other's media outlets.

## The limits of Gulf autonomy and American retrenchment

Gulf activism of recent years has been remarkable in its intensity and reach. State crises in Iraq, Syria and Libya, as well as political upheaval in Egypt, have created disturbances in the Middle East order that the Gulf states have sought to shape to their benefit. But their responses have proven tentative, costly and inconclusive.

Rather than uniting the monarchies against perceived threats, US retrenchment has involuntarily exposed the deep divisions among them, and aggravated their competition with one another. An intensification of the rivalry between Saudi Arabia and Iran has coincided with a rise in toxic sectarianism, a struggle for leadership among the Sunni monarchies and a contest over the future of political Islamism. These complex fault lines do not allow for steady alliances, and instead facilitate opportunistic, volatile alignments.

Disagreements between Gulf states over regional strategies and ambitions have had a major influence on the Middle East order. Qatar's alliance with the Brotherhood has been countered by Saudi Arabia and the UAE, who have helped reverse the movement's initial success in Egypt and sought to weaken Hamas. Riyadh and Doha have sponsored rival groups in Syria, exacerbating the fragmentation of the Syrian opposition.

The Gulf states' infighting, and the perception that they have contributed to the radicalisation of the war against Assad, has damaged their global credibility and exposed them to international criticism. The expansion of the Islamic State of Iraq and al-Sham (ISIS), often blamed on Gulf recklessness and complacency, has revived a debate in the West about the wisdom of allying with the monarchies.

The Gulf states' greater activism in countries undergoing civil strife has also revealed their lack of experience, expertise and strategic patience, particularly in comparison to Iran. Their limited diplomatic, intelligence and power-projection capabilities have not been enough to translate massive financial investment into tangible political or security gains.

Saudi and Emirati anxiety about engagement with Iran has run against a cautiously optimistic international mood on the country, stemming from the prospect of a comprehensive nuclear deal with a pragmatic Rouhani government. Perhaps unfairly, Saudi Arabia is now seen as a particularly inflexible opponent to any such agreement. In contrast, Qatar and Oman have welcomed diplomacy with Iran, while the UAE has adopted a cautious tone. Gulf concerns have therefore failed to coalesce around a common, constructive approach that could potentially sway Western diplomacy.

Grand ambitions to develop the GCC into a security alliance have also stalled. The Saudi plan for a Gulf Union has fuelled fears among other members of the organisation that their sovereignty and domestic politics will be compromised. Leaders and important constituencies in Qatar, Kuwait and Oman have therefore balked at increased integration. Omani Minister in Charge of Foreign Affairs, Yusuf bin Alawi, offered a blunt rebuttal during the 2013 Manama Dialogue, stating 'we are against a union, but we will not prevent it'.[35] As a consequence of such statements, rhetoric about the union has been scaled back and corresponding plans revised.

Even the strategy of diversifying partnerships has been mostly dissatisfying for the Gulf states. Despite the promise of these relationships, new friends are both reluctant and unable to make major security commitments to the monarchies. Such a move would require them to take sides in the Middle East's complex politics, and to expend resources and political capital on missions that are currently carried out by the US (and from which they benefit). The Gulf states' own free-riding makes potential security partners unwilling to significantly change their role. This speaks to the fundamental, sobering dilemma for the Gulf states: whereas their economic future lies in the East, their security depends on the West. Indeed, ambivalent Asian countries remain imperfect substitutes for Western powers willing to provide security commitments, deploy troops and sell high-end weaponry.

The perception of a diminished American role in the Gulf has confounded Asian powers that ostensibly benefit from the US rebalance (through security improvements to Asia-Pacific sea lanes). They worry that an ill-managed change in US posture will make the Middle East more volatile, affecting energy supply, and will damage America's international credibility.

Events of the past few years have also shown Washington the limits and complexities of disentanglement. America's diminished involvement in the Middle East means that it is less able to counter Gulf policies that run against its interests. The disregard for Washington's preferences shown by Riyadh and Abu Dhabi in Bahrain and Egypt highlighted US weakness, and incurred no cost. Moreover, the unintended effects of the monarchies' behaviour have complicated Washington's effort to extricate itself from the region, and to stay away from crises such as that in Syria. From the US perspective, Saudi and Qatari policies in the country have amounted, intentionally or otherwise, to entrapment. This has forced Obama to increase the US role in Syria and Iraq.

The Gulf states' expressions of anxiety have compelled Washington to acknowledge their concerns, and to demonstrate its commitment to its allies by assuring them that a comprehensive nuclear deal with Iran would not affect US policy on other regional issues. Fears of secret arrangements and even realignment have pervaded Gulf thinking. In response, Kerry has sought to emphasise the strength of the relationship with Saudi Arabia, stating 'the United States will do nothing in negotiating with Iran that will change that relationship'.[36] The campaign to steady US–Gulf relations culminated in Obama's visit to Saudi Arabia in March this year. However, the Gulf states remain convinced that there is an intrinsic link between nuclear diplomacy with Iran, the war in Syria and the flawed strategy to defeat ISIS. Yet, despite the Gulf states' frustration with Washington and exploration of partnerships to the East, the monarchies continue to treat American policy as their strategic compass.

## Notes

1   Jimmy Carter, 'State of the Union Address 1980', 23 January 1980, Jimmy Carter Library and Museum, http://www.jimmycarterlibrary.gov/documents/speeches/su80jec.phtml.

2   Author interview with a senior Gulf official, the UAE, January 2007.

3   Embassy of the Kingdom of Saudi Arabia to the United States, 'King Abdullah Begins Asian Tour with Visit to China', 24 January 2006, http://www.saudiembassy.net/archive/2006/news/page879.aspx.

4   Matthew Saltmarsh, 'France Opens First Military Bases in the Gulf', New York Times, 26 May 2009, http://www.nytimes.com/2009/05/27/world/europe/27france.html.

5   Author interview with a senior Gulf official, the UAE, January 2007.

6   Christopher M. Blanchard and Richard F. Grimmett, 'The Gulf Security Dialogue and Related Arms Sale Proposals', Congressional Research Service, 8 October 2008, http://fas.org/sgp/crs/weapons/RL34322.pdf.

7   'Key Judgments from a National Intelligence Estimate on Iran's Nuclear Activity', New York Times, 4 December 2007, www.nytimes.com/2007/12/04/washington/04itext.html.

8   Josh Rogin, 'How the Obama Administration Bungled the Iraq Withdrawal Negotiations', Foreign Policy, 21 October 2011, http://thecable.foreignpolicy.com/posts/2011/10/21/how_the_obama_administration_bungled_the_iraq_withdrawal_negotiations.

9   Sam Dagher, 'Transcript: Maliki on Iraq's Future', Wall Street Journal, 28 December 2010, http://online.wsj.com/articles/SB100014240529702035

1320457604780411203090.

10 US Department of State, 'U.S. Relations with Syria', 20 March 2014, http://www.state.gov/r/pa/ei/bgn/3580.htm.

11 Chuck Hagel, 'Global Security Priorities for the US', speech delivered at the IISS Manama Dialogue, 7 December 2013, https://www.iiss.org/en/events/manama%20dialogue/archive/manama-dialogue-2013-4e92/plenary-1-a895/chuck-hagel-80d9.

12 *The Military Balance 2011* (Abingdon: Routledge for the IISS, 2010), p. 48.

13 Eyder Peralta, 'Citing Uncertainty, Pentagon Will Not Deploy Aircraft Carrier to Persian Gulf', National Public Radio, 6 February 2013, www.northcountrypublicradio.org/news/npr/171300433/citing-uncertainty-pentagon-will-not-deploy-aircraft-carrier-to-persian-gulf.

14 David Larter, 'US Navy Chief: Two Carriers in the Gulf Region is Unlikely', *Defense News*, 8 October 2014, http://www.defense-news.com/article/20141008/DEFREG02/310080035/CNO-Two-Carriers-Gulf-Region-Unlikely?odyssey=nav|head.

15 US Energy Information Administration, 'U.S. Imports by Country of Origin', http://www.eia.gov/dnav/pet/pet_move_impcus_a2_nus_epoo_imo_mbbl_a.htm.

16 Keith Crane et al., 'Imported Oil and U.S. National Security', RAND Corporation, 2009, http://www.rand.org/pubs/monographs/MG838.html.

17 Chuck Hagel, 'The United States' Contribution to Regional Stability', speech delivered at the IISS Shangri-La Dialogue, 31 May 2014, http://www.iiss.org/en/events/shangri%20la%20dialogue/archive/2014-c20c/plenary-1-d1ba/chuck-hagel-a9cb.

18 *Ibid.*

19 US Committee on Foreign Relations, 'Re-Balancing the Rebalance: Resourcing U.S. Diplomatic Strategy in the Asia-Pacific Region', 17 April 2014, http://www.foreign.senate.gov/imo/media/doc/872692.pdf.

20 *Ibid.*

21 US Committee on Foreign Relations, 'Re-Balancing the Rebalance'.

22 Saudi–US Relations Information Service, 'Diplomacy and Romance: A Conversation with Prince Turki Al-Faisal', 16 December 2013, http://susris.com/2013/12/16/diplomacy-and-romance-a-conversation-with-prince-turki-al-faisal/.

23 Yousef Al Otaiba, 'The Asia Pivot Needs a Firm Footing in the Middle East', *Foreign Policy*, 26 March 2014, http://www.foreign-policy.com/articles/2014/03/26/us_uae_saudi_arabia_relations.

24 Michael R. Gordon, 'Accord Reached with Iran to Halt Nuclear Program', *New York Times*, 23 November 2013, http://www.nytimes.com/2013/11/24/world/middleeast/talks-with-iran-on-nuclear-deal-hang-in-balance.html.

25 Hagel, 'Global Security Priorities for the US'.

26 Chuck Hagel, 'SecDef Hagel Remarks at US–GCC Defense Dialogue', speech delivered at the US–GCC Defense Dialogue, Jeddah, 14 May 2014, http://susris.com/2014/05/20/secdef-hagel-remarks-at-us-gcc-defense-dialogue/.

27 Mohammed bin Nawaf bin Abdulaziz Al Saud, 'Saudi Arabia Will Go It Alone', *New York Times*, 17 December 2013, http://www.nytimes.com/2013/12/18/opinion/saudi-arabia-will-go-it-alone.html.

28 James R. Clapper, 'Worldwide Threat Assessment of the US Intelligence Community', Senate Select Committee on Intelligence, 29 January 2014, http://www.dni.gov/files/documents/Intelligence%20Reports/2014%20WWTA%20%20SFR_SSCI_29_Jan.pdf.

29 David D. Kirkpatrick and Eric Schmitt, 'Arab Nations Strike in Libya, Surprising U.S.', *New York Times*, 25 August 2014, http://www.nytimes.com/2014/08/26/world/africa/egypt-and-united-arab-emirates-said-to-have-secretly-carried-out-libya-airstrikes.html.

30 Nicolas Parasie, 'Bahrain, Russia Funds in Deal to Pursue Investments', *Wall Street Journal*, 1 May 2014, http://blogs.wsj.com/middleeast/2014/05/01/bahrain-russia-funds-in-deal-to-pursue-investments/.

31 Sh Khalid Bin Ahmed Al Khalifa, 'Priorities for Regional Security', speech delivered at the IISS Manama Dialogue, 8 December 2012, https://www.iiss.org/~/media/Documents/Events/Manama%20Dialogue/MD2012/Plenary%202%20QA.pdf.

32 Ellen Knickmeyer and Adam Entous, 'Saudi Arabia Replaces Key Official in Effort to Arm Syria Rebels', *Wall Street Journal*, 19 February 2014, http://online.wsj.com/news/articles/SB10001424052702303775504579392942097203608.

33 Steve Clemons, '"Thank God for the Saudis": ISIS, Iraq, and the Lessons of Blowback', *Atlantic*, 23 June 2014, http://www.theatlantic.com/international/archive/2014/06/isis-saudi-arabia-iraq-syria-bandar/373181/.

34 Awad Mustafa, 'GCC Announces a Joint Military Command', *Defense News*, 11 December 2013, http://www.defensenews.com/article/20131211/DEFREG04/312110011/GCC-Announces-Joint-Military-Command.

35 Wafa El Sayed, 'Oman Says No to Gulf Union', IISS, 9 December 2013, http://www.iiss.org/en/manama%20voices/blogsections/2013-e202/alawi-oman-281a.

36 John Kerry and Abdallah bin Zayid Al Nuhayyan, 'Remarks with Emirati Foreign Minister Abdallah bin Zayid Al Nuhayyan after their Meeting', speech delivered in Abu Dhabi, 11 November 2013, http://www.state.gov/secretary/remarks/2013/11/217438.htm.

# CHAPTER SEVEN

# Obama and the Middle East: The Politics, Strategies and Difficulties of American Restraint

Dana H. Allin

At a September 2014 IISS conference in Oslo, Chinese businessman Eric Li gave an impressive performance. He cast Chinese claims for a revised Asia-Pacific order in terms that seemed both reasonable and inevitable. The world order set up after the Second World War, in large part through the exertions of the United States, was not a bad one, but it was set up without the participation of China, and now that China has arrived at a stage of much greater wealth and considerably greater power, its demand for a larger share of the pie was simply in the nature of things. The only real question was whether China has the clout to achieve this larger share, and Li's answer was yes:

> The US is, of course, much more powerful than China in all respects, but it is not when considering the sizes of their respective objects at the moment. China's objectives in Asia are modest, relative to its national capabilities. It is punching below its weight. America's objectives in the world are enormous, compared to its national capabilities and the internal problems it faces. It is punching above its weight.[1]

Li's performance was impressive, not least because he was articulating nationalist, unsettling and potentially dangerous claims in the most reasonable tones. But his core analysis of America's intrinsic overextension – and the opportunities this presents to rising powers like China – was persuasive. Whether the United States is in a condition of resurgence or decline at any given moment, it seems undeniable that its responsibilities, ambitions and pretensions in the global order make it difficult for the US leadership to set priorities and adequately attend to the domestic sources of American strength.

There is no reason to doubt the sincerity of President Barack Obama's repeated assertions that American decline is a 'myth', or that the United States is an 'exceptional' nation with exceptional global responsibilities. Still, the past six years have amply demonstrated that the president's core strategic instincts favour restraint (if not retrenchment), and that these instincts derive from a keen understanding of the chronic overstretch that Li expressed so succinctly. From his December 2009 West Point speech to his policies in Syria, Obama has shown in words and action that he considers the main problem and central mistake of the past decade or so to have involved strategic overcommitment and military entanglement. 'Don't do stupid stuff' (if 'stuff' is the word he used) may not inspire, but it still seems a sensible prescription for avoiding more self-inflicted wounds after the reckless wars of the George W. Bush era.

And yet – Obama becomes the fourth president in succession to order military action in Iraq, and he has now extended that action to Syria. Is it simply impossible to orchestrate a managed retrenchment from what was rightly seen as debilitating overextension?

Grappling with this question requires attention to three considerations. Firstly, what is the reasonable balance of domestic and foreign responsibility? In insisting that the latter should not crowd out the former, Obama has been attentive to what John

F. Kennedy called the 'substance' rather than the 'shadow' of power.[2] But working on the substance has been difficult, to put it mildly, in an American political context where the conservative minority rejects the very legitimacy of his presidency.

Secondly, how have Obama's efforts at retrenchment and restraint fit with previous efforts to avoid being drawn into military commitments? Dwight Eisenhower in regard to Suez and Hungary; Kennedy's Bay of Pigs and Cuban Missile Crisis (and, arguably, his determination to avoid a ground war in Vietnam); even Ronald Reagan after the Marine barracks bombings in Lebanon – these and other examples show that Obama's restraint can only be considered radical in the context of the George W. Bush wars of the preceding decade.

Thirdly, and perhaps most problematic: prior efforts at restraint did not, in the end, work out very well. Kennedy, whatever his own instincts, did lay the basis for escalation in Vietnam (not to mention a counterproductive 60-year embargo of Cuba). The Reagan administration's hyper-realist, if not cynical, strategy of supporting Ba'athist Iraq against revolutionary Iran did not preserve the United States from grave moral compromise, nor did it provide a stability that saved Reagan's successors from the commitment of air power, collective economic punishment, ground wars and disastrous occupation in Iraq. In recent months, Obama has genuinely confronted the choice between allowing genocide or deploying military force. His decision for using but also circumscribing air power seems necessary but also fraught with future problems. The strategic and moral commitments of American power remain extensive and, arguably, debilitating.

## Unfinished business

To grasp the implications of this reinsertion of military power in the Middle East, it is useful to remember the administration's positions and assumptions just a few months ago, before the

Islamic State of Iraq and al-Sham (ISIS) overturned them with its capture of Mosul and brutal sweep towards Baghdad. The main premise was that the George W. Bush administration had devoted too much blood, treasure and attention to the Middle East, with counterproductive, not to say catastrophic, results. The 'pivot' to Asia, an arguably botched strategic-rebranding exercise, together with a general retrenchment to focus on domestic demands, flowed from this premise. Peter Beinart was among the many analysts who identified a recognisable administration strategy of 'offshore balancing', which was to say, 'the idea that America can best contain our adversaries not by confronting them on land, but by maintaining our naval and air power and strengthening those smaller nations that see us as a natural counterweight to their larger neighbors'.[3] Thus, America might be able to balance its continued responsibilities against limited resources and capabilities.

These residual responsibilities included, to be sure, substantial, continuing exposure and commitment in the Middle East. The number one commitment was to somehow stop Iran's nuclear programme from leading to a weapon. There was considerable scepticism about what Israeli or American military action against Iran's nuclear facilities could achieve. Yet, if negotiations were to fail, such action would remain a real possibility.

The Iran nuclear problem is in fact an excellent case for considering the ambiguities and difficulties of trying to maintain a more restrained military posture in the Middle East. In the run-up to the 2012 election, President Obama stated unambiguously that the United States would not permit Iran to develop nuclear weapons.[4] This statement came in the midst of months of acrimonious debate and pressure – from the Israeli government, from the Saudis and other Gulf allies, and from Republican critics at home, all of whom argued that the administration was fecklessly permitting Iran to continue developing its nuclear capabilities. In making such a clear statement about Iranian nuclear *weapons*, Obama probably considered himself to be acting with restraint; his critics generally want the United States to prevent Iran from developing even a latent nuclear capability, a capability that could be said to exist well before actual weaponisation. Obama, by contrast, was drawing a line quite a few steps back, and one that Tehran might be shrewd enough not to cross even as it endowed itself with most of the attributes of a 'virtual' nuclear power.

But, of course, nobody knows for sure. The president had made a commitment that he or his successor might very well be required to fulfil. The administration in any event believed that weaponisation would be an irrevocable step change in the strategic environment. And there were obvious limits to what the United States could do about it. The Obama administration was, in fact, hugely successful in organising international sanctions – the unity and steadfastness of the Europeans had perhaps been a pleasant surprise – and the White House took some justifiable pride in keeping that alliance together. Direct negotiations between the US and Iran were considered another achievement, but the two sides remained far apart. Obviously, there was serious disagreement between the US, on the one hand, and Israel, Saudi Arabia and other states in this region, on the other hand, about what could be achieved. The US simply did not buy the view that zero enrichment was a viable negotiating position.

Measured on the basis of diplomatic investment, the second priority had been the Israel–Palestine peace effort. (This was a particular enthusiasm of Secretary of State John Kerry, but it still reflected an enormous amount of energy and time from the administration.) At the outset of Kerry's effort, critics questioned whether this was a justifiable use of the secretary's time. Those critics would now have the extra advantage of being able to say that the peace effort has, once again and fairly predictably, failed. So will the US now face reality? Probably not. To begin with, as intractable as Israel–Palestine may appear, it is logically false to argue that the US has less traction there than in nearby disaster areas such as Syria and Iraq. Secondly, Israel–Palestine is not a normal foreign-policy problem – it is a crucial and visceral American domestic issue. It goes to the heart of America's view of itself as a democracy at the hub of an alliance system of other democracies. The relationship with Israel is America's real 'special relationship' – special in good ways and bad. (Whereas the British relationship is mainly a good one, and therefore not so special.) Israel is becoming a polarising issue in American domestic politics, in a way that it never has before. So, even though hard-headed realism might suggest that we should walk away from the problem, it is not clear that we can.

The civil war in Syria came lower on the list of Middle East problems for which US military or diplomatic engagement could provide a plausible answer: this at least seemed to be the admin-istration's judgement by late spring 2014. America had been engaged in the Syrian civil war from the beginning, but not effec-tively and not to the satisfaction of those who, in anguish, called for us to do more. Though there was considerable dissent within the administration, the president seemed determined to avoid an open-ended commitment to bringing down the Assad regime. For various reasons, Syria was considered different from Bosnia, different from Libya and, in the opposite sense, different from our overarching confrontation with Iran, though obviously it is also a part of that confrontation.

## In defence of restraint

On the eve of Obama's commitment to an air war against ISIS, prevailing assessments of his foreign policies were trending nega-tive.[5] It was alleged that he did not channel enough support to 'moderate' rebels against the Syrian regime at a time when such support (it is argued) might have tipped the balance in the rebellion away from extreme jihadists. He set a rhetorical 'red line' against the regime's use of chemical weapons, but then opted for a Russian-brokered deal to remove those weapons from Syria instead of launching retaliatory air-strikes. His administration, according to critics, did not work hard enough with Iraq's government to negotiate a Status of Forces Agreement for keeping a residual US military force in the country, and hence was unable to shape the country's political terrain to prevent the emergence of a Sunni extremist force that went on to capture much of the country. All of this reluctance, and especially the choice of diplomacy over military action against Syrian chemical-weapons use, was said to have nourished in Russian President Vladimir Putin a justified contempt for American resolve, emboldening Moscow to annex Crimea and stir civil conflict in the rest of Ukraine.

The overall picture was of a president and administration averse to the necessary use of American leadership and military power, watching passively as the world unravelled on his watch. But there were a few problems with this picture. Firstly, it required a lot of faith in the directed application of military force to satisfying political ends. The notion that early and more robust military support for the Syrian opposition would have shaped a different, more humane civil war is impossible to disprove but also a bit hard to believe. Calls for a deeper American engagement often relied on strategic arguments, but at bottom their appeal was a moral one. The moral problem that is Syria and Iraq is huge, but the strategic judgement of the administration – and this appears to come down to the president himself – is that the United States should not be dragged into an asymmetrical engagement where its interests are insufficient to justify a prolonged commitment. There was also a debate to be had about whether intervention really would serve the moral imperative. It would only do so if it led to a speedier end to the war or, in any event, to a just and lasting stability. Since this could not really be achieved in Iraq with a vastly greater commitment of resources and lives – Iraqi in greater numbers than American – it was at least uncertain that it could be achieved in Syria.

Secondly, the notion that American abdication has precipitated a general unravelling of world order required greatly overstating, if not completely inventing, both the abdication and the unravelling. Robert Kagan, one of the more thoughtful critics of this administration's instincts for foreign-policy restraint, has long argued that when America tires of its world role, increasing chaos will follow. At the outset of the first George W. Bush administration, Kagan in my journal criticised the outgoing Clinton administration for having failed to appreciate the enduring American responsibility:

> It is too easily forgotten that the plans for world order devised by American policy-makers in the early 1940s were not aimed at containing the Soviet Union, which many of them still viewed as a potential partner. Rather, those policy-makers were looking backward to the circumstances that had led to the catastrophe of global war. Their purpose was to construct a more stable international order than the one that collapsed in the 1930s: an economic system that furthered the aim of international stability by promoting growth and free trade; and a framework for international security that, although it placed some faith in the ability of the great powers to work together, rested ultimately on the keystone of American power.[6]

Kagan has repeated this basic theme over the ensuing 13 years, conceding along the way that the Bush administration made some mistakes, but always warning against overlearning the lessons of those mistakes. In a recent *New Republic* article, he continued the argument, observing that 'signs of the global order breaking down are all around us'. He attributes the breakdown not to American incapacity to shape events, but to 'an intellectual problem, a question of identity and purpose'.[7]

But Boston University professor Andrew Bacevic objects that Kagan is conjuring a halcyon post-war order that didn't remotely exist:

> Disruptions to a 'world order' ostensibly founded on the principle of American 'global responsibility' included the 1947 partition of India (estimated 500,000 to one million dead); the 1948 displacement of Palestinians (700,000 refugees); the exodus of Vietnamese from north to south in 1954 (between 600,000 and one million fled); the flight of the pied noir from Algeria (800,000 exiled); the deaths resulting directly from Mao Tse Tung's quest for utopia (between 2 million and 5 million); the mass murder of Indonesians during the anti-Communist purges of the mid-1960s (500,000 slaughtered); the partition of Pakistan in 1971 (up to 3 million killed; millions more displaced); genocide in Cambodia (1.7 million dead); and war between Iran and Iraq (at least more 400,00 killed [sic]). Did I mention civil wars in Nigeria, Uganda, Burundi, Ethiopia, Mozambique, Sudan, Congo, Liberia, and Sierra Leone that killed millions? The list goes on.[8]

This post-war world was in fact a 'disorderly conglomeration', and if it contained any kind of order, its main achievement 'was to avoid a cataclysmic third world war'. Here, to the extent America deserves some credit, it should be more for its restraint than its assertiveness. For evidence, Bacevic returns to Kennedy and Cuba, where, in October 1962, 'Khrushchev's rashness handed John F. Kennedy the chance to liberate Cuba from communism'.

But Kennedy abjured. 'Rather than confrontation', Bacevic notes, 'he opted for negotiation, offering the Soviets an unearned concession – in exchange for their missiles out of Cuba, ours would come out of Turkey. Cubans remained unliberated.'[9]

There is a third category of criticism against the Obama administration that can hardly be taken as seriously as the previous two. But, since it is ubiquitous in the general commentary, it requires some attention. This is the accusation that Obama has fallen disastrously short in some ineffable element of 'leadership', such that he has proved unable to shape events through the power of his personality. Commentator Matthew Yglesias has parodied the idea brilliantly as the 'Green Lantern Theory of Geopolitics' (he was referring to a comic-book hero whose boundless willpower is channelled and unleashed through a transformative ring).[10]

The critique of failed leadership relies in part on a fuzzy notion of 'credibility'. Obama's critics argue that because he didn't bomb Syria after saying he would, credibility was lost: Iran no longer takes the United States seriously, and even Putin was emboldened in Ukraine. Yet credibility doesn't really work that way. There is plenty of research to support the very different notion that credibility is a function of a putative adversary's understanding of one's capabilities and interest in any particular face-off.[11] Moreover, taking military action for the purpose of bolstering credibility ignores the very significant opportunity costs of such action. Invading Iraq, and watching it go horribly wrong, didn't give the US extra credibility and deterrent power in that region; quite the opposite. Each intervention has an opportunity cost that makes the next intervention more, rather than less, difficult, and less, rather than more, likely. Hence Libya made it harder, not easier, to intervene in Syria. Intervening in Syria would make it harder, not easier, for the United States to enforce its red line regarding Iranian nuclear weaponisation.

## Domestic success

Obama's failure of leadership is said to define both foreign- and domestic-policy paralysis. In domestic policy, it is alleged, better leadership skills would have overcome the Republican Party's sharp turn rightwards and strategy of general obstruction of policy measures that were once the stuff of bipartisan compromise, such as health-care reform based on the system introduced by Governor Mitt Romney in Massachusetts.

Obviously, if the administration has failed to make any progress on the problems that have ailed America's domestic political economy, then foreign-policy restraint will have served limited purpose. But the administration has not failed domestically.

In June of this year *New York Magazine* writer Jonathan Chait posted on his blog a piece with the following headline: 'Obama Promised to Do 4 Big Things as President. Now He's Done Them All.'[12] In the piece, Chait supplied the following quote from the president's first inaugural address: 'homes have been lost, jobs shed, businesses shuttered. Our health care is too costly, our schools fail too many, and each day brings further evidence that the ways we use energy strengthen our adversaries and threaten our planet.' Those two sentences encapsulated the list of problems to fix: economic meltdown, failed education, health care and climate change. The striking thing to which Chait points is that the administration has now made serious progress on all of them. Against the financial and economic meltdown there was an $800 billion stimulus package, passed while Democrats still had control of both houses of Congress. The amount was insufficient, but it seemed unimaginably huge at the time, and it probably averted a catastrophic depression. At this writing America's unemployment rate is under 6%, and its economy is growing faster than that of any other major industrial country.

Health-care and insurance reform was the big domestic fight of Obama's first term. He won it also thanks to Democratic control of both houses; and while the result was complicated and messy, it has withstood Supreme Court challenge, and so far its positive results have exceeded predictions.[13]

By itself, this achievement makes Obama the most consequential domestic reformer since Lyndon Johnson. While Obamacare doesn't immediately make health coverage universal, it does establish the principle that affordable health insurance is a right rather than a privilege. It thus fills a gaping hole in the American welfare state, fulfilling a liberal ambition going back to President Harry Truman, and bringing the United States closer into the community of other rich democracies. Republicans, for reasons unfathomable to this author, have promised to continue their war against it, and the Supreme Court had agreed, at the time of writing, to hear another argument against it based on a tendentious reading of some arguably sloppy legislative drafting. So the achievement may still be precarious. Even so, it is difficult to believe that America will willingly go back to a situation in which its citizens can so easily be bankrupted by illness, or denied coverage (which in some cases leads to their deaths), because of pre-existing medical conditions.

Just as expanding health care was the great fight of Obama's first term, the battle over carbon regulation is likely to dominate the final two years of his second. What is interesting here is that, on arguably the most important threat and challenge both foreign and domestic, the current administration has given a text-book demonstration of what 'leadership' can mean in concrete rather than magical terms. In spring 2014 the administration unveiled new Environmental Protection Agency (EPA) regulations for limiting carbon emissions by coal-fuelled power plants. This executive action was necessary because there is precisely zero chance of legislation from a Republican-controlled House of Representatives. It was possible because the Supreme Court ruled in 2007 that the EPA under current law has not only the authority but also the obligation to regulate greenhouse gases as pollutants.[14] And it could very possibly be effective in keeping US carbon emissions to a level consistent with the commitments that successive US administrations have undertaken in international negotiations.

It is undeniably the case that the United States cannot by its own actions do anything significant to affect climate change. But it is also the case that the necessary international policies are unimaginable if America refuses to take part. If the new regulations stand – and they will certainly be challenged in court – then America will at least be in a position of 'leadership' for the necessary, and excruciatingly difficult, negotiations with other large polluters. Indeed, in November 2014, Obama reached an agreement with Chinese President Xi Jinping matching a US commitment to cut emissions by 26–28% from 2005 levels by 2025 with China's intention that its emissions should peak in 2030, by which point it aims to have increased the share of non-fossil fuels in primary energy consumption to 20%. Together, the two countries account for more than four-tenths of global carbon emissions, so their agreed restraint would be important in itself. But it should also have a political and technological cascade effect on economic powers such as India, which is reluctant to commit itself to reducing emissions, and the European Union, which is already fully committed. Aside from diplomatic pressure, having the world's two largest economies and biggest polluters seriously regulating greenhouse gases will have economic and technological feedback effects that should encourage innovation and make low-carbon energy more feasible on a global basis.

The state of its economy, the health and education of its citizens, the nurturing of its human and natural resources — these are, in Kennedy's terms, elements of the substance rather than shadow of America's power. In similar terms, the future prospects for global security will be determined in a big way by whether this generation finds effective measures to avert irreversible and catastrophic climate change, and only negligibly, if at all, by ephemeral concepts such as 'credibility'.[15]

## Between West Point and Oslo

A policy of realistic restraint in foreign military policy, as part of an effort to set priorities and to concentrate on domestic needs, was always going to be held hostage to ideals and events. Both have now intervened to frustrate the president's hopes for turning the page on the wars of the George W. Bush era.

Obama has admitted that he underestimated the capabilities of ISIS, and it is also clear that there was a general overestimation of the state of Iraqi military forces. As ISIS overran much of Iraq, it also perhaps undermined Obama's assumptions about how weary Americans were of war. Videos depicting the grisly beheadings of two Americans were enough to shift US public opinion dramatically on whether it was an American interest and responsibility to seek out more war with the Sunni extremists. As Beinart observed, channelling Walter Russell Mead's famous categories, these heinous acts revived America's 'Jacksonian' instincts – 'the peculiar combination of jingoism and isolationism forged on the American frontier'.[16] All of a sudden, Vice President Joe Biden, not the most jingoistic among America's current crop of politicians, was vowing to follow the perpetrators 'to the gates of hell'.[17]

Beinart was warning that the American mood had changed abruptly, even though little had changed in the assessment of how direct a threat ISIS posed to American security or even America's broader interests, and so the new jingoism was a fertile field for more policy blunder. He was not, however, arguing that the proper American course would be to stand passive against ISIS advances and atrocities. These jihadists' record of beheadings, crucifixions, immolation, rape, enslavement and genocidal determination against religious minorities posed a challenge to American identity and purpose that could not be discounted simply by more rigorous accounting of American interests.

Every American president, at least since the Second World War, has had to balance realist against idealist traditions, and the current one is no exception. Indeed, Obama, being especially articulate, has fully presented both traditions in what might be called his West Point Declaration and his Oslo Declaration.

The West Point Declaration was delivered to US military cadets in June 2009. Obama was announcing an escalation – a 'surge' – of 30,000 more troops to fight the war in Afghanistan. But he was at the same time taking great care to delineate the limits of America's commitment to that country, dictated by competing interests and limited resources:

> As President, I refuse to set goals that go beyond our responsibility, our means, or our interests. And I must weigh all of the challenges that our nation faces. I don't have the luxury of committing to just one. Indeed, I'm mindful of the words of President Eisenhower, who – in discussing our national security – said, 'Each proposal must be weighed in the light of a broader consideration: the need to maintain balance in and among national programs.'[18]

This speech was a classic expression of Obama's small-c conservatism, concerned with restoring a balance between international commitments on the one hand, and American capabilities and resources on the other. He delivered it at a tricky moment in his relationship with senior military commanders, whom he felt were trying to box him into a more open-ended escalation.[19]

The Oslo Declaration was crafted in response to a rather different political problem: the fact that so many considered his Nobel Peace Prize in the early months of his presidency to be some kind of bad joke. Obama signalled that he got the joke, but rather than decline the award he decided to confound the prize-givers by accepting it with a statement on why American exceptionalism is intrinsically tied up with the sometimes greater American understanding of the need for organised violence:

> Make no mistake: Evil does exist in the world. A non-violent movement could not have halted Hitler's armies. Negotiations cannot convince al Qaeda's leaders to lay down their arms ... The world must remember that it was not simply international institutions – not just treaties and declarations – that brought stability to a post-World War II world. Whatever mistakes we have made, the plain fact is this: The United States of America has helped underwrite global security for more than six decades with the blood of our citizens and the strength of our arms.[20]

In respect to ISIS, the Obama administration is now trying to balance between the calculated caution of the West Point Declaration and the grim but noble imperative of the Oslo Declaration. In seeking this balance, the administration has indeed pursued a strategy that looks a lot like offshore balancing. It has local allies to fight on the ground, which it supports with training, intelligence and air power. The strategy makes sense, insofar as this author at least has not heard anyone propound a better one. But its flaws are nonetheless obvious. Two of ISIS's most potent enemies, Iran and the Assad regime in Syria, are, for different but related reasons, unfit for the coalition. Even America's preferred partners, such as Saudi Arabia and Turkey, have different and sometimes conflicting goals. Ankara, for example, has stated that it will fully join battle against ISIS only when Washington commits itself to also toppling Assad. Yet, while there is truth to the Turkish view that the Syrian regime's mass murders have fuelled and will continue to fuel unending jihadism, there is as much truth to the

American view that fighting two contending sides in a vicious civil war is a recipe for strategic incoherence.

And yet – strategic coherence will be difficult to maintain. Former White House official Steven Simon poses a key question:

> What happens if one of the non-jihadist opposition groups that the United States is aiding in the fight against ISIS requests urgent assistance against the Assad regime? If the United States fails to come to the group's aid, the support the United States enjoys among these groups by virtue of its airpower and train-and-equip efforts would swiftly fade. But if the United States accedes to the request, then it unequivocally becomes a combatant in the civil war. And if the United States consents to Turkey's proposal for a safe haven within Syria for refugees and possibly as a base for an opposition army – essentially a tethered goat stratagem designed to trigger regime attacks that American planes would then have to repel – Washington would become even more deeply engaged in the conflict.[21]

Like the war against ISIS itself, the president's balancing between the principles of the West Point and Oslo declarations is an act that his successor will almost certainly have to continue. And that successor, like Obama, will find this a very difficult task.

## Notes

1  Eric Li, 'A New Cold War in Asia?', IISS Global Strategic Review, Oslo, Norway, 21 September 2014, http://www.iiss.org/en/events/gsr/sections/global-strategic-review-2014-281a/plenary-4-9b37/discussion-38a2.

2  Kennedy to Arthur Schlesinger, Jr, quoted in Gordon M. Goldstein, *Lessons in Disaster: McGeorge Bundy and the Path to War in Vietnam* (New York: Henry Holt and Company, 2008), p. 41.

3  Peter Beinart, 'Obama's Foreign

Policy Doctrine Finally Emerges With "Offshore Balancing"', *Daily Beast*, 28 November 2011, http://www.thedailybeast.com/articles/2011/11/28/obama-s-foreign-policy-doctrine-finally-emerges-with-off-shore-balancing.html#.

4   Jeffrey Goldberg, 'Obama to Iran and Israel: "As President of the United States, I Don't Bluff"', *Atlantic*, 2 March 2012, http://www.theatlantic.com/international/archive/2012/03/obama-to-iran-and-israel-as-president-of-the-united-states-i-dont-bluff/253875/; Barack Obama, 'Remarks by the President at AIPAC Policy Conference', Washington DC, 4 March 2012, http://www.whitehouse.gov/photos-and-video/video/2012/03/04/president-obama-2012-aipac-policy-conference#transcript.

5   This section is adapted in part from Dana H. Allin, 'Letting Things Go', *Survival*, vol. 56, no. 4, August–September 2014, pp. 215–24.

6   Robert Kagan, 'The World and President Bush', *Survival*, vol. 43, no. 1, Spring 2001, p. 8.

7   Robert Kagan, 'Superpowers Don't Get to Retire', *New Republic*, 26 May 2014, http://www.newrepublic.com/article/117859/allure-normalcy-what-america-still-owes-world.

8   Andrew J. Bacevich, 'The Duplicity of the Ideologues: U.S. Policy & Robert Kagan's Fictive Narrative', *Commonweal Magazine*, 4 June 2014, https://www.commonwealmaga-zine.org/duplicity-ideologues.

9   *Ibid*.

10  Ezra Klein, 'The Green Lantern Theory of the Presidency, Explained', Vox, 20 May 2014, http://www.vox.com/2014/5/20/5732208/the-green-lantern-theory-of-the-presidency-explained.

11  Peter Beinart, 'The U.S. Doesn't Need to Prove Itself in Ukraine', *Atlantic*, 5 May 2014, http://www.theatlantic.com/international/archive/2014/05/us-credibility-fallacy-ukraine-russia-syria-china/361695/2/; Theodore G. Hopf, *Peripheral Visions: Deterrence Theory and American Foreign Policy in the Third World, 1965–1990* (Ann Arbor, MI: University of Michigan Press, 1994); Daryl G. Press, *Calculating Credibility: How Leaders Assess Military Threats* (Ithaca, NY: Cornell University Press, 2005).

12  Jonathan Chait, 'Obama Promised to Do 4 Big Things As President. Now He's Done Them All', *New York Magazine*, 8 June 2014, http://nymag.com/daily/intelligencer/2014/06/obama-has-now-fulfilled-his-4-big-promises.html.

13  'Is the Affordable Care Act Working?', *New York Times*, 26 October 2014, http://www.nytimes.com/interactive/2014/10/27/us/is-the-affordable-care-act-working.html?_r=0#/.

14  Robert Barnes, 'Supreme Court: EPA Can Regulate Greenhouse Gas Emissions, with Some Limits', *Washington Post*, 23 June 2014, http://www.washingtonpost.com/politics/supreme-court-limits-epas-ability-to-regulate-green-house-gas-emissions/2014/06/23/c56fc194-f1b1-11e3-914c-1fb-d0614e2d4_story.html.

15  Dana H. Allin and Steven Simon, 'Ukraine and Obama's "Credibility"', Politics and

Strategy, 6 March 2014, http://www.iiss.org/en/politics%20and%20strategy/blogsections/2014-d2de/march-1ef8/ukraine-and-obama-bcc4.

16 Peter Beinart, 'Pursuing ISIS to the Gates of Hell', *Atlantic*, 4 September 2014, http://www.theatlantic.com/international/archive/2014/09/why-americas-pursuing-isis-to-the-gates-of-hell/379622/?single_page=true.

17 Wesley Lowery, 'Biden to Islamic State: We Will Follow You "To the Gates of Hell"', *Washington Post*, 3 September 2014, http://www.washingtonpost.com/blogs/post-politics/wp/2014/09/03/biden-to-islamic-state-we-will-follow-you-to-the-gates-of-hell/.

18 Barack Obama, 'Remarks by the President in Address to the Nation on the Way Forward in Afghanistan and Pakistan', West Point, NY, 1 December 2009, http://www.whitehouse.gov/the-press-office/remarks-president-address-nation-way-forward-afghanistan-and-pakistan.

19 Bob Woodward, 'McChrystal: More Forces or "Mission Failure"', *Washington Post*, 21 September 2009, http://www.washingtonpost.com/wp-dyn/content/article/2009/09/20/AR2009092002920.html.

20 Barack Obama, 'Remarks by the President at the Acceptance of the Nobel Peace Prize', Oslo, Norway, 10 December 2009, http://www.whitehouse.gov/the-press-office/remarks-president-acceptance-nobel-peace-prize.

21 Steven Simon, 'Staying Out of Syria', *Foreign Affairs*, 26 October 2014, http://www.foreignaffairs.com/articles/142295/steven-simon/staying-out-of-syria.

# CHAPTER EIGHT

# Is Russia an Outside Power in the Gulf?

Samuel Charap

When Russia is invoked in analysis of outside powers' role in the Middle East, it is often thought of in two related ways: either as a shrunken Soviet Union or as a potential regional security guarantor should the United States abdicate that role. Following the 2013 IISS Manama Dialogue, a Gulf leader was quoted as saying: 'the Russians have proved they are reliable friends … As a result, some states in the region have already started to look at developing more multilateral relations, rather than just relying on Washington.'[1] This particular statement was alleged to have been fabricated, but the sentiment contained therein is broadly reflective of regional elite opinion about Russia.[2] The implication is that Russia seeks clients, as the Soviet Union did; is active in the region largely to compete with the US; and could, if asked, step in to displace or supplement the US regional role. Despite all of the headlines generated by the Ukraine crisis, however, Russia is not a shrunken Soviet Union, nor is it in a position to replace the US in the region.

While the Soviet Union had global ambitions and reach, Russia has neither. The Soviet Union was engaged in a global ideological competition with the US that created imperatives to seek influence and connections everywhere. That ideology also gave it a presence in many regions via communist parties, workers' movements, or governments with anti-Western policies. In contrast, post-Soviet Russia lacks both the ideological impetus and the geopolitical imperative to compete with the US in every region. Moreover, despite the country's economic recovery during the Putin era, it lacks the resources to project power – be it hard power, economic power or soft power – in the way that the Soviet Union did.

Post-Soviet Russia is a qualitatively different kind of outside power for the Middle East than the US. Firstly, it does not value what could be called 'regional public goods' enough to sacrifice for and provide them on its own – beyond its immediate neighbourhood, that is. Russia has not created military alliances, nor even offered security guarantees, beyond its neighbourhood. Moreover, it has no interest in doing so. This means that Russia does not have to balance its national interests in the region against broader objectives, a dilemma the US faces regularly due to its focus on regional public goods and its commitment to allies' security. For the US, goals such as maintaining stability in energy markets and countering Iran often trump worries about extremism or human-rights concerns. For Russia, however, there are no similar balancing factors that prevent it from pursuing its more narrow national priorities. While extremism is arguably an equal threat to both the US and Russia, the two countries focus on this problem in completely different ways.

Unlike the US, Russia is opportunistic and practical, rather than principled or ideological in its regional engagement. It does not use domestic politics or regime type as a criterion for judging how to engage with regional states: it will work with governments ranging from new democracies to old monarchies. Nor do Russian officials ask questions about what governments do to their domestic opposition. Part of the reason, of course, is that they do not like being asked the same questions about their own government's monopolisation of the political space at home.

Indeed, Moscow will speak to any country or entity that it does not consider a direct threat to Russia, even if some of those countries and entities are threats to one another. While its relationship with Israel is better than ever, it also has strong ties to Iran, and talks to Hamas. In other words, unlike the US, it will not adopt the threat perceptions of its regional partners, nor will it cater to them. Russia will not take sides in what it sees as the disputes of others.

This refusal to meddle arises in part from another aspect of Russian opportunism: the country's readiness to take advantage of regional displeasure with the US to make a buck, particularly in the military-industrial sphere. The military-industrial sector is a large employer at home, with a shrinking customer base worldwide. So, for example, if Egypt wants to demonstrate its displeasure with Washington by buying Russian kit, Moscow will be happy to sell. But this readiness stems from the weakness of Russia's market position globally, not its strength.

## Countering extremism at home

Russia's own Muslim citizens, who constitute 10–15% of the country's population, are a major factor in its engagement with the Gulf states.[3] Moscow demonstrates its credentials to that community by engaging with majority-Muslim countries and international groupings, such as by becoming an observer in the Organization of Islamic Cooperation.

Mostly, however, Moscow's regional engagement on this issue is defined by its 20-year struggle with Islamist extremism and terrorism at home, Russia's most significant domestic-security challenge. What began as a separatist conflict in Chechnya in the early 1990s evolved into a brutal Islamist insurgency, spreading violence to other republics in the North Caucasus and leading to spectacular acts of terror in Moscow and other large cities. The killing of Chechen rebel leader Aslan Maskhadov in 2005 was a watershed in the conflict, marking the shift away from nationalist separatism to an effort to establish what Dmitry Gorenburg has called a 'pan-regional Islamic state'.[4] In 2007, Doku Umarov, Maskhadov's successor, announced the creation of the 'Caucasus Emirate', a militant jihadist group aiming to establish an independent Islamic state in the greater Caucasus region.

Although violence in the Chechen republic itself has greatly decreased in recent years under the Kremlin-backed leadership of Akhmad Kadyrov, and later his son Ramzan, the Caucasus Emirate has found fertile ground in other regions of Russia's North Caucasus. Indeed, the epicentre of violence is now in Dagestan, the republic to Chechnya's east. Meanwhile, the reach of the organisation has extended all the way to Russia's core. In November 2009, the Caucasus Emirate took responsibility for a bombing on the Moscow–St Petersburg express train, which killed 27 people and injured 130. In 2010 the group carried out a subway bombing in Moscow that killed 40, and in 2011 a suicide attack at Domodedovo Airport that killed 37. The group carried out two suicide bombings in Volgograd in December 2013, weeks before the start of the Sochi Winter Olympic Games, killing 34.

The Russian government has long alleged that extremists in the North Caucasus have been funded and aided from abroad, particularly from entities in the Gulf. Specifically, Moscow has alleged that Gulf-based Islamic charity organisations both inject radical Islam into the region and bankroll extremist groups. Officials have fingered a range of Gulf-based groups, including the International Islamic Relief Organization, Al-Haramayn (The Two Holy Places), El-Hairiya (Charity), Jamiat Ihia Al-Turath Al-Islamiya (Revival of Islamic Heritage Society) and the Benevolence International Foundation.[5]

After the collapse of the Soviet Union, the North Caucasus, along with other Russian regions populated by Muslims (such as Tatarstan on the Volga river), experienced an Islamic revival. The Gulf-based charities were seen as the driving force behind that revival, financing the sudden boom in the construction of mosques in the North Caucasus and Volga regions – 300 such buildings in 1991 had grown to over 4,000 by 2001.[6] Some of the foundations sent Salafist clerics to oversee these institutions, with a mandate to bring traditionally moderate local practices into conformity with the Salafist tradition. Most of these clerics were expelled from Russia by the end of the 1990s, as the government came to equate those who practiced Salafism with Islamist extremists.[7]

In the early 2000s, Russian security officials reported that Gulf states were sending as much as $1.5–3 million per month in support of the foundations' activities.[8] Despite a crackdown on terrorist financing, Russian intelligence reported that, in 2003, charity organisations were delivering $500,000–1m a month to Chechnya.[9]

This linkage between extremism in Russia and the Gulf has coloured Russia's relations with the region. For example, the relationship with Kuwait came under strain in February 2003 when Moscow accused two NGOs tied to the Kuwaiti government, the Social Reform Society and the Society of the Revival of Islamic Heritage, of sponsoring terrorism. Moscow put both on a federal list of terrorist organisations and banned their operations in Russian territory.[10] Kuwait insisted that the two groups supported only charitable activities and were not involved in sponsoring terrorism.[11]

Regional states have also provided shelter to insurgents from the North Caucasus. On 13 February 2004, Zelimkhan Yandarbiyev, the former president of the self-proclaimed Chechen separatist government – the so-called 'Republic of Ichkeria' – was killed when a bomb ripped through his car in Doha, Qatar. Yandarbiyev had been accused by the Russian government of financing Chechen separatists and organising high-profile terrorist attacks in Moscow. Russia had repeatedly requested Yandarbiyev's extradition, but the Qatari government granted him asylum three years prior to his death. Two Russian intelligence officers were arrested for the bombing, convicted by a Qatari court and sentenced to life in prison. They were eventually extradited to Russia, where they were released from custody.

In short, Russia has come to see the Gulf countries as contributors to its most significant domestic security problem. This has not only created tensions between Russia and regional governments, particularly when Moscow has decided to act on its own to counter perceived threats, but also served to limit the extent to which Russia is willing to engage with the region on other issues.

Russian Islamist extremists have also participated in Middle Eastern conflicts in recent years. The presence of these insurgents compounds Russia's problems at home in two ways. Firstly, these jihadists are likely to return to Russia at some point, bringing all of their battlefield experience with them. Secondly, they have attempted to mobilise the global jihadist movement against the Russian government.

In 2012 reports surfaced that Russian Muslims had appeared in Syria and were fighting on behalf of various Syrian rebel groups. Estimates of the exact number of fighters from the North Caucasus have varied from as few as 150 to as many as 1,700.[12] Syrian opposition sources have indicated that Chechens (it should be noted that, in the Syrian conflict, the term 'Chechen', or 'Shishani' in Arabic, has been applied to any jihadist from the North Caucasus region) comprise the second-largest force of foreign fighters in Syria, coming after Libyans.[13]

Militants from the Caucasus region have even assumed top leadership positions in groups such as the Islamic State of Iraq and al-Sham (ISIS). For instance, Abu Umar al-Shishani, an ethnic Chechen from Georgia's Pankisi Gorge who fought against Russia in the Second Chechen War and the 2008 Russia–Georgia War, began his career in Syria as the emir of the al-Qaeda-inspired Jaish al-Muhajirin wal-Ansar (The Army of the Emigrants and Helpers). He subsequently swore the group's allegiance to ISIS. Since then, he has established himself as a tactical mastermind, reportedly rising in rank to become one of ISIS's top military commanders.[14]

ISIS has turned its sights on Russia as a future target, though its ability to carry out attacks on Russian soil seems limited. In a video released in early September 2014, an ISIS fighter sitting in a seized Russian military jet in Raqqa, the group's seat of power, said:

> This message is for you, Vladimir Putin! These are the aircraft you sent to Bashar [al-Assad], and we're going to send them to you. Remember that! We will with the consent of Allah free Chechnya and all of the Caucasus! The Islamic State is here and will stay here, and it will spread with the grace of Allah! … Your throne has already been shaken, it is under threat and will fall with our arrival … We're already on our way with the will of Allah![15]

Although these threats may amount to little more than propaganda for recruitment, or mere bluster, Russian security services blocked the video in Russia and launched a criminal investigation.[16] Ramzan Kadyrov took to Instagram to voice his disgust, posting: 'these bastards have no relation to Islam. They are outspoken enemies of Muslims around the world. Naive people chose to threaten Chechnya and all of Russia with two planes. They can send two thousand planes, but they will not reach Russia.'[17] Shishani has since placed a $5m bounty on Kadyrov's head.[18] He has also threatened to directly attack Russia. In a recording of an alleged phone call with his father, who still lives in Georgia's Pankisi Gorge, he said: 'don't worry Dad, I'll come home and show the Russians. I have many thousands following me now and I'll get more. We'll have our revenge against Russia.'[19]

It is unclear whether ISIS has the operational capacity to make good on these threats. Still, Russia now faces a declared threat from an organisation with demonstrated military capabilities, voiced by an Islamist leader from its insecure periphery who has vowed to bring his followers home to fight Russia.

## Making a buck

Moscow has made efforts to bolster economic engagement with the Middle East over the past decade, although overall the region still represents a relatively small portion of Russia's global trade and investment flows. Russia is also a marginal participant in the Gulf states' economies. In 2013 the value of total Gulf Cooperation Council (GCC) trade with the world was $1.47 trillion. The same year, Russia–GCC trade was valued at $3.74 billion, or 0.25% of GCC total trade and 0.45% of Russia's total trade. For comparison, China accounted for $165bn, or 11.24%, of total GCC trade that year.[20]

Growth in economic ties has centred on three areas: arms sales, upstream energy projects and mutual investment. In the period 2005–12, the Middle East as a whole accounted for 14.3% of Russia's arms-export contracts, or $8.2bn. As such, the region is the second-largest arms-export market for Russia, behind the Asia-Pacific.[21]

Following the British and French governments' decisions to revoke security-equipment export licenses to Bahrain after the monarchy's 2011 crackdown on protesters, Russia stepped in to fill the void. A source told Bloomberg that Rosoboronexport, Russia's arms-export monopoly, signed a multimillion-dollar contract to sell modernised Kalashnikovs with grenade launchers and ammunition to Bahrain. A Bahraini government spokesman said: 'the relationship between Russia and Bahrain has been increasingly getting stronger. We are looking to cooperate with Russia in trade and technical services. One of the fields is in the area of light arms.'[22]

Although ostensibly competitors, Russia and the Gulf states have developed some joint energy projects in the Middle East. In December 2010, Stroytransgaz completed the construction of the Taweelah–Fujairah gas pipeline in the United Arab Emirates, worth $417m.[23] In May 2014, Reuters reported that Russia's Lukoil would start drilling for unconventional gas in Saudi Arabia's 'Empty Quarter' desert region in 2015.[24]

While investment numbers are harder to find, that is clearly where the most significant engagement is currently occurring. Funds from the UAE, Kuwait, Qatar and Bahrain have made investments in Russia, ranging in size from hundreds of millions to billions of dollars, including in infrastructure projects and power companies, and in the Russia Direct Investment Fund, a government-managed fund targeting high-growth sectors of the economy. Inward foreign direct investment in Russia from Gulf states nearly quintupled during 2007–13.[25]

## Global imperatives

Despite all this, Russia is not a wholly pragmatic actor in the region, limiting itself to the pursuit of regional interests and conducting realpolitik. In fact, what can be called the primary global imperative of Russian foreign policy – the neutralisation of threats to 'regime stability' at home – will always trump Russia's regional interests in the Middle East (or any other region, for that matter) when the two conflict. At times, however, these two sets of interests can be mutually reinforcing. Much depends on the particular circumstances, and the attitudes of regional states towards those circumstances.

Russia's prioritisation of its own regime stability is manifest in its resistance to US-led regime-change efforts in the Middle East, whether real or imagined. Moscow has consistently argued that US military intervention is a major source of instability and extremism in the region; recently, for example, the Ministry of Foreign Affairs blamed US intervention for the rise of ISIS: 'the surge in terrorist threats in Iraq and the Middle East as a whole are largely the result of external unlawful military intervention in the internal affairs of states in order to address selfish geopolitical objectives.'[26] Moscow has also come to the conclusion that the West's allegedly irrepressible urge to topple inconvenient governments has at times trumped its efforts to counter extremism. At the International Conference on Peace and Security in Iraq, held in Paris on 15 September 2014, Russian Foreign Minister Sergei Lavrov said:

> The core of international efforts to combat terrorism has always been a willingness to address all of its forms and manifestations, not dividing terrorists into 'bad' and 'good' ones. Unfortunately, in the MENA [Middle East and North Africa] region, this fundamental principle began to falter. It has repeatedly been sacrificed to the aspirations for overthrowing a regime in a given country.[27]

He went on to cite Western actions in Libya and Iraq as examples.

But Moscow's justification of its opposition to Western-led regime change on regional grounds, while an accurate reflection of Russian thinking, is mostly convenient, rhetorical window dressing for a much more parochial concern. Many in the Russian foreign-policy establishment believe that the string of US-led interventions that have resulted in regime change since the end of the Cold War – Kosovo, Afghanistan, Iraq and Libya – set extremely dangerous precedents that could be used against Russia itself and its autocratic allies in its neighbourhood. Russia has wielded its veto to prevent the UN Security Council from giving its imprimatur to any intervention it suspected of being motivated by a stated or unstated intention to remove a sitting government. Above all else, Moscow wants to avoid legitimising US-led regime change or attempts to pick winners in internal conflicts.[28]

By prioritising this resistance to forcible regime change, Russia often appears to 'support' regimes in US cross hairs. But analysts should not confuse a by-product for a directed policy. Unfortunately, many have done just that when it comes to Russia's approach to the crisis in Syria. In the initial years of the conflict, journalists and policymakers alike focused on the ties (including military, military-industrial and intelligence-sharing) that allegedly bound Russia to the Assad regime. Western newspapers regularly published stories on Russian arms sales to Syria and its naval facility at Tartus. When it became clear that Moscow was still intent on resisting attempts to overthrow Assad even after these ties were literally destroyed by the civil war, observers settled on the more generic 'support' label: Russia supports Assad, so the argument goes, and therefore will do whatever it takes to keep him in office for as long as possible.

If Russia were indeed driven to keep Assad in power at all costs, its behaviour thus far would have been quite different. Like Iran, it would have supplied the regime with boatloads of mortars, artillery and tanks, and sent uniformed military advisers. Instead, its arms sales are largely confined to sophisticated air-defence systems, which are useless against the rebels. The terms of these deals are commercial – cash on delivery – without any below-market-rate state-bank loans to support the purchases (as per Russian practice elsewhere), let alone, as with Russia's allies, via an assistance package. Russia would have vetoed UN Security Council Resolutions 2042 and 2118, both of which called for a 'political transition' in Syria, instead of voting in favour of both. It would not have sponsored the Geneva communiqué, which requires that the opposition sign off on the composition of a future Syrian leadership, an implicit endorsement of a transition that does not include Assad himself. Senior officials would have explicitly stated their support for Assad, rather than repeatedly saying that they do not care about his fate.[29] For an example of what Russian support for a repressive regime really looks like, see how Russia backs Alexander Lukashenko's government in Belarus.

The September 2013 US–Russia deal to remove Syria's chemical weapons proves the point about the drivers of Russia's Syria policy. At the time, it was a major concession, considering that

Moscow had, just weeks before, rejected far less ambitious proposals. Why the major policy reversal? The Russian leadership was convinced that the US was on the verge of military strikes, and recognised that the chemical-weapons agreement could prevent these from proceeding. By putting forth the proposal, Russia succeeded in heading off US military action, but forced the Assad regime to give up its most potent weapon in its fight for survival.

Russia has paid a price, in terms of its regional interests, for its policy on the Syria crisis. Its stance has created friction in its relationships with all regional governments, with the exception of Iran. Yet this regional backlash has done little to sway Moscow. During a February 2012 meeting at the United Nations, the Qatari ambassador reportedly told his Russian counterpart, Vitaly Churkin, that Russia would lose the support of all Arab countries for its stance on Syria. Churkin allegedly retorted, 'If you talk to me in this tone Qatar will cease to exist as early as tomorrow.'[30] The next month, tensions between Russia and Saudi Arabia broke out into the open with a series of disparaging tit-for-tat statements. On 4 March the Russian Ministry of Foreign Affairs issued a statement accusing the Saudis of supporting terrorism in Syria, calling Riyadh's behaviour 'dangerous and irresponsible'.[31] The Saudi Ministry of Foreign Affairs responded by accusing Russia of giving the Assad regime 'license to commit more crimes' against the Syrian people 'in a way that is contrary to human morality and all international laws and norms'.[32] At the 2013 IISS Manama Dialogue, Prince Turki bin Faisal Al Saud, the former director of Saudi Arabia's intelligence service, said that Russia's 'manoeuvring' was tainted by 'the blood of the Syrian people'.[33] He went on to question whether Russia even had the right to attend the Geneva II conference on Syria.

A March 2014 decision by the Saudi government to supply MANPAD systems to Syrian rebels proved another occasion for a public airing of differences. Moscow said it was 'deeply concerned' by the move, which prompted the Saudi government to lash out: '[Russian] support is the principal reason for the barbarity of the Syrian regime and for the conflict dragging on for three years without hope of a settlement or of an end anytime soon to one of the most serious humanitarian crises of our time.'[34] In itself, such a 'dialogue' means little in terms of policy. However, it speaks volumes about the current tenor of Russia's relations with the Gulf states.

Russia's economic interests in the Gulf have also suffered as a result of its Syria policy. In June 2012, Saudi trade bodies twice refused a visit from Russian delegations in protest at Russia's support for Assad. According to Abdul Rahman Al Jaraisi, the head of the chamber of commerce in Riyadh, 'we refused to meet because we wanted to convey the message from the Saudi business community and from Saudi Arabia that we have reservations about the unfair and unjust way they have been dealing with Syria'.[35] In July 2012, Saudi tycoon Mubarak Swaikat responded to Russia's policies in Syria by cancelling large contracts with more than 20 Russian oil and gas companies. 'This is the least that I can do to support our brothers in Syria', he said.[36]

Arab populations, many of which were traditionally sympathetic to Russia due to the Soviet Union's support for Arab states, have reacted to Russia's Syria policy just as poorly as their governments. Following Russia's UN Security Council veto of a draft resolution on Syria in February 2012, hundreds of protesters gathered in front of Russian embassies in Tripoli, Amman and Doha.[37] Protesters in Tripoli were so incensed that a number of them climbed onto the roof of the Embassy and tore down the Russian flag.[38] There were also calls for boycotts of Russian goods in Arab countries. Beginning as grassroots movements on social media, these calls received support from the heads of the International Union of Muslim Scholars and the Jordanian Muslim Brotherhood. The Saudi press ran a number of articles supporting the calls for a boycott.[39]

According to the Pew Global Attitudes Project, Russia's reputation in Egypt, Jordan and Lebanon (the only Middle Eastern countries regularly polled) has steadily declined since the Syria crisis began. From 2010 to 2012, Russia's unfavourable ratings increased from 58%, 58% and 40% in those three countries to 65%, 70% and 48% respectively.[40]

Thus, the Syria case demonstrates that Russia's regional interests have suffered due to Moscow's adherence to the global imperative of resisting Western-led regime-change efforts. Russia's position on Syria undermined its position in the region and damaged its material stake there. Clearly, those regional ties have been given lower priority in the hierarchy of Russian foreign-policy decision-making.

## Libya: lessons learned

Developments since the fall of Muammar Gadhafi in Libya have taught Moscow that there is no upside to playing nice with the West on the intervention question. Although Russia did not foresee a regime-change effort when it abstained on UN Security Resolution 1973, and complained bitterly when it materialised, it did nothing to stop the NATO operation. Nevertheless, after Gadhafi's ouster, it lost lucrative contracts, and its interests in Libya have been largely ignored both by the West and the new government.

Russia held $8bn worth of contracts with Gadhafi's Libya, most of which have not been honoured.[41] A representative of the Libyan oil firm AGOCO told reporters in August 2011 that 'we don't have a problem with Western countries like the Italians, French and UK companies. But we may have some political issues with Russia, China and Brazil.'[42] This attitude seems to have been widespread among the new authorities. In addition, the Russian Embassy in Libya was attacked by armed gunmen in the evening of 2 October 2013, provoked by a Libyan citizen's alleged murder by a Russian citizen. The following day, the Embassy was completely evacuated, and it has remained closed ever since.[43]

In short, if there were any doubts left in Moscow that US intervention in the region can only cause problems for Russia, developments in Libya have put an end to them.

*     *     *

The crisis in and around Ukraine that began in February 2014 demonstrates the limits of Russia's 'outside power' status in the Gulf. For Moscow, not all regions are created equal. The Ukraine crisis is an all-consuming issue for Russian foreign policy because Ukraine and, more broadly, Russia's immediate neighbourhood, is the region in which Russia most commonly behaves like an outside power, in the sense that this term is often used in the Gulf. In its neighbourhood, Russia does seek to balance US influence, and it can provide such a counterweight. Moreover, doing so is a security imperative that trumps almost all other priorities. For example, Deputy Defence Minister Anatoly Antonov, when given an opportunity to address a plenary session at the May 2014 IISS Shangri-La Dialogue on Asia-Pacific security, spoke almost exclusively about the Ukraine crisis and the security threat that such 'coloured revolutions' pose to all regions, including the Asia-Pacific. His audience, after two days of focusing on the myriad challenges to regional security, was somewhat mystified by the choice of subject matter. By contrast, the US can 'multitask', dealing, for example, with the Ukraine crisis while simultaneously ramping up its anti-ISIS campaign.

The bottom line is that Russia has neither the means nor the desire to displace the United States in the Middle East, or to replicate the Soviet Union's role in the region. Both its material stake in the Middle East and its ability to influence events there are limited. Moreover, in the same way that the invasion of Afghanistan eroded the gains the Soviet Union had made in the region from the 1950s to the 1970s, Moscow's support for the Assad regime in Syria has threatened to spoil the steps Putin took to engage with the Middle East from 2000 onward.

## Acknowledgements

The author is extremely grateful to John Drennan and Hannah Alberts for their research assistance.

## Notes

[1] Con Coughlin, '"Schizophrenic" US Foreign Policy Pushing Arab States Toward Russia, Bahrain Warns', *Telegraph*, 8 December 2013, http://www.telegraph.co.uk/news/worldnews/middleeast/10504011/Schizophrenic-US-foreign-policy-pushing-Arab-states-toward-Russia-Bahrain-warns.html.

[2] 'Statement by Court of Crown Prince Regarding Daily Telegraph Article', Bahrain News Agency, 12 September 2013, http://www.bna.bh/portal/en/news/592477.

[3] Data supplied by the 'Russia' section of the CIA *World Factbook*, 2014, https://www.cia.gov/library/publications/the-world-factbook/geos/rs.html.

[4] Dmitry Gorenburg, *Russia's Muslims: A Growing Challenge for Moscow* (Washington DC: PONARS Eurasia, December 2006), p. 3, http://www.ponarseurasia.org/sites/default/files/policy-memos-pdf/pm_0421.pdf.

[5] Aleksei Malashenko and Akhmed Yarlykapov, 'Radicalisation of Russia's Muslim Community', MICROCON Policy Working Paper, 9 May 2009, p. 30, http://www.microconflict.eu/publications/PWP9_AM_AY.pdf.

[6] Gorenburg, *Russia's Muslims*, p. 1.

[7] *Ibid.*, p. 2.

[8] Nick Paton Walsh, 'Chechen Rebels Phone Gulf During Siege', *Guardian*, 4 December 2002, http://www.theguardian.com/world/2002/dec/05/chechnya.nickpatonwalsh.

[9] Sharon LaFraniere, 'How Jihad Made Its Way to Chechnya: Secular Separatist Movement Transformed by Militant Vanguard', *Washington Post*, 26 April 2003.

[10] Edinii federal'nii spisok organizatsii, 'Priznannykh terroristicheskimi Verkhovnym Sudom Rossiiskoi Federatsii', 14 February 2003, http://www.fsb.ru/fsb/npd/terror.htm.

[11] 'Posol Kuveyta: otnosheniyam mezhdu nashimi stranami dan "zelenii svet"', IslamNews, 28 August 2006, http://www.islamnews.ru/news-6125.html.

[12] 'How Many Chechens Are Fighting In Syria?', Radio Free Europe/Radio Liberty, 19 June 2013, http://www.rferl.org/content/chechen-syria-fighting-kadyrov/25022321.html.

13  Thomas Grove and Mariam Karouny, 'Militants from Russia's North Caucasus Join "Jihad" in Syria', Reuters, 6 March 2013, http://www.reuters.com/article/2013/03/06/us-syria-crisis-russia-militants-idUSBRE9251BT20130306.

14  Bassem Mroue, 'Omar al-Shishani, Chechen in Syria, Rising Star in ISIS Leadership', *Christian Science Monitor*, 3 July 2014, http://www.csmonitor.com/World/Latest-News-Wires/2014/0703/Omar-al-Shishani-Chechen-in-Syria-rising-star-in-ISIS-leadership.

15  'Islamskoe gosudarstvo: poslanie Putinu. "My osvobodim Chechnyu i ves' Kavkaz"', YouTube video posted by 'RusVideo63', 2 September 2014, https://www.youtube.com/watch?v=M244nSFJXe8.

16  'V Rossii zapreshchen dostup k videoobrashcheniyu boevikov "Islamskogo gosudarstva", ugrozhavshikh razvyazat' voinu v Chechne', NEWSru, 4 September 2014, http://www.newsru.com/russia/04sep2014/ig.html.

17  Ramzan Kadyrov, Instagram, 3 September 2014, http://instagram.com/p/seyn7uiRl5/?modal=true.

18  'Umar as-Shishani (Tarkhan Batirashvili)', *Kavkaz Uzel*, 26 September 2014, http://www.kavkaz-uzel.ru/articles/249731/.

19  Michael Winfrey, 'Islamic State Grooms Chechen Fighters Against Putin', Bloomberg, 9 October 2014, http://www.bloomberg.com/news/2014-10-08/how-islamic-state-grooms-chechen-fighters-against-putin.html.

20  Data supplied by the IMF, Direction of Trade Statistics, http://elibrary-data.imf.org.

21  'Ezhegodnik: Statistica i analiz mirovoi torgovli oruzhiem', Tsentra analiza mirovoy torgovli oruzhiem, 2013, http://www.armstrade.org/files/yearly_2013_3_1.pdf.

22  'Russia Strikes First Bahrain Arms Deal', Bloomberg, 25 August 2011, http://www.bloomberg.com/news/2011-08-25/russia-strikes-first-bahrain-arms-deal-after-u-k-french-bans.html.

23  Ministry of Foreign Affairs of the Russian Federation, 'Rossiisko-emiratskie otnosheniya', 10 October 2011, http://www.mid.ru/bdomp/ns-rasia.nsf/1083b79%2037ae580ae432569e7004199c2/ea9fc49475782a0a43256d-d3002cc34b.

24  'Russia's Lukoil to Drill for Tight Gas in Saudi Desert', Reuters, 15 May 2014, http://www.reuters.com/article/2014/05/15/saudi-lukoil-gas-idUSL6N0O034G20140515.

25  Central Bank of the Russian Federation, 'Russian Federation: Inward Foreign Direct Investment, by Geographical Allocation, 2007–2013', http://www.cbr.ru/Eng/statistics/print.aspx?file=credit_statistics/inv_in-country_e.htm&pid=svs&sid=ITM_48993.

26  Russian Ministry of Foreign Affiars, 'O spetsial'noi sessii Soveta OON po pravam cheloveka (SPCh) po voprosu o massovykh narusheni-yakh prav cheloveka v rezul'tate deyatel'nosti terroristicheskoi organizatsii "Islamskoe gosudarstvo Iraka i Levanta" (IGIL) na territorii Iraka', 2 September 2014, http://www.mid.ru/brp_4.nsf/newsline/D8BAD016AA1963FA44257D47002CAE94.

27  Russian Ministry of Foreign Affairs, 'Vystuplenie Ministra inostran-nykh del Rossii S.V. Lavrova na Mezhdunarodnoi konferentsii po obespecheniyu mira i bezopasnosti v Irake, Parizh', 15 September 2014, http://www.mid.ru/brp_4.nsf/news line/4CB0FB5E61731E5844257D540 03BB730.

28  See Samuel Charap, 'Russia, Syria and the Doctrine of Intervention', *Survival,* February–March 2013, vol. 55, no. 1, pp. 35–41.

29  See Jeremy Shapiro and Samuel Charap, 'Winning the Peace by Failing in Geneva', *Foreign Affairs,* 9 January 2014, http://www. foreignaffairs.com/articles/140641/ jeremy-shapiro-and-samuel-charap/ winning-the-peace-by-failing-in-geneva; Samuel Charap and Jeremy Shapiro, 'How the US Can Move Russia on Syria', Al-Monitor, 22 July 2014, http://www.al-moni-tor.com/pulse/originals/2013/07/ syria-russia-geneva-engagement-peace-process-us-interests.html#.

30  Corey Flintoff, 'Does Russia Have A Cogent Middle East Strategy?', NPR, 9 February 2012, http://www. npr.org/2012/02/09/146622704/ does-russia-have-a-cogent-middle-east-strategy.

31  'Saudi Official Rejects Russia's "False" Claims of Terrorism in Syria', BBC Monitoring Newsfile, 8 March 2012.

32  Ministry of Foreign Affairs of Saudi Arabia, 'Ministry of Foreign Affairs Rejects and Condemns the Statements Issued by the Spokesperson of the Russian Foreign Ministry', 10 March 2012, http://www.mofa.gov.sa/sites/ mofaen/ServicesAndInformation/ news/MinistryNews/Pages/ ArticleID201231010421303.aspx.

33  Statement by Prince Turki bin Faisal Al Saud, 'The Future of the Middle East: Conflict and Change', Sky News Arabia Opening Televised Panel, IISS Manama Dialogue 2013, Bahrain, 6 December 2013, https:// www.youtube.com/watch?v=8b3xb gf53fI&list=UUYygxNuTTlq2neh6F u6rP4Q.

34  'Saudi Arabia Hits Back at Russia Criticism on Syria Arms Deal', *Daily Star,* 1 March 2014, http:// www.dailystar.com.lb/News/ Middle-East/2014/Mar-01/248916-saudi-arabia-hits-back-at-russia-criticism-on-syria-arms. ashx#axzz3D7WQWTQw.

35  Habib Toumi, 'Saudi Tycoon Cancels Russia Contracts', Gulf News, 28 July 2012, http:// gulfnews.com/news/gulf/ saudi-arabia/saudi-tycoon-cancels-russia-contracts-1.1054408.

36  *Ibid.*

37  Joseph Logan and Patrick Worsnip, 'Russia, China Veto of Syria UN Resolution Sparks Outrage', Reuters, 5 February 2012, http://www. huffingtonpost.com/2012/02/05/ russia-china-veto_n_1255990. html; Muath Freij, 'Syrians Gather Outside Russian Embassy in Amman to Protest Support for Assad', *Jordan Times,* 5 February 2014, http://jordantimes.com/ syrians-gather-outside-russian-embassy-in-amman-to-protest-support-for-assad; 'Syrians Protest Outside Russian Embassy', *Peninsula,* 8 February 2012, http:// thepeninsulaqatar.com/news/ qatar/182617/syrians-protest-outside-russian-embassy.

38 Logan and Worsnip, 'Russia, China Veto of Syria UN Resolution Sparks Outrage'.

39 Y. Yehoshua, 'Following Russian–Chinese Veto in Security Council, Increasing Calls in Arab World to Boycott Russian, Chinese Goods', Report No. 794, Inquiry & Analysis Series, The Middle East Media Research Institute, 7 February 2012, http://www.memri.org/report/en/0/0/0/0/0/0/6059.htm.

40 Data supplied by the Pew Research Center's Global Attitudes Project, http://www.pewglobal.org/. The Pew Research Center bears no responsibility for the analyses or interpretations of the data presented here.

41 Dmitri Trenin, *The Mythical Alliance: Russia's Syria Policy* (Moscow: Carnegie Moscow Center, 12 February 2013), http://carnegie.ru/2013/02/12/mythical-alliance-russia-s-syria-policy/ffl4#.

42 Svetlana Kovalyova and Emma Farge, 'UPDATE 4-ENI Leads Libya Oil Race; Russia, China May Lose Out', Reuters, 22 August 2011, http://www.reuters.com/article/2011/08/22/libya-oil-idUSL5E7JM17F20110822.

43 Russian Ministry of Foreign Affairs, 'Zayavlenie ofitsial'nogo predstavitelya MID Rossii A.K. Lukashevicha v svyazi s evakuatsiei sotrudnikov Posol'stva Rossii v Livii', 3 October 2013, http://www.mid.ru/brp_4.nsf/newsline/6778F4FE3EFCF18244257BF90049511A.

# CHAPTER NINE

# China and the Middle East

## Alexander Neill

China is sometimes described as a reluctantly growing power in the Middle East, due to the wariness with which Chinese leaders view the political turmoil and many wars of the region.[1] Beijing is particularly unsettled by the Arab Spring, which it believes has a demonstration effect that could inspire a 'Jasmine revolution' at home, and by the spread of Islamic radicalism from al-Qaeda fighters in Pakistan's tribal areas to Uighur separatists in the restive Turkic Muslim region of Xinjiang.

Against a background of hesitant Western policy on the Middle East, China's more consistent approach to the region has allowed it to operate in states in which the interests of America and its allies have diminished, such as Libya, Sudan and Iraq. The concurrent rise in political tension between Washington and Riyadh has led to strengthened Saudi–Chinese ties, reflected in the latter's alleged recent purchase of the Chinese-made DF-21 missile, among other deals.

Washington's attempt to relinquish its traditional leadership role in the Gulf creates a strategic opportunity for Beijing, albeit a problematic one. Many Chinese strategists are intrigued by America's manoeuvres in the region as an indication of its future behaviour in the Asia-Pacific, and some have advocated a more assertive approach to the Middle East based on cultural links, and even cooperation with European powers in the Gulf. Regardless of whether it chooses this specific course, China will inevitably be pushed further into the Middle East arena by its burgeoning energy needs.

Beijing created new alliances in the region during the Cold War, but was initially unable to capitalise on these relationships due to the turmoil of the Cultural Revolution. This started to change after Chinese President Deng Xiaoping enacted the reform and opening policies of the early 1980s, and particularly after 1993, when China became a net oil importer.[2] Having theretofore taken an amoral, mercantilist approach to the Middle East, China began in the 1990s to see the region as fertile ground for the promotion of multipolarity, a policy furthered in particular by then-Special Envoy on the Middle East Wu Sike during the 2000s and 2010s. Although rising demand has led China to diversify its oil supplies, the Middle East remains the country's main source of the product. America's energy independence from the region has encouraged Middle East leaders to increasingly look to China, a shift that has been compounded by their anxiety over Washington's 'rebalance' to Asia. (This concern is shared by their counterparts in Europe, some of whom may have started to hedge in the same way.) China accounted for more than 60% of the growth in global oil consumption in 2011–13. The country imports more oil than the United States, and is projected to consume more of the product than its rival by 2030.[3]

Much recent strategic discourse has focused on China's need for energy from the Middle East, and has underplayed the country's interest in exporting to the region, as well as the enthusiasm for Chinese investment there. The value of China's exports to the Middle East grew from $6.47 billion in 1999 to $121bn in 2012, and large-scale infrastructure and other construction projects have become a major feature of the Chinese economic activity in the region, as have services such as telecommunications and finance.[4] Companies such as Huawei, ZTE and China Unicom have played a major role in the establishment of mobile networks and digital infrastructure in the Middle East.

Hence, the region has enticing yet complicated prospects for China. Unlike the country's newfound influence in the Asia-Pacific – where its rise has been shaped by rivalry with Washington's 'hub and spokes' network of alliances – Chinese power in the Middle East has often been ill-defined.[5] Beijing's turn westward has long been explained in terms of establishing resource arteries across the Indian Ocean and Central Asia, but it is only recently that it has produced a narrative on the link between the Middle East and core Chinese interests. The vision of the Chinese leadership involves two new versions of the 'Silk Road': the first of these is a maritime route across the Indian Ocean, the Red Sea and the Mediterranean to Greece; the second extends overland from Xinjiang to Europe, via Central Asia and the Middle East.

## Beijing's history of engagement with the Middle East

From the founding of the People's Republic in 1949 to its acquisition of a permanent seat on the UN Security Council in 1971, China largely engaged with the Middle East through front organisations. Following the 1955 Bandung Conference, which brought together Asian and African countries, China was able to open a small number of diplomatic missions in the Levant and North Africa. The royal families of the Middle East, which at the time included monarchs in Iran and Iraq, were wary of republican China. However, Baghdad established relations with Beijing soon after the 1958 revolution in Iraq, led by Abd al-Karim Qasim. This helped to offset the deterioration of the relationship between China and Egypt caused by Egyptian President Gamal

Abdel Nasser's support for Moscow in a Sino-Soviet dispute over a border in Xinjiang. The subsequent break between the Chinese leadership and the Kremlin damaged many of China's alliances in the Middle East, with the result that Beijing had little leverage in the region, and could provide only moral support for Arab revolutionary movements.

By 1972, the year of the historic visit to China by US President Richard Nixon, a common interest in curbing Soviet influence had improved some of Beijing's relationships in the Middle East. China's admission to the UN Security Council had allowed it to open trade and diplomatic missions in the region, laying the groundwork for Deng's reforms a decade later. By the time of the 1979 Iranian Revolution, China had abandoned its ideological zeal and sketched out policies on the Middle East that have remained largely intact to this day. Beijing's approach has been based on the principles that China should not involve itself in the internal affairs of other states, and should avoid becoming a hegemon in the region, thereby avoiding costly responsibilities.

China's enthusiasm for trade drove it to sell weapons to both sides of the Iraq–Iran War (1980–88). Beijing's provision of arms to Tehran has been a key element of the Sino-Iranian relationship ever since, and proliferated Chinese weapons systems have often appeared on the modern-day battlefields of Syria and Iraq.

The improvement in Cold War relations between Beijing and Middle East governments was interrupted by the fallout of Tiananmen Square and the instability in the Gulf that followed Iraq's 1990 invasion of Kuwait. Taking to heart Deng's advice to 'bide one's time, hide one's talents', Beijing shifted the focus of its foreign policy to the Asia-Pacific, acquiescing to US preferences in the Gulf.

Nonetheless, the relationship with Iran remained strong for many years; exports of Chinese weapons to the country steadily increased and Tehran received Beijing's assistance in the development of its civilian nuclear programme. Following the rapid growth of China's economy and need for energy throughout the 1990s, Iran had by 2000 become the largest exporter of crude to China. This energy demand caused Beijing to view Central Asian states as not a buffer to the Middle East but an extension of it, and to centre its Gulf policy on the Sino-Iranian relations.[6] In recent years, China has sought to balance the relationship with its wider strategic interests, particularly in the wake of Tehran's increasing intervention in Shia-majority states and the onset of its confrontation with the US over the Iranian nuclear programme. This adjustment was reflected in Beijing's support for UN sanctions on Iran over the nuclear issue, even while it maintained beneficial Sino-Iranian trade and energy agreements.

After the 2005 accession of Abdullah bin Abdul Aziz Al Saud to the Saudi throne, Riyadh began to pay more attention to Asia. In 2008 China's trade with Saudi Arabia was valued at $42bn, the highest such figure for any Middle East state. Three years later, Riyadh had become China's largest crude-oil supplier, providing the country with close to 1.1 million barrels per day.[7] Leaders in Beijing and Riyadh regularly undertake state visits to each other's countries, and have developed their relationship around shared security concerns, such as Islamic extremism and instability in Pakistan. Spurred by Saudi Arabia's doubts about the US commitment to its security, Riyadh's relations with Beijing have entered an intriguing new phase that includes tentative cooperation on defence.

## Chinese policy on the Middle East

In light of Beijing's traditionally apolitical, mercantilist approach to the Middle East, the debate on the region among Chinese strategists has focused on the impact of US intervention and the role that China should play as a stakeholder in the security there.[8] However, with Beijing's development of a more assertive brand

of leadership, which includes a 'new type of great-power relations' with the US, many in China have questioned whether their
country is prepared to challenge core American interests in both
the Asia-Pacific and the Middle East.[9] China's ongoing reluctance
to act as a security guarantor in the latter region contrasts with
its policy on security in Asia, which President Xi Jinping envi-
sions as controlled by Asians alone. Speaking on a recent trip to
Cairo, Gong Xiaosheng, China's new special envoy on the Middle
East, repeated the familiar refrain: Middle East issues should be
resolved by the people of the region.

When criticised for this approach, Beijing responds that
China has contributed front-line UN peacekeeping troops for the
first time in Lebanon; provided warships to protect sea lines of
communication in the Gulf of Aden; and deployed military vessels
in the Mediterranean as part of the mission to dispose of Syria's
declared chemical arms coordinated by the Organisation for the
Prohibition of Chemical Weapons.

As a permanent member of the UN Security Council, China has
taken a distinctly pro-Arab position and often impeded Western
interests, abstaining from the 2011 vote on intervention in Libya
and subsequently vetoing three resolutions on Syria, in tandem
with Russia. Beijing's voting behaviour has consistently adhered
to what it describes as the five principles of peaceful coexis-
tence.[10] Yet, despite its decade-long habit of challenging American
policy on the Middle East, China supported the 2003 UN vote to
recognise the US–British occupation of Iraq, and has persistently
opposed Iran's nuclear programme.

Beijing is thought to have vetoed the UN resolutions on Syria
due its principle of non-intervention and its belief that foreign
military action exacerbates radicalisation in Middle East societies. China has steadfastly refused to join US-led coalitions, with
the exception of the George W. Bush administration's 'coalition
of the willing', established in the wake of 9/11. (In return for this

show of support, the US Department of State agreed to back the inclusion of the East Turkestan Islamic Movement on the UN list of terrorist organisations.)

Chinese commentators often describe Beijing's ability to cross the great political rifts of the Middle East as 'baggage-free diplomacy'. China has traded with Saudi Arabia and Iran alike, and invested in both Israel and Palestine; it seems to view the threat of regime change in the Middle East as the cost of doing business there.[11] In Egypt, China maintained close links with the regime of Hosni Mubarak for three decades. Beijing also engaged with the Muslim Brotherhood government that succeeded him, and has maintained good relations with the military government currently in power. In Syria, China has retained its links to President Bashar al-Assad while establishing a relationship with the opposition.

China's economic strength appears to have made it impervious to the political concerns of its Gulf trading partners. Both Doha and Riyadh were annoyed by Beijing's approach to Syria at the UN, but have not allowed their discontent to affect the economic relationship. China's increasingly adroit and well-funded diplomacy in the Middle East is directed towards winning support in a multipolar system, and advocacy for developing countries in the region. After the onset of the global financial crisis in 2008, Beijing made even greater calls for multipolarity and South–South cooperation, enhancing its influence in the Middle East through the Forum on China–Africa Cooperation and the China–Arab States Cooperation Forum. (The latter organisation provides a forum for members of the Arab League to negotiate international initiatives such as large-scale infrastructure projects.) Beijing appointed an envoy on Syria in 2012, ten years after nominating its first special envoy on the Middle East, whose primary role had been to seek a resolution to the Israel–Palestine conflict.

## Military development

The drive to modernise China's military was not inspired by the strength of American forces in the Asia-Pacific, but by the display of US and allied military power during the First Gulf War. In the early 2000s, the remit of the People's Liberation Army (PLA) was expanded to include the protection of Chinese interests far from home, as President Hu Jintao promoted the idea that the military had 'new historic missions'. This more ambitious role was reflected in China's 2011 operation to evacuate 36,000 Chinese citizens from Libya, which required the deployment of a warship, and in recent anti-piracy missions in the Gulf of Aden.[12] These latter operations have been far less problematic than China's naval activity in the Asia-Pacific, where its military rivalry with the US, Japan and smaller Asian powers carries the risk of inter-state conflict. China has contributed to anti-piracy efforts in order to prevent the hijacking of Chinese-flagged ships, a problem that came to light in 2008. Beijing regards such operations as a valuable opportunity to target non-state actors alongside, if not under the command of, international missions by states who share its security concerns.[13]

But these initiatives have also highlighted the Chinese military's lack of permanent bases and established centres of influence in the Middle East. They are therefore something of an experiment for China, allowing it to test its capacity to protect sea lines of communication in cooperation with other states. Beijing's willingness to relax its principle of non-intervention for these missions is driven by self-interest that could also lead it to deploy its first aircraft carrier, the *Liaoning*, to the Persian Gulf. The ship could potentially make its port call in the Gulf at the Doha Port facility currently being constructed by a Chinese company.

China's maritime interests in the region extend beyond countering piracy, however, and it has voiced concern about the possibility that Tehran will deny access to the Strait of Hormuz. Nonetheless, its weapons exports to the Middle East, which in

2012 were valued at $45m, have included arms supplies to Iran that could be used to implement such a blockade.[14] Although China has in recent years accounted for only 5% of arms exports to the Middle East, a market dominated by Western firms, it has come under international scrutiny for certain deals, particularly its sale of missiles to Iran during the 1980s and 1990s.[15] The extent to which Chinese weapons have proliferated was shown during the 2006 war between Israel and Hizbullah, when the group successfully struck an Israeli corvette, the INS *Hanit*, using a Chinese-made C-802 missile.

Beijing's arms exports to the region have been a point of contention in Sino-American relations for three decades, and, like its diplomacy, have transcended local rivalries. Washington has been particularly displeased with its attempts to procure advanced weapons technologies from the Israelis, such as the *Phalcon* early-warning system (the sale of which the US objected to in the late 1990s) and those related to unmanned aerial vehicles. The Chinese air force participated in the 2010 Turkish military exercise *Anatolian Eagle*; three years later, Ankara unsettled its NATO allies by announcing that it would purchase China's HQ-9 long-range surface-to-air missile system.

The Middle East is no longer a dumping ground for cheap Chinese versions of Soviet arms, as China's share of international defence markets increases and the country develops new weapons systems for export. Chinese defence companies such as Norinco and the Poly Technologies are less constrained than their Western competitors by domestic political scrutiny of their relationships and marketing campaigns in the region. Saudi Arabia appears to be particularly interested in purchasing Chinese arms: in April this year, Riyadh for the first time displayed the Chinese-made DF-3 ballistic missiles that it had purchased during a frosty period in US–Saudi relations in the 1980s. Rumours have circulated that Riyadh is willing to buy JF-17 fighters, built jointly by China and

Pakistan (although such a purchase would be politically motivated, and would not address a military need). The creation of Saudi Arabia's strategic rocket force may also provide China with a reliable export market.

The kingdom's reported purchase of the more advanced DF-21 missile from China, in 2007, allegedly took place with the consent of the US.[16] (The Pentagon is likely to take a particular interest in the deployment of this weapon, which it regards as an anti-access/area-denial system that could be used by China in the Asia-Pacific theatre.) If such collusion on the purchase of the DF-21 has taken place, the obvious focus of the deterrent would be Iran's nuclear programme. This would indicate that Beijing is becoming more willing to share the burden of maintaining the Middle East security order, a trend also suggested by its deeper involvement in UN peacekeeping operations, which have included a growing PLA deployment to southern Lebanon. However, the purchase could also compel Iran to pursue a nuclear weapon more energetically, out of fear that the DF-21 will be used as a delivery system for a Saudi nuclear device, developed in cooperation with Pakistan.

## China's economic strategy

In May 2014, China's Xinhua news agency unveiled Beijing's strategy for promoting China's economic growth and interconnectivity with Europe and Africa.[17] The Chinese leadership centred the plan on Xi's 'Chinese Dream' and two trade routes, adopting the slogan 'New Silk Road, New Dreams'.[18] Both of these routes pass through large swathes of the Middle East, but China has avoided designating key Middle East cities as waypoints on the routes.

For most of the last decade, commentary on China's economic rise has focused on the country's littoral as the key to its success. Beijing has been right to link national power to maritime trade and logistics, as shown by the rapid growth of China's coastal economic zones. Historically, the provinces of Guangdong and Fujian have served as a gateway not only for trade but for Chinese emigration. Many of China's current politburo members built their careers on careful stewardship of coastal regions. Beijing's conception of a maritime Silk Road has allowed it to link three of the most economically vibrant maritime regions in the world: the South China Sea, the Persian Gulf and the Mediterranean.

But the success of China's coastal regions has not been replicated in Xinjiang, the western hinterland that makes up around half of the country's landmass and whose name means 'new frontier'. Xinjiang has traditionally served as the transit point for trade and cultural exchange between Chinese civilisation and the Middle East. Judaism, Islam and early Christian sects spread from the Middle East to China via the ancient Silk Road through Xinjiang. At the turn of the millennium, Beijing launched the Great Western Development Strategy, designed to revitalise China's west through investment.

A potential complication for both the land and maritime versions of the new Silk Road is China's limited capacity to secure them. This problem is indicated by the fact that Tehran is the only Middle East city marked as a waypoint on Chinese maps of the routes. The sea route relies on the Red Sea for transit to the Mediterranean, and does not include a loop into the Persian Gulf, while the land route largely travels to the north of the Arab states, only briefly skirting through northern Iraq.

Since abandoning its ideological courtship of Middle East regimes, Beijing has developed a pragmatic approach to the region designed to improve Chinese energy security, thereby underpinning rapid economic growth at home and, by extension, the legitimacy of Communist Party rule. As China's oil consumption nears 10m b/d, the country is becoming an increasingly important source of goods for the Middle East, while the Gulf states are providing progressively more capital to the Chinese financial-services sector.[19] The continued prosperity of several Gulf states depends on China. Simon Williams, an HSBC economist, has commented that:

> As a consequence of this China-driven surge in oil receipts, the energy exporters of the Gulf have seen their aggregate GDP increase by $1 trillion in a decade to $1.7tn, lifting per capita GDP to an average of $35,000 and close to $100,000 in Qatar and Abu Dhabi.[20]

China's energy diversification has been to the detriment of Iran. The declining Iranian oil industry has become more reliant on Beijing, as Chinese enterprises have taken over from European companies forced by sanctions to abandon upstream development of Iran's oil resources. By 2010, Iranian oil exports to China had fallen to less than 200,000b/d, prompting some analysts to ask whether the fall-off resulted from a strategic decision by Beijing. This development occurred during the period in which China became both the largest buyer of Saudi crude and the main source of exports to the Middle East. Beijing also reconfigured the Chinese refining industry to focus on Saudi Arabia's crude products around the same time, and Saudi companies have invested heavily in related ventures. Benefiting from the availability of petrochemical derivatives in the Gulf, China has expanded its operations into the Middle East's medical and pharmaceuticals industries, as well as its agrochemicals sector.

Given the perceived decline of US influence in the Gulf and doubts about the viability of Washington's rebalance to Asia, has China 'pivoted' towards the Middle East? The importance that Riyadh places on its relationship with Beijing is indicated by the fact that the Saudi monarch's first state visit was to China, as well as the frequency with which Chinese leaders have travelled to Saudi Arabia.[21] While the US looks to Asia for domestic and global economic growth, China regards Europe as its biggest market. Against this background, the Middle East becomes a key link in the economic and political interests of both great powers. In 2011 China's trade with Europe and the US was valued at $567bn and $446bn respectively. Beijing views the Middle East as a trade, logistics and financial hub, and in 2014 Chinese trade with the Arab states was worth more than $300bn.[22]

The United Arab Emirates has particularly benefited from Chinese economic expansion: more than 3,000 Chinese companies operate in the country, supporting 200,000 Chinese residents.[23] In the financial sector, the UAE has become a centre for trading in the renminbi; organisations there and in the wider Middle East provide access to markets in Africa, which are thought to employ more than one million Chinese traders and to generate $120bn in trade with China.[24] China's exports to the Middle East have included consumer electronics, textiles, light machinery and automobiles. In 2012 its top markets for such goods were the UAE ($30bn), Saudi Arabia ($18bn), Turkey ($16bn), Iran ($11bn) and Egypt ($8bn).[25] Middle East states' enthusiasm for investing in Chinese interests was shown in the July 2010 public offering by the Agricultural Bank of China, which raised $23bn, almost $4bn of which came from the Qatar and Kuwait investment authorities.[26] Gulf Cooperation Council investors are gaining confidence in China's growth, and will continue to play an important role in the country's financial sector.

Chinese state-owned energy firms have broadened their ambitions beyond satisfying China's immediate energy requirements. For example, in the wake of the 2003 invasion of Iraq, they secured three of the country's 11 major oil-extraction contracts, including one for the development of the enormous Rumaila oil field. Operating primarily at sites south of Baghdad, within the Shia sphere of influence, Chinese energy firms may have sought to avoid investing in the more politically controversial northern fields run by the Kurdistan Regional Government. What interests China has in the north are threatened by the advances of the Islamic State of Iraq and al-Sham (ISIS), particularly the group's capture of the oil-rich city of Mosul; nonetheless, some analysts have argued that Iraq could become China's largest supplier of crude by 2020.

In 2011 Chinese activity in the Middle East construction market was valued at more than $21bn, and China's largest customers in the region were Saudi Arabia ($4.4bn), Algeria ($4.1bn), Iran ($2.2bn), the UAE ($1.9bn) and Iraq ($1.8bn). (This is in sharp contrast to Chinese overseas direct investment in the region, which amounted to only $1.3bn in 2010.)[27] In line with Beijing's Silk Road vision, Chinese contractors are involved in more than half of the transport and infrastructure construction projects in the Middle East.[28] In Saudi Arabia, China is investing heavily in new rail links across the Arabian Peninsula, and is close to completing the Haramain High Speed Rail project, which will link Mecca to Medina, via Jeddah. China Civil Engineering Construction Corporation is building a north–south rail line that will connect the kingdom's mineral-rich north with Riyadh and Jubail. Beijing has also invested $4bn in a five-year project to build a high-speed Eilat–Haifa rail link, which will bypass the Suez Canal.[29] Chinese companies have assisted in the development of Libya's rail infrastructure, and Iran's east–west railway. Beijing has invested in Egypt's Tianjin Economic and Technological Development Area (TEDA), where there are also plans to establish high-speed rail lines. China's Electric Power Construction Corporation has started work on a desalination and power plant at Ras al-Khair, Saudi Arabia, and China Harbour Engineering is building a bauxite-processing facility nearby. Along with their work on the Doha Port project, Chinese companies are involved in the development of Boubyan Port, Kuwait.

In digital communications, Huawei has 4,000 employees in the Middle East. The firm generates $2.5bn in revenues there, a figure that increases by almost 20% annually, and it provides 4G mobile Internet access across large parts of Saudi Arabia.[30] As early as the mid-1990s, Beijing assisted in Iraq's construction of a hardened fibre-optic network for national air-defence systems. After the 2003 invasion of the country (in which the US destroyed that network), Chinese companies were the first to assist in the rebuilding of the telecommunications infrastructure. Huawei has won more than 600 contracts in Iraq since 2004, leading one US official to claim that the firm 'owned' Iraqi telecommunications.[31]

## Islamic extremism

Like Washington and its allies, Beijing is growing more concerned about the threat to domestic security posed by ISIS. Abu Bakr al-Baghdadi, the group's leader, has referred to China as a country that persecutes Muslims, and his imagined caliphate extends into Xinjiang. The appearance of Chinese Uighurs within the ranks of ISIS has coincided with an increasingly sophisticated and elusive insurgency in China's west. For almost two decades, militants from the East Turkestan Islamic Movement have found sanctuary in Pakistan's tribal areas, joining the Islamic Movement of Uzbekistan and other al-Qaeda affiliates. Uighurs made up part of Osama bin Laden's entourage, and a small number of them were captured by US forces during the invasion of Afghanistan. The leadership of the East Turkestan Islamic Movement has been targeted by American drone strikes.

More recently, Uighur militants who adhere to al-Qaeda's philosophies have distanced themselves from the East Turkestan secessionist movement, reorganising as the Turkestan Islamic Party, with the intent of waging war on the Han population in Xinjiang. In the last two years, well-planned terrorist attacks have been carried out in Xinjiang and even Tiananmen Square. Despite draconian measures by the Chinese security forces and a broad campaign to suppress Muslims in the region, the group has persisted in its campaign. The territory held by ISIS in Syria and northern Iraq may provide a new base for the Turkestan Islamic Party, and there is some evidence that the former group has established a unit comprised of Chinese Uighurs. Should the international campaign against ISIS drive back the group in coming months, China could face the prospect of battle-hardened Uighurs returning to Xinjiang.

In private, Washington and some of its allies have lamented Beijing's lack of engagement with interventions in the Middle East and Afghanistan, especially in light of growing Chinese military capabilities.[32] The threat posed by ISIS could therefore create a new opportunity for security cooperation between China and the West. However, it is more likely that Beijing will take a similar approach to Moscow, repeating its non-interventionist mantra and strictly limiting its participation.

Beijing remains concerned about Turkey, where a sizeable Uighur population actively campaigns for the establishment of a breakaway republic that would include Xinjiang. In 2009 then-President Abdullah Gül delivered a warmly received speech in Turkish to Uighur students at Xinjiang University, underlining their cultural ties. Gül emphasised the 1,500-year relationship between Xinjiang and Turkey, proclaiming that regional capital Urumqi was a new gateway for the Silk Road. Just days later, the city was hit by the worst riots in the region for decades. The response of the Chinese security forces resulted in the deaths of hundreds of demonstrators, an event that then-Turkish Prime Minister Recep Tayyip Erdogan described as 'tantamount to genocide', causing Beijing to immediately demand an apology.[33]

Given Turkey's position as an entry point to Syrian battlefields, it is plausible that Uighur jihadists will travel through the country to join the conflict in Syria and Iraq, eventually posing a threat to Chinese interests in the Middle East. Possible targets include Dubai's Dragon Mart, the world's largest foreign-based trading centre for Chinese goods, which in 2009 was the subject of a planned bombing by two Uighur militants.[34] The many Chinese workers involved in large-scale infrastructure projects and upstream oil production in the Middle East could also be vulnerable to attacks similar to that at Algeria's Tigantourine gas facility in January 2013.

## A period of adjustment?

As Jon Alterman argued in 2011, there is something inherently unstable about a Middle East order that relies on the West for its security and the East for its prosperity.[35] Beijing will face an increasingly complex set of policy challenges as it develops closer relationships with states in the region, which may require an adjustment by Chinese strategists accustomed to focusing on the Asia-Pacific and the relationship with Washington. Nevertheless, the groundwork for this shift was laid in the early 2000s, when Hu tasked Chinese research institutes with planning around a Chinese periphery that extended to West Asia. Although Beijing's main concern remains its 'near abroad', Chinese leaders now view interdependency with the Middle East as vital to national interests.

Having been preoccupied with the American military presence, complex great-power relations and intractable conflicts in the Middle East, China will be forced to dedicate far more attention to its relationship with Saudi Arabia, while closely watching US policy in the region and maintaining its business interests in Iran. In the UN Security Council, Chinese diplomats will need to vote in such a way as to reassure their Gulf partners, observe China's core principles and distinguish Beijing's behaviour from that of Moscow, particularly after Russia's challenge to the sovereignty and territorial integrity of Ukraine. According to Yitzhak Shichor, Chinese diplomats in the Middle East are being forced to abandon the Daoist principle of *wu wei*, which teaches that inaction produces dividends.[36]

Washington continues to be frustrated by Beijing, which it regards as largely free-riding on American efforts to improve Middle East security, such as the war in Afghanistan. In contrast, Chinese leaders maintain the position that US-led interventions in the region have only caused further instability, a view that is widely backed by the Chinese public. Yet Xi's new National Security Commission will need to deal with the jihadist threat in the absence of any significant Chinese contribution to the international coalition that opposes ISIS. China also needs to consider how it might be affected by the rising costs of exporting to, and operating in, the Middle East. Beijing appears eager to avoid assuming the traditional US leadership role in the region, but its policy of non-intervention and economic incentivisation may become untenable as the war in Syria and Iraq continues.[37] Although China and the Middle East can appear to be culturally distant from each other, they often have a shared interest in opposing Western interests. Political and business leaders in Beijing will prioritise pragmatism, flexibility and economic success over tradition and accountability in the region. As China's influence in the Middle East grows, it is unclear whether they will be able to maintain their neutrality.

## Notes

[1] John B. Alterman, 'China's Balancing Act in the Gulf', Center for Strategic and International Studies, August 2013, http://csis.org/files/publication/130821_Alterman_ChinaGulf_Web.pdf.

[2] Brad Plumer, 'China Now Gets More Oil from the Middle East than the US Does', 3 September 2013, http://www.vox.com/2014/9/3/6101885/middle-east-now-sells-more-oil-to-china-than-to-the-us.

[3] Erica S. Downs, 'China–Middle East Energy Relations', Brookings Institution, 6 June 2013, http://www.brookings.edu/research/testimony/2013/06/06-china-middle-east-energy-downs.

[4] 'Hearing on "China and the Middle East"', testimony of Dawn C. Murphy before the US–China Economic and Security Review Commission, 6 June 2013, http://www.uscc.gov/sites/default/files/MURPHY_testimony.pdf.

[5] Shannon Tiezzi, 'Why China Won't

Lead in the Middle East', *Diplomat*, 28 July 2014, http://thediplomat.com/2014/07/why-china-wont-lead-in-the-middle-east/.

6 Wu Bingbing, 'Strategy and Politics in the Gulf as Seen from China', in Bryce Wakefield and Susan L. Levenstein (eds), *China and the Persian Gulf: Implications for the United States* (Washington DC: Woodrow Wilson International Center for Scholars, 2011).

7 Downs, 'China–Middle East Energy Relations'.

8 Stig Stenslie and Wang Luyao, 'Volume 7/1: China the "Next U.S." in the Middle East?', National University of Singapore, http://mei-nus.com/publications/the-singapore-middle-east-papers/volume-71-china-the-next-u-s-in-the-middle-east-2.

9 Andrew S. Erickson and Adam P. Liff, 'Not-So-Empty Talk: The Danger of China's "New Type of Great-Power Relations" Slogan', *Foreign Affairs*, 9 October 2014, http://www.foreignaffairs.com/articles/142178/andrew-s-erickson-and-adam-p-liff/not-so-empty-talk#cid=soc-twitter-at-snapshot-not_so_empty_talk-000000.

10 Chinese Ministry of Foreign Affairs, 'China's Initiation of the Five Principles of Peaceful Co-Existence', http://www.fmprc.gov.cn/mfa_eng/ziliao_665539/3602_665543/3604_665547/t18053.shtml.

11 'Understanding China's Role in Changing Middle East', lecture delivered by Pan Guang at the National University of Singapore, 24 September 2014, http://mei-nus.com/events/understanding-chinas-role-in-changing-middle-east.

12 Andrea Ghiselli, 'Could Iraq Be Another Libya for China?', *Diplomat*, 24 June 2014, http://thediplomat.com/2014/06/could-iraq-be-another-libya-for-china/.

13 Andrew S. Erickson and Austin M. Strange, 'No Substitute for Experience: Chinese Antipiracy Operations in the Gulf of Aden', *China Maritime Studies*, no. 10, November 2013, https://www.usnwc.edu/Research---Gaming/China-Maritime-Studies-Institute/Publications/documents/CMS10_Web_2.aspx.

14 Murphy, 'Hearing on "China and the Middle East"'.

15 'Hearing on "China and the Middle East"', testimony of Yitzhak Shichor before the US–China Economic and Security Review Commission, 6 June 2013, http://origin.www.uscc.gov/Hearings/hearing-china-and-middle-east-webcast.

16 'China's Reported Ballistic Missile Sale to Saudi Arabia: Background and Potential Implications', testimony of Ethan Meick before the US–China Economic and Security Review Commission, 16 June 2014, http://origin.www.uscc.gov/sites/default/files/Research/Staff%20Report_China%27s%20Reported%20Ballistic%20Missile%20Sale%20to%20Saudi%20Arabia_0.pdf.

17 Xinhua, 'New Silk Road, New Dreams', http://www.xinhuanet.com/world/newsilkway/index.htm.

18 Shannon Tiezzi, 'China's "New Silk Road" Vision Revealed', *Diplomat*, 9 May 2014, http://thediplomat.com/2014/05/chinas-new-silk-road-vision-revealed/.

19 US Energy Information Administration, 'Despite Decline in Some Regions, World Oil Consumption Still Seen Rising', 11 September 2014, http://www.eia.gov/todayinenergy/detail.cfm?id=17931.

20 Tom Arnold, 'China–Russia Gas Deal Likely to Challenge Middle East's Grip over Beijing', *National*, 1 June 2014, http://www.thenational.ae/business/industry-insights/energy/china-russia-gas-deal-likely-to-challenge-middle-easts-grip-over-beijing.

21 Emile Hokayem, 'Looking East: A Gulf Vision or a Reality?', in Wakefield and Levenstein (eds), *China and the Persian Gulf*.

22 'China and the Middle East', testimony of Bryant Edwards before the US–China Economic and Security Review Commission, 6 June 2013, http://www.uscc.gov/sites/default/files/EDWARDS_testimony.pdf.

23 *Ibid.*

24 *Ibid.*; Terence McNamee et al., 'Africa in Their Words – A Study of Chinese Traders in South Africa, Lesotho, Botswana, Zambia and Angola', Brenthurst Foundation, April 2013, http://www.thebrenthurstfoundation.org/files/brenthurst_commisioned_reports/Brenthurst-paper-201203-Africa-in-their-Words-A-Study-of-Chinese-Traders.pdf.

25 Murphy, 'Hearing on "China and the Middle East"'.

26 'Qatar Said to Invest $2.8 Billion in AgriBank IPO', Bloomberg, 20 June 2010, http://www.bloomberg.com/news/2010-06-20/qatar-said-to-invest-2-8-billion-in-agribank-ipo.

html.

27 Murphy, 'Hearing on "China and the Middle East"'.

28 Edwards, 'China and the Middle East'.

29 *Ibid.*

30 *Ibid.*

31 Shaun Waterman, 'Chinese Firm "Owns" Telephone System in Iraq', *Washington Times*, 21 February 2011, http://www.washingtontimes.com/news/2011/feb/21/chinese-telecom-end-ties-us-high-tech-start-/.

32 Wu Sike, 'The Fight Against Terror Will Entail Joint Efforts', *China–US Focus*, 14 September 2014, http://www.chinausfocus.com/peace-security/the-fight-against-terror-will-entail-joint-efforts/.

33 'China Tells PM Erdogan to Withdraw Uighur Genocide Remark', *Today's Zaman*, 15 July 2009, https://www.todayszaman.com/_china-tells-pm-erdogan-to-withdraw-uighur-genocide-remark_180954.html.

34 Hassan Hassan, 'Uighur Terrorists Jailed for DragonMart Bomb Plot', *National*, 1 July 2010, http://www.thenational.ae/news/uae-news/courts/uighur-terrorists-jailed-for-dragonmart-bomb-plot.

35 Jon B. Alterman, 'The Vital Triangle', in Wakefield and Levenstein (eds), *China and the Persian Gulf*.

36 Shichor, 'Hearing on "China and the Middle East"'.

37 James M. Dorsey, 'China and the Middle East: Embarking on a Strategic Approach', S. Rajaratnam School of International Studies, 16 September 2014, http://www.rsis.edu.sg/wp-content/uploads/2014/09/CO14183.pdf.

# CHAPTER TEN

# India: Gulf Security Partner in Waiting?

Rahul Roy-Chaudhury

India's historical connection with the Gulf dates back more than five thousand years, to trading between the ancient civilisations of the Indus Valley and the Dilmun (linked with present-day Bahrain).[1]

Over the centuries, the Arabian Peninsula served as a major centre of commerce for Indian merchants, some of whom settled in Oman during the Middle Ages. In the eighteenth century, Tipu Sultan, ruler of the south Indian state of Mysore, had an extensive relationship with the Imam of Oman, posting emissaries to Muscat and receiving the Imam's in Mangalore.[2] As the Hajj pilgrimage took place yearly from the seventh century onwards, so India's Gulf links expanded.[3] Britain's imperial interests in the Gulf were also determined, pursued and administered from the Bombay Presidency.[4]

In the last century, India's first treaty with an Arab state was concluded in 1953 with Oman, where an Indian consulate was established in 1955. The Indian rupee was legal tender in Kuwait, Bahrain, Qatar, the Trucial states – now the United Arab Emirates (UAE) – and Oman until the early 1960s. And with control over Gwadar (in present-day Baluchistan, Pakistan), Oman was a near-neighbour of India on land until the late 1950s.

Today, the Gulf is an integral part of India's 'extended neighbourhood', both by way of geographical proximity and as an area of expanded interests and growing Indian influence. Historic maritime and cultural links have developed into strong relationships of 'energy, expatriates and economy'. These are currently diversifying into security and defence cooperation, and India today has a strong and growing stake in Gulf stability. Tensions in the Gulf are a threat to India's security. Moreover, as Indian nationals make up the Gulf states' largest expatriate community, a stable South Asia is also in the interests of the Gulf.

Yet, strangely, the Gulf does not get the attention it deserves from India's leadership. Despite it being the single geographical region that could adversely affect India's vital interests in a contingency short of conflict, India has no publicly articulated, comprehensive Gulf policy. Although some Gulf countries are now recognised as 'strategic partners', reciprocal leadership visits are rare, and India's diplomatic missions in the Gulf are small. Notwithstanding recent attempts to build defence links, the Indian embassies in Bahrain and Kuwait, for example, still do not have resident defence attachés; nor, until March 2013, did the Indian embassy in the UAE.

The Gulf also remains neglected by the Indian media, except for coverage of the plight of semi-skilled Indian workers in the region. There are but a handful of Gulf experts in Indian academia and government, despite some exceptional ambassadors, past and present, having been posted to the region. In short, India's new prime minister, Narendra Modi, urgently needs to prioritise India's relations with the Gulf.

## India's core interests
### Energy
India is dependent on the six Gulf Cooperation Council (GCC) states for 42% of its overall oil imports; adding Iran, Iraq and

Yemen brings the total to 60%.[5] Three of the top five oil suppliers to India are Gulf states, with Saudi Arabia, the largest, providing 20% of total oil imports. The fourth- and fifth-largest suppliers are Kuwait and the UAE respectively, together providing another 20% of total oil imports (with Iraq and Venezuela the second- and third-largest respectively). In addition, Qatar is India's dominant supplier of liquefied natural gas (LNG), and has provided as much as 85% of total LNG imports since making its first shipment, in 2004. Qatar agreed to supply 5 million tonnes of LNG per annum for 25 years, beginning in January 2004, and an additional 2.5m tonnes per annum for 25 years, from 2009. India sought in November 2008 to double the total to 15m tonnes, but pricing issues have remained unresolved. Energy imports account for almost all of India's imports from Saudi Arabia, Qatar and Kuwait, but India has diversified trade with the UAE (where oil now accounts for less than half of total imports), Bahrain and Oman.

The Gulf is thus acknowledged as an 'indispensable pillar of India's energy security'.[6] Consequently, any disruption of energy supplies imperils Indian economic growth and security. During the 1973–74 oil shocks, for instance, India had to significantly increase its exports to oil-rich countries, in order to prevent a balance-of-payments crisis. During the 1991 Gulf War, India had to sharply step up its oil imports from Saudi Arabia to compensate for the loss of those from Iraq and Kuwait.[7]

**Expatriates**

Although neither the Gulf states nor their Indian embassies have a reliable figure for the number of Indian nationals working or living in the region, Indians are now widely acknowledged to constitute the largest expatriate community in all Gulf states. The Indian expatriate community in the Gulf is also the largest such community anywhere in the world. According to official Indian sources, Saudi Arabia hosts the largest expatriate Indian population (2.8m), followed by the UAE (2.6m), Kuwait (762,000), Oman (705,000), Qatar (500,000) and Bahrain (350,000). Indian expatriates in Bahrain, Qatar and the UAE reportedly constitute about a third of the countries' total population, with Indian expatriates numbering more than the local population in the UAE and Qatar.[8] The volume of traffic between India and the Gulf states is considerable: there are over 100 flights per day between India and the UAE, for example, with an average flying time of only three hours. Roughly 70% of Indian expatriates in the Gulf originate from the southwestern province of Kerala.

India is home to the world's second-largest Muslim population, meaning that the annual Hajj pilgrimage is an important aspect of its relationship with Saudi Arabia. India provides the second- or third-largest number of foreign pilgrims performing Hajj, numbering 171,671 in 2010.[9]

While 70% of Indian expatriates in the Gulf are blue-collar workers, about 20% are professionals such as IT experts, doctors and engineers.[10] According to resident Indian ambassadors, they are considered a 'preferred community' in the Gulf, and indeed a 'factor for stability' in the region, due to their expertise, law-abiding tendencies and non-involvement in local or regional politics.

However, the Indian expatriate community is not problem-free. Official counts of Indians in the Gulf are rendered inaccurate by the large numbers of them who are on tourist and visitor visas, and are known to overstay. Several criminal cases have also involved Indian expatriates. Moreover, a considerable part of Indian diplomatic missions' work involves labour issues, including alleviating difficult working conditions, standardising model employment contracts and the practice of employers retaining their employees' passports.

On occasion, the Indian government has had to evacuate expatriates living in the Gulf and the wider Middle East, due to conflict or political turmoil. The most high-profile incident of this kind is the controversial evacuation of over 100,000 Indian nationals from Iraq and Kuwait in 1990, following the Iraqi invasion. More recently, during the conflict in Lebanon in July 2006, 1,768 Indians were evacuated from Beirut by Indian naval ships,[11] along with 436 Sri Lankan, 69 Nepalese and seven Lebanese nationals. In February–March 2011, at the height of the conflict in Libya, New Delhi was able to safely evacuate more than 15,000 Indians from the country.[12] Even though such incidents are rare, it is important to acknowledge that there can be no realistic contingency plan for the large-scale evacuation of the many Indian nationals in the Gulf.

## Economy

India's largest regional-bloc trading partner is the GCC, which accounted for $145 billion of trade in 2011–12, nearly a 75% increase from the $84bn of two years earlier.[13] This is far above the level of India–ASEAN trade ($76bn)[14] or India–EU trade ($90bn).[15] By comparison, GCC–China trade is currently $160bn.[16] Two of India's top five trading partners in 2013–14 were from the Gulf: third-largest was the UAE ($60bn), having been India's largest trading partner a year earlier, and fourth-largest was Saudi Arabia ($49bn).[17] The GCC also provides over $30bn in foreign-exchange remittances from Indian expatriates, accounting for over 40% of the total.[18] The relationship with the GCC is therefore an important factor in India's external finances.

India's largest joint venture abroad is in Oman: the $969m Oman India Fertilizer Company, formally inaugurated in Sur in January 2006. India imports the plant's entire output of granulated urea and ammonia under a long-term buy-back agreement.[19] Additional Indian projects in Oman raise its total investment there to approximately $4.5bn. At the same time, Oman's 26% holding in Bharat–Oman Refineries at Bina comprises a 6m-tonne refinery and a crude-oil-storage terminal in Jamnagar, and a crude-oil pipeline from Jamnagar to Bina.[20] Dubai-based DP World is also involved in the development of five ports in India, with an esti-mated investment of $2.4bn.[21]

However, there are several severe shortcomings in this bilateral-trade and commercial relationship. There is still no India–GCC Free Trade Agreement, although a framework agreement on economic cooperation was signed in August 2004. Two rounds of talks have been held to finalise the details, including those related to tariff rules and rules of origin, although they have made little progress.[22] Foreign direct investment from the GCC to India also remains well below potential, estimated at roughly $3.2bn during 2000–14, with the UAE India's 11th-largest investor, providing $2.7bn.[23] India has not been able to attract sovereign-wealth funds from the Gulf.[24]

Moreover, some of India's economic decisions have caused concern for Gulf investors. The cancellation of the 2G spectrum allocation by the Indian supreme court in February 2012 led to the withdrawal of Emirati firm Etisalat from the Indian market, wiping out $827m of prospective investment in India after the company decided not to take part in revised bidding held in November 2012. Bahrain Telecommunications also sold its 43% stake in its Indian telecoms affiliate.[25]

## Indian inattention

Given these interests, it was no surprise that the first compre-hensive review of India's security mechanisms, carried out by a previous Bharatiya Janata Party (BJP) government in February 2001, noted the country's 'vital interest in the security and stability of the [sea lines of communication] in the Indian Ocean'.[26] This was followed by the maritime doctrine (INBR 8) of April 2004, which formally stated, for the first time, that India's 'legitimate area of interest' was in the Indian Ocean, stretching 'from the Persian Gulf to the Straits of Malacca'.[27] The updated maritime doctrine of 2009 defined India's 'primary' maritime areas of interest as including 'the Arabian Sea and the Bay of Bengal, [and] the Persian Gulf, which is the source of [the] majority of our oil supplies and is also home to a considerable population of expatriate Indians'.[28]

However, in broader terms, the strategic importance of the Gulf has rarely been reflected in Indian policy. The political leadership in New Delhi does not pay the Gulf the attention it deserves. There is, for example, no formal expression of a Gulf or West Asia policy, despite the region being of greater strategic importance than Southeast and East Asia, which enjoy an official 'Look East' (now 'Act East') policy, focusing on enhancing trade and security ties. India also has regional policies such as 'Connect Central Asia'; India as a 'net security provider' for Indian Ocean island states; and, most recently, 'Link West', aimed at the United States. India lacks an integrated perspective on the energy, trade, expatriate, political, defence and security dimensions of its Gulf links. Although the bilateral relationships with Saudi Arabia, Oman and Qatar have been elevated to the level of a 'strategic partnership', there is no discernible impact in terms of top-level policy attention to these countries, who join a group of 25 with such a status.

India's political inattention to the Gulf derives from its foreign and security priorities, which lie in its immediate or near neighbourhood. These are marked by tensions with Pakistan, border stand-offs with China, and uncertainties in Afghanistan, all of which have negative implications for India's security. These are followed in importance by India's focus on the West, especially the US; and Southeast and East Asia, where strategic dynamics between the US, China, Japan and India intersect.

Notwithstanding its historical ties with the Gulf, India's post-independence ideological stance favoured secular Arab nationalists, such as Egypt's Gamal Abdul Nasser, over the monarchical political order of the newly independent Gulf states in the 1960s and 1970s.[29] During the Cold War, the Gulf countries were suspicious of India's non-alignment and its proximity to the Soviet Union, especially given their own strong ties with the United Kingdom and the US.

India's relative neglect of the Gulf is most vividly shown by the lack of leadership visits over the last decade. During this period, then-Prime Minister Manmohan Singh made bilateral visits to only three Gulf countries: Oman and Qatar in November 2008, and Saudi Arabia in February 2010. Although the visit to Qatar was the first by an Indian prime minister, these visits were still not an adequate reflection of India's high stakes in the region.[30] In terms of the broader Middle East, Singh went only to Iran and Egypt, on multilateral visits. This contrasts with the four Indian prime ministerial visits to Brazil in the last 11 years, both bilaterally and multilaterally, along with four Brazilian presidential visits to India during the same period.

Reciprocal leadership visits to India from the Gulf have similarly remained scarce. The visit of King Abdullah bin Abdulaziz Al Saud in January 2006 was the first by a Saudi monarch in more than five decades (and his second foreign visit after ascending to the throne five months earlier). King Abdullah is the only Gulf head of state to have been honoured as the 'chief guest' at India's annual Republic Day celebrations. The emir of Kuwait, Sabah al-Ahmad Al Sabah, visited India in June 2006, and the emir of Qatar, Hamad bin Khalifa Al Thani, has visited twice, in May 2005 and April 2012. Dates are yet to be finalised for the visit of Sultan Qaboos bin Said of Oman, during which the Sultan will be formally bestowed with the Jawaharlal Nehru Award for International Peace he won in 2004, India's highest honour to a foreign leader. The first state visit of King Hamad bin Isa Al Khalifa of Bahrain to India in February 2014 built upon visits by Crown Prince Salman bin Hamad Al Khalifa in May 2012 and March 2013.

There also continue to be staffing shortages and a lack of Arabic-speaking foreign-service officers at India's diplomatic missions in the Gulf. Until recently, India had only two defence advisers resident in Saudi Arabia and Oman, who covered all the Gulf states and Yemen. This has now increased to four military officers, although Kuwait continues to be covered by the Indian defence adviser based in Riyadh, and Bahrain by the defence adviser based in Muscat.

## Diversifying relationships

Despite these shortcomings, the traditional relationships of 'energy, expatriates and economy' have begun to diversify. Moreover, although upgrading bilateral ties to the level of 'strategic partnerships' has not brought with it top-level political input, it has nevertheless led to defence and security cooperation on counter-terrorism, money laundering, cyber issues, organised crime, human trafficking and anti-piracy.

Bilateral relations with Oman were upgraded to a 'strategic partnership' during Singh's visit in November 2008, building on the annual India–Oman Strategic Consultative Group meetings held by foreign-ministry secretaries since 2003. Singh's visit to Qatar in November 2008 inaugurated another 'strategic partnership', and set up ongoing ministerial-level consultations. The 'Delhi Declaration' signed during King Abdullah's visit to India in 2006 established a joint Saudi–Indian focus on counter-terrorism, and was followed by the 'Riyadh Declaration' signed during Singh's February 2010 visit, which confirmed the upgrade in relations to a 'strategic partnership', and strengthened defence cooperation.

A newly formed India–Bahrain High Joint Commission is to be co-chaired by foreign ministers, serving as an umbrella framework for bilateral cooperation. An annual security dialogue between deputy national-security advisers has also been agreed, along with strengthened information- and intelligence-sharing. A first dialogue between India's National Security Council Secretariat and Kuwait's National Security Bureau also took place in October 2013.

## Counter-terrorism

India's counter-terrorism cooperation with Saudi Arabia and the UAE has expanded to become a key feature of both bilateral relationships. Despite official Indian concerns over Saudi funding to fundamentalist Muslim institutions in India,[31] the two countries are developing a coordinated approach towards counter-extremism. In the 2006 Delhi Declaration, they agreed to 'actively cooperate to fight the menace of terrorism and other transnational crimes like money laundering, drugs and arms smuggling in a sustained and comprehensive manner'. A memorandum of understanding (MoU) on 'combating crime', signed during the visit, was to help in the fight against terrorism, extremism and criminal elements.[32] Concerns later emerged over the Gulf network of Pakistan-based terror group Lashkar-e-Taiba (LeT), including its possible role in the 2008 Mumbai attacks.[33] The 2010 Riyadh Declaration subsequently sought to 'enhance cooperation in exchange of information relating to terrorist activities, money laundering, narcotics, arms and human trafficking, and develop joint strategies to combat these threats'.[34]

Notably, a Saudi–Indian extradition treaty and an agreement for the transfer of sentenced persons were also signed – and, two years later, their first major success was made public. After considerable effort by India's intelligence agencies, Indian national Zabiuddin Ansari, also known as Abu Jundal, the alleged 'handler' of the ten terrorists involved in the Mumbai attacks, was deported from Saudi Arabia and arrested on arrival at Delhi airport on 21 June 2012; significantly, he reportedly held a Pakistani passport.[35] Soon afterwards, Saudi Arabia also deported A. Rayees, a suspected LeT operative wanted in connection with a 2009 explosives case, and Fasih Mohammad, a member of the Indian Mujahideen.[36]

There has also been significant cooperation with the UAE. In February 2002, Abu Dhabi swiftly deported Aftab Ansari, the alleged mastermind of the attack on the US consulate in Kolkata the previous month. Ansari's deportation took place without invoking the India–UAE treaty, a strong demonstration of political will by the UAE authorities.[37] Muthappa Rai, another figure sought by the Indian authorities, was also deported. The subsequent bilateral security-cooperation agreement of November 2011 focused on combating terrorism, organised crime, drug trafficking, weapons smuggling, money laundering, and economic and cyber crimes. In early May 2014, the UAE deported to India Faizan Ahmad Sultan, allegedly an important organiser in the Indian Mujahideen.[38]

India signed an extradition treaty with Oman in December 2004. In early 2009, Oman deported Sarfaraz Nawaz, an Indian national who played a key role in the serial blasts in Bangalore on 25 July 2008.[39] An Omani national, Ali Abdul Aziz al-Hooti, had also allegedly procured some of the SIM cards used in the Mumbai attacks.[40]

**Anti-piracy**

India has played an active role in enhancing the stability and security of the Gulf's sea lanes through its participation in anti-piracy patrols off the coast of Somalia. As then-Minister of External Affairs Salman Khurshid told the 2013 Manama Dialogue, since October 2008 the Indian Navy has continuously deployed one ship in the Gulf of Aden for anti-piracy duties, with operational turnarounds at Salalah, Oman.[41] Indian Navy vessels have escorted 1,104 ships (139 Indian- and 965 foreign-flagged, from 50 countries) through the Internationally Recommended Transit Corridor.[42] In its first five years of this activity, the Indian Navy reportedly captured 100 pirates and foiled over 40 piracy attempts.[43] Although India is not engaged in Combined Task Force 151 on counter-piracy efforts in the Gulf of Aden, it has begun coordinating patrols with China, Japan and South Korea.[44] It also interacts with other naval representatives involved in anti-piracy through the Bahrain-based Shared Awareness and Deconfliction mechanism, formed in December 2008 for sharing 'best practices'.

India's participation in these anti-piracy patrols came despite some initial reluctance on the part of the civilian leadership, though not the navy. The Singh government procrastinated for over a year, until finally moved to action by Somali pirates' hijacking of the Japanese-owned but largely Indian-crewed chemical tanker MT *Stolt Valor* in the Gulf of Aden, in September 2008.[45]

### Defence cooperation

India's relations with the Gulf have begun, with a fair degree of success, to encompass defence and naval cooperation, including joint exercises, regular Indian ship visits and broad-based MoUs.[46] Gulf armed-forces personnel are also trained in Indian defence and military academies. All the Gulf states are members of the Indian Navy-conceived Indian Ocean Naval Symposium (IONS), which was established in 2008 as a biennial forum for navy chiefs of the Indian Ocean littoral. The IONS, which currently has 35 member states (including France, in acknowledgement of its Indian Ocean interests), has held meetings in India, the UAE, South Africa and, most recently, Australia.

India's most notable (but equally low-key) defence cooperation has been with Oman. An MoU on defence cooperation was signed in December 2005; visits to Oman by Indian Navy ships have since increased, and Royal Navy of Oman sailors have travelled to India for training in hydrography, diving and dockyard management.[47] Then-defence minister A.K. Antony travelled to Oman in May 2010, a rare overseas visit. India's state-owned Goa Shipyard delivered three 12-tonne tugboats to Oman in 2010, amid global competition, with the expectation of further defence orders.[48] The bilateral defence relationship was extended for another five years when Omani defence minister Sayyid Badr bin Saud bin Harib al-Busaidi visited India in December 2011.[49]

The first bilateral naval exercise with the Royal Navy of Oman was carried out in 1993. Since then, a series of biennial naval exercises named *Naseem Al Bahr* has been developed, held in the waters off Mumbai, on India's west coast, and in the Gulf of Oman. The ninth *Naseem Al Bahr* took place in September 2013; four Indian naval ships, including the destroyer *Mysore* and the replenishment and repair ship *Aditya*, exercised alongside Omani naval vessels and air-force combat aircraft, focusing on surface warfare, search and seizure, anti-air warfare, air operation, advanced helicopter operations and maritime-interdiction operations.[50] The Omani government also provides critical support to Indian Navy ships at Salalah, to sustain their deployment for anti-piracy patrols in the Gulf of Aden. In October 2009, India and Oman also conducted their first joint air exercises, *Eastern Bridge*, at the Omani air-force base at Thumrait. The second in this series was held in Jamnagar in October 2011, and the third in October 2013 at Masirah Island, Oman.[51]

The Riyadh Declaration of February 2010 welcomed the existing level of Saudi–Indian defence cooperation, and agreed to strengthen it. Antony's visit to Saudi Arabia in February 2012 resulted in the establishment of a joint committee of service chiefs, designed to deal with ship visits and naval exercises. An MoU on hydrographic cooperation was to be explored.[52] A further MoU on defence cooperation, involving greater information exchange and training, was signed in February 2014, on the occasion of the visit of Crown Prince Salman bin Abdulaziz Al Saud to India.[53]

The first India–UAE MoU on defence cooperation was signed in June 2003.[54] Subsequently, there have been regular high-level exchanges between service chiefs, port calls by ships of both navies and joint naval exercises. An annual bilateral defence dialogue has been held. The first India–UAE joint air-force exercise took place in September 2008. In November of that year, Singh signed a defence-cooperation agreement with Qatar that involved joint exercises, the training of personnel and maritime cooperation.[55]

## China and Pakistan

India's policies towards the Gulf are not motivated by competition with China or Pakistan. Although China's presence in the region may well be growing with its greater dependence on energy imports, Indians far outnumber Chinese nationals in the region.

Meanwhile, Pakistan continues to develop its links with the Gulf: the country has nearly 3m expatriates in the region, most of whom are in Saudi Arabia and the UAE; and $21bn in trade with the Gulf states. It is also dependent on energy imports from the region, and has long-standing defence and security ties with the Gulf that involve troop training, joint exercises and the secondment of Pakistani personnel to the Saudi Arabian and Bahraini security forces. The Pakistan Navy participates in Combined Task Force 150 (on counter-terrorism operations in the Gulf) and Combined Task Force 151. Gulf states have also served as willing hosts for senior Pakistani politicians during difficult times. After being deposed as prime minister of Pakistan, Nawaz Sharif lived in exile in Saudi Arabia for nearly seven years, from December 2000 to August 2007, and Benazir Bhutto lived in self-imposed exile in the UAE for several years.

In view of its strong ties with both India and Pakistan, the GCC has in the past expressed concern over bilateral tensions between the two countries. During the 1999 Kargil conflict and the 2001–02 military confrontation, the GCC urged them to resolve their disputes amicably. The Gulf has no desire to pick sides in the tense India–Pakistan relationship[56] – although the deportation of Abu Jundal was a significant victory for Saudi–Indian cooperation.

## Gulf policy under Modi

The May 2014 election of a new centre-right BJP government under Modi could provide impetus to India–Gulf relations. With a stable leadership at the centre and a majority in the lower house of parliament, the Modi government has the potential for bold foreign- and security-policy initiatives in the Gulf. Gulf states such as the UAE have made financial investments in Gujurat, despite privately expressing concern over Modi's tenure as chief minister of the province during the anti-Muslim riots of 2002. Gulf leaderships have also welcomed Modi's election as prime minister.

Yet the BJP election manifesto failed to mention the Gulf – indeed, it failed to mention most of the rest of the world, with only a few paragraphs on foreign and security policy appearing towards the end.[57] Nor, unfortunately, was the region mentioned in the Indian president's inaugural address to the joint houses of parliament on 9 June, the first official indicator of the Modi government's top priorities. This neglect was made even more pronounced when the president specifically mentioned China, Japan, Russia and the US, along with regional organisations such as the South Asian Association for Regional Cooperation (SAARC) and the European Union.[58]

Nonetheless, the foreign minister of Oman was the first overseas visitor to call on Modi after the leaders of SAARC and Mauritius had met him during his swearing-in ceremony in New Delhi. External Affairs Minister Sushma Swaraj's first visit to the Gulf took place in early September 2014, in the form of a trip to Bahrain for a meeting of the Indian diaspora and bilateral talks, and was followed by a visit to the UAE in early November 2014.

Indeed, the Modi government's first foreign-policy crisis arose in the Middle East, with the need to protect Indian nationals caught up in the advance of the Islamic State of Iraq and al-Sham (ISIS). Among the 10,000 Indians in Iraq, several hundred were airlifted home in June and July 2014, even as 39 Indian workers in Mosul, in the north of the country, were taken hostage by ISIS.[59]

## Time to focus on the Gulf

The US 'rebalance' from the Gulf to the Asia-Pacific comes amid regional concerns over the shelf life of American engagement, and at a time when domestic US shale-gas discovery and cost-effective extraction could lead to a dramatic decline in US energy dependence. At the same time, China, as an increasingly energy-dependent great power, is seeking to position itself favourably for a larger role in the Gulf, even as it diversifies into Central Asian and Russian energy sources. Russia remains distracted by the Ukraine crisis and its fallout. The current Iran–US 'rapprochement' could also have an impact on Gulf-related dynamics vis-à-vis Saudi Arabia and Iran.

Amid such fluid regional security developments, India's dependency on Gulf oil is expected to increase from the current 70% of total demand to an estimated 90% within the next ten years.[60] India will therefore continue to remain a long-term market for Gulf energy, as will China, Japan and South Korea. New supply options include the construction of a $5bn, 1,130km deep-sea Oman–India pipeline across the Arabian Sea, to bring natural gas from Iran to India; this has already begun to be explored trilaterally, at the foreign-ministerial level. The number of Indian expatriates living and working in the Gulf could also increase, depending on prospective economic growth and infra-structure projects in the region. India's external finances will also continue to be dependent in large part on trade and remittances from the Gulf.

It was therefore not surprising that at the 2013 Manama Dialogue Khurshid emphatically stated that:

> The region sits astride strategic Sea Lines of Communications (SLOCs) and any disruption to these SLOCs can have a serious impact on the Indian economy, including in terms of energy supplies. It is important to keep the region out of bounds for pirates and other nefarious non-state actors. India has the *capabilities and the will* to not only safeguard India's own coastline and

island territories, but also *contribute to keeping our region's SLOCs open and flowing.*[61]

Yet, in a subsequent interview, Khurshid also made clear that, despite its deepening defence and security links with the region, India had no intention of becoming a US-style protector of the Gulf states, even if they asked it to do so.[62]

This qualification was in line with India's long-standing policy of not joining alliances or military groups, and of avoiding foreign military deployments not mandated by the United Nations. But it also reflects a key dilemma – namely, that if India were to expand its role and influence in the Gulf, there could be negative repercussions for its core interests in the region and beyond. A key determinant of India's Gulf policy is the safety and security of its largest expatriate community. Intervention or other military involvement in the region could result in unforeseen blowback for Indian nationals – whether as the targets of terrorist attacks, by earning the political displeasure of specific Gulf states or through the radicalisation of a section of the community. Any high-profile Indian involvement in Middle East politics could also serve to exacerbate sectarian divisions among Muslims at home.

Although India is a vibrant democracy, it does not seek to impose this framework on the region. India has repeatedly stated its opposition to Western military intervention to resolve regional political issues, and its concern over the exacerbation of extremist and sectarian divides in Iraq, Libya and Syria.[63] In these circumstances, India's preference is to follow a pragmatic, status quo policy towards the Gulf, avoiding the risk of any political or security misadventures.

India's perspective on the Gulf has also been deeply influenced by the nature of its complex set of relationships in the Middle East – with Saudi Arabia and Iran, Israel and Palestine, and Shi'ites and Sunnis. While India has been able to successfully balance its relations with adversarial countries and ideological factions in the region – a rare occurrence – this has so far taken place at the cost of taking on a more active role. In an unusual admission of this aspect of India's policy, then-National Security Adviser Shivshankar Menon said in March 2014:

> We have stayed out of these dichotomies, tried to insulate ourselves and our people from growing extremism and radicalism in the region, and worked with all the major actors to defend our security and economic interests. We may be one of the few powers able to do so with Iran, Saudi Arabia, Egypt, and Turkey, all at the same time. This balancing is not easy or pretty *but it is necessary.*[64]

Nonetheless, amid evolving security dynamics and India's direct interest in the Gulf's security and stability, influential Indian experts have recently begun to advocate a more active strategic role for India. This could take place through participation in a cooperative regional security arrangement, along with the three other major Asian economies dependent on Gulf energy (China, Japan and South Korea) and others.[65] But it is also argued that, while such a new cooperative framework may be welcome, its time has not yet come: such a grouping would need to overcome intra-Asian competition and inherited disputes.

In essence, despite India's growing stakes in the Gulf on defence and security cooperation, alongside its vital interests in 'energy, expatriates and economy', it will be wary of taking on a more assertive role, for fear that risky interventions or misadventures might harm those very interests it seeks to protect. Nevertheless, there is still sufficient scope for the new Modi government to pay greater policy attention to the Gulf – and to ensure a prime-ministerial visit during his first year in office.

# Notes

1   Mushtaq Hussain, 'Bahrain', in P.R. Kumaraswamy (ed.), *Persian Gulf 2013: India's Relations with the Region* (New Delhi: Sage, 2014), p. 46.

2   Marimuthu Ulaganathan, 'Oman', in Kumaraswamy (ed.), *Persian Gulf 2013: India's Relations with the Region*, p. 151.

3   P.R. Kumaraswamy, 'Introduction', in Kumaraswamy (ed.), *Persian Gulf 2013: India's Relations with the Region*, p. 3.

4   *Ibid.*

5   *Ibid.*

6   Anil Wadhwa, keynote address to the 6th IISS–MEA Dialogue, New Delhi, 4 March 2014, http://www.iiss.org/en/research/south%20asia%20security/south%20asia%20conferences/sections/2014-ba9a/sixth-iiss-mea-foreign-policy-dialogue-5724/anil-wadhwa-address-b5cf.

7   Manjeet S. Pardesi and Sumit Ganguly, 'India and Energy Security: A Foreign Policy Priority', in Harsh V. Pant (ed.), *Indian Foreign Policy in a Unipolar World* (New Delhi: Routledge, 2009), pp. 103–4.

8   For estimated numbers of Indian expatriates, see the websites of Indian embassies in the Gulf.

9   Md. Muddassir Quamar, 'Saudi Arabia', in Kumaraswamy (ed.), *Persian Gulf 2013: India's Relations with the Region*, p. 212.

10  Mukund Narvenkar, 'Iran and the Gulf', in David Scott (ed.), *Handbook of India's International Relations* (London: Routledge, 2011), pp. 169–70.

11  Indian Ministry of Defence, 'Operation Sukoon for the Evacuation of Indian Nationals from Lebanon', 24 August 2006, http://pib.nic.in/newsite/erelease.aspx?relid=20224.

12  Suhasini Haidar, 'Over 15,000 Indians Safely Evacuated from Libya', CNN–IBN, 12 March 2011, http://ibnlive.in.com/news/over-15000-indians-safely-evacuated-from-libya/145637-3.html.

13  Ministry of Commerce and Industry, 'Trade with Gulf Countries', Press Information Bureau, 6 March 2013, http://pib.nic.in/newsite/erelease.aspx?relid=93100.

14  Press Trust of India, 'India, ASEAN Can Be Great Partners, "No Irritants" in Relationship: Modi in Myanmar', *First Post*, 12 November 2014, http://www.firstpost.com/world/india-asean-can-great-partners-irritants-relationship-modi-myanmar-1799483.html.

15  'European Union, Trade in Goods with India', European Commission, 27 August 2014, http://trade.ec.europa.eu/doclib/docs/2006/september/tradoc_113390.pdf.

16  Stasa Salacanin, 'GCC–China Rising Trade Value', *BQ Doha*, 23 March 2014, http://www.bqdoha.com/2014/03/gcc-china-rising-trade-value.

17  'Total Trade: Top 25 Countries', Export Import Data Bank, Indian Department of Commerce, 21 November 2014, http://commerce.nic.in/eidb/iecnt.asp.

18  Speech by Salman Khurshid to the 2013 Manama Dialogue, 8 December 2013, https://www.iiss.org/en/events/manama%20dialogue/archive/manama-

dialogue-2013-4e92/plenary-5-fbc6/khurshid-632c.

19  'India–Oman Trade Relations', Embassy of India in Oman, 23 June 2013, http://www.indemb-oman.org/inner.aspx?type=Menu&id=16.

20  Debjit Chakraborty, 'Oman Oil to Buy New Stake in BPCL–JV', DNA Analysis, 26 November 2009, http://www.dnaindia.com/money/report-oman-oil-to-buy-new-stake-in-bpcl-jv-1316508.

21  'Dubai Firms Eye More Investments in India', Rediff, 14 May 2008, http://www.rediff.com/money/report/dubai/20080514.htm.

22  Huma Siddiqui, 'FTA Talks Between India, Gulf Council to Resume Soon', Financial Express, 6 November 2013, http://archive.financialexpress.com/news/FTA-talks-between-India--Gulf-council-to-resume-soon/1191211.

23  Biswajit Nag and Mohit Gupta, 'The Rise of Gulf Investment in India: Searching for Complimentarity and Synergy', Middle East Institute, 9 October 2014, http://www.mei.edu/content/map/rise-gulf-investment-india-searching-complementarity-and-synergy.

24  Victor Mallet, 'Old Ties Between India and the Gulf are Renewed', Financial Times, 29 June 2014, http://www.ft.com/cms/s/0/577314ce-f856-11e3-815f-00144feabdc0.html?siteedition=uk#axzz3HXaBZEIK.

25  'UAE's Etisalat Takes $827 Million Charge against Indian Ops', Reuters, 9 February 2012, http://www.reuters.com/article/2012/02/09/etisalat-india-writedown-idUSL5E8D950F20120209.

26  Government of India, 'Recommendations of the Group of Ministers: Reforming the National Security System', February 2001, p. 10.

27  Indian Navy, Indian Maritime Doctrine (INBR 8), April 2004, p. 56.

28  Ibid., pp. 65–8.

29  Kumaraswamy, 'Introduction', p. 3.

30  C. Raja Mohan, 'Look Middle East Policy', Indian Express, 2 June 2014, p. 10.

31  Harsh V. Pant, 'India and the Middle East: A Re-Assessment of Priorities?', in Pant (ed.), Indian Foreign Policy in a Unipolar World, pp. 258, 271.

32  'Delhi Declaration, Signed by King Abdullah bin Abdulaziz Al Saud of the Kingdom of Saudi Arabia and Prime Minister Dr. Manmohan Singh of India', Consulate General of India, Jeddah, 27 January 2006, http://cgijeddah.mkcl.org/Content.aspx?ID=26453&PID=683; and Press Trust of India, 'India, Saudi Arabia Sign Four Accords', Times of India, 25 January 2006, http://timesofindia.indiatimes.com/india/India-Saudi-Arabia-sign-four-accords/articleshow/1386965.cms.

33  Josy Joseph, 'LeT's Gulf Arm Funded 26/11, Bangalore Blasts?', Times of India, 15 May 2010, http://timesofindia.indiatimes.com/india/LeTs-Gulf-arm-funded-26/11-Bangalore-blasts/articleshow/5932847.cms.

34  'Riyadh Declaration: A New Era of Strategic Partnership', Prime Minister's Office, 28 February 2010, http://pib.nic.in/newsite/erelease.aspx?relid=58617.

35  Quamar, 'Saudi Arabia', in Kumaraswamy (ed.), Persian Gulf 2013: India's Relations with the Region, p. 208.

36  'Saudi Arabia Deports Alleged

Terrorist Wanted by Kerala', Press Trust of India, 22 October 2012, http://www.ndtv.com/article/india/saudi-arabia-deports-alleged-terrorist-wanted-by-kerala-283105.

37  Vinay Kumar, 'A Milestone in India–UAE Ties', *Hindu*, 10 December 2002, http://www.thehindu.com/2002/12/10/stories/2002121004251200.htm.

38  Praveen Swami, 'Alleged IM Operative Deported from UAE', *Hindu*, 3 May 2014, http://www.thehindu.com/news/national/alleged-im-operative-deported-from-uae/article5971265.ece.

39  Praveen Swami, 'Hyderabad Plot Casts Light on Renewed Lashkar Threat', *Hindu*, 4 May 2010, http://www.thehindu.com/todays-paper/hyderabad-plot-casts-light-on-renewed-lashkar-threat/article761099.ece.

40  Joseph, 'LeT's Gulf Arm Funded 26/11, Bangalore Blasts?'.

41  Speech by Salman Khurshid to the 2013 Manama Dialogue, 8 December 2013.

42  Angana Guha Roy, 'Indian Navy's Anti Piracy Operations', Indian Council of World Affairs, 5 March 2012, http://www.icwa.in/pdfs/Ang6032012.pdf.

43  Sunil K. Vaidya, 'Oman Plays Key Role in Solving Piracy Problem', *Gulf News*, 21 September 2013, http://gulfnews.com/news/gulf/oman/oman-plays-key-role-in-solving-piracy-problem-1.1233553.

44  N. Manoharan, 'Anti-piracy Activity in the Gulf of Aden: The Role of the Japan Maritime Self-Defence Force', National Maritime Foundation, 14 October 2013, http://www.maritimeindia.org/Archives/ANTI-PIRACY.html.

45  Vice Admiral Pradeep Chauhan (retd), 'Oceanic Moves', *Force*, February 2014, p. 24.

46  Speech by Salman Khurshid to the 2013 Manama Dialogue, 8 December 2013.

47  Indian Ministry of Defence, '20 Years of Indian Navy–Royal Omani Navy Partnership: Ninth "Naseem Al Bahr" Bienniel Naval Exercise', 22 September 2013, http://pib.nic.in/newsite/erelease.aspx?relid=99552.

48  Ritu Sharma, 'Goa Shipyard Limited Eyes Global Market', *India Strategic*, May 2010, http://www.indiastrategic.in/topstories610.htm.

49  Marimuthu Ulaganathan, 'Oman', in Kumaraswamy (ed.), *Persian Gulf 2013: India's Relations with the Region*, p. 153.

50  Indian Ministry of Defence, '20 Years of Indian Navy–Royal Omani Navy Partnership'.

51  'IAF, RAFO Wargame Jaguar Together, Grow Closer', *SP's Aviation*, 28 October 2013, http://www.sps-aviation.com/exclusive/?id=12&h=IAF-RAFO-wargame-Jaguar-together-grow-closer.

52  Sitanshu Kar, 'India and Saudi Arabia Agree to Set up a Joint Committee on Defence Cooperation', Indian Ministry of Defence, 15 February 2012, http://pib.nic.in/newsite/erelease.aspx?relid=80322.

53  'India, Saudi Arabia Seek to Deepen Business, Strategic Ties', India Abroad News Service, 1 March 2014, http://www.gulf-times.com/region/216/details/382951/india,-saudi-arabia-seek-to-deepen-business,-strategic-ties.

54  Jatung Raja Philemon Chiru, 'UAE', in Kumaraswamy (ed.), *Persian Gulf 2013: India's Relations with the Region*, p. 236.

55  Manjari Singh, 'Qatar', in Kumaraswamy (ed.), *Persian Gulf 2013: India's Relations with the Region*, p. 176.

56  C. Raja Mohan, 'Look Middle East Policy', *Indian Express*, 2 June 2014, p. 10.

57  Bharatiya Janata Party Election Manifesto, 2014, http://bjpelection-manifesto.com/pdf/manifesto2014.pdf.

58  'Address by the President of India to the Joint Sitting of Parliament', 9 June 2014, http://cdnpmindia.nic.in/wp-content/uploads/2014/06/President_Address.pdf.

59  '39 Indians Abducted in Iraq Still in Captivity', *Hindustan Times*, 13 August 2014, http://www.hindustantimes.com/world-news/iraqonthebrink/39-indians-abducted-in-iraq-still-in-captivity/article1-1251801.aspx.

60  Talmiz Ahmad, 'The Gulf Security Imbroglio: Shaping an Asian Initiative for a New Regional Cooperative Security Architecture', in Tim Niblock and Yang Guang (eds), *Security Dynamics of East Asia in the Gulf Region* (Berlin: Gerlach Press, 2014), p.53.

61  Speech by Salman Khurshid to the IISS Manama Dialogue, 8 December 2013.

62  William Maclean, 'Rising Power India Sees No US-style Gulf Security Role', Reuters, 7 December 2013, http://uk.reuters.com/article/2013/12/07/uk-gulf-security-india-idUKBRE9B60DV20131207. See also Indrani Bagchi, 'Can India Take on a Bigger Role in the Persian Gulf?', *Times of India*, 14 December 2013, http://timesofindia.indiatimes.com/india/Can-India-take-on-a-bigger-role-in-the-Persian-Gulf/articleshow/27363253.cms.

63  Anil Wadhwa, keynote address to the 6th IISS–MEA Dialogue, New Delhi, 4 March 2014, http://www.iiss.org/en/research/south%20asia%20security/south%20asia%20conferences/sections/2014-ba9a/sixth-iiss-mea-foreign-policy-dialogue-5724/anil-wadhwa-address-b5cf.

64  Shivshankar Menon, 'India's Security Environment', address to the Kerala State Planning Board, 19 March 2014, http://southasiamonitor.org/detail.php?type=emerging&nid=7606. Italics added.

65  See Ahmad, 'The Gulf Security Imbroglio', in Niblock and Guang (eds), *Security Dynamics of East Asia in the Gulf*, pp. 58–9; and Talmiz Ahmad, 'New Silk Roads of the 21st Century: GCC–Asia Economic Connectivities and their Political Implications', paper presented to the workshop 'India–Gulf Strategic Partnership in a Pan-Asian Cooperative Paradigm', Cambridge, 12 July 2012, p. 4.

# CHAPTER ELEVEN

# Securing Middle East Oil

## Pierre Noël

China's reliance on globally traded oil has increased dramatically over the past decade, while America's has declined. Both trends look likely to continue. Maintaining steady exports of Middle East oil is a major strategic concern for Beijing, yet Washington remains the guarantor of security in the Gulf. Could China replace the United States in this role? The answer to that question depends on three factors: Beijing's willingness to secure the Gulf; the Chinese military's capacity to do so; and the likelihood that an oil-independent US would lose interest in acting as guarantor.

If the US retreated from the Gulf before credible alternative security architecture had been put in place, China would have no choice but to try to fill the gap. In this scenario, Beijing would increase its investment in naval and other power-projection capabilities, and would strengthen its diplomatic engagement with the region. It is likely that a China forced to play an active role in securing Middle East oil production and exports would acquire the military capability to so in a matter of years, rather than decades. This essay focuses on the issue of whether oil independence would cause the US to abandon its security commitments in the region.

## Less oil for America, more for Asia

An important shift is under way in the geography of world oil trade. Due to growing production and stagnating consumption, US oil imports have steadily declined since 2007, in a reversal of long-standing trends. During this period, American imports have fallen from more than 600 million tonnes per year to 300mt/y, and from 60% of consumption to 33%. Simultaneously, there has been a boom in Asian petroleum consumption and imports. Chinese oil imports are almost as large as those of America, grow by more than 10% per year and meet 60% of domestic consumption. Between 2002 and 2012, China accounted for just under 50% of world oil-consumption growth (or nearly 75% in combination with India and Southeast Asian countries), compared with -30% for the European Union and the US, taken together. Between 1992 and 2002, the figures were 50% for China, India and Southeast Asia combined, and 34% for the US and EU. The focal point of global oil trade is rapidly moving from the Atlantic to the Asia-Pacific, and it remains to be seen how this change will affect strategy.

Figure 1. **Contribution to world oil-demand growth (ten-year moving interval)**

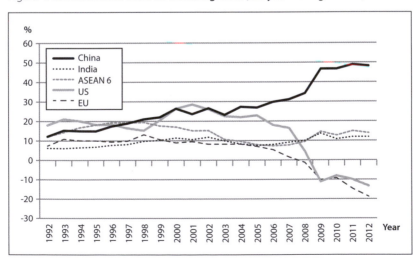

Figure 2. **Net oil imports: US and China**

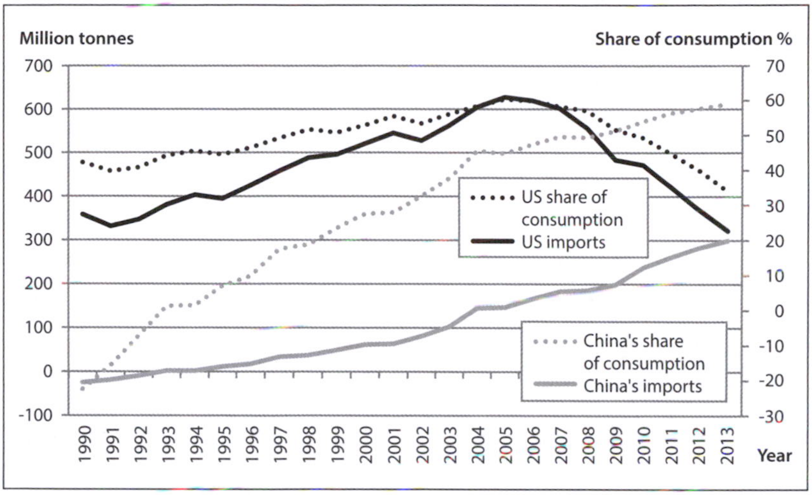

Sources: US Energy Information Administration; BP Statistical Review of World Energy 2012

## Why secure Middle East oil?

It is taken as a given, in the strategic literature and wider public discourse, that the need to secure oil supplies is an important driver of America's policy in the Middle East, especially its military presence and strategic posture there. But what does it mean to secure the oil supply, exactly?

One rationale for US policy in the region identifies a need for Washington to maintain access to, or control of, Gulf energy through political and military means. If this was the case, there would be a strong argument that America's sharply diminished demand for imported oil necessitated the retreat of US power from the Middle East. However, this reasoning overlooks the fact that Washington has no control over where Middle East oil is refined and consumed, or even the mixture of different crudes and products that meet American import needs. There is a single global oil market that is supplied by all sources of production worldwide, and from which all consumers draw – what the late oil economist Morris Adelman once called the 'one great pool'.[1] In light of various crude qualities, product specifications and logistical constraints, the relationship between supply and demand is determined by decentralised market processes, including private contracts, the price mechanism, and physical and paper arbitrage. There has never been a 'soft pipeline' linking the Middle East to US refineries. It is possible to show how much oil from the region has been imported by America, but the figures would not demonstrate US dependence on the supply; rather, they would show that the Middle East has played a role in supplying the global oil market, on which America relies.

Another popular rationale for Washington's strategy in the Middle East centres on a sort of grand bargain between the US and the oil-exporting monarchies of the Gulf, particularly Saudi Arabia. In this conception, America provides security in exchange for an accommodating oil policy from its Gulf partners. Some see evidence of such a bargain in Riyadh's willingness to maintain spare production and export capacity; rapidly increase its exports when the oil price spikes during a crisis; and maintain 'oil-market stability' (a vague term often used by exporting governments). Yet, looking at the era of oil-industry nationalisation in the early 1970s, one would struggle to find an energy-policy decision by Riyadh that was inconsistent with its economic interests or would make sense only in the context of a grand bargain with Washington. Like other members of the Organization of the Petroleum Exporting Countries, Saudi Arabia has consistently defended the highest possible price for the commodity, constrained in the short term by the need to avoid choking off economic growth and in the long term by a desire to prevent the emergence of substitutes. Saudi Arabia's spare capacity results from production cuts when the market is weak; maintaining this costs little, and gives Riyadh the option to serve a tight market. This spare capacity is therefore akin to a large asset with low storage costs and high option value.

The US government may be more or less pleased with Riyadh's oil policy, but the Saudi approach is not a form of payment for American security guarantees. If Washington ceased to act as guarantor – because of reduced oil imports or some other reason – the Gulf monarchies' oil policy would stay the same.

The only credible oil-related rationale for America's Middle East security guarantees is the perceived need to prevent large and enduring disruptions in the flow of oil to the global market. Such disturbances could result from regional wars or internal political destabilisation. American forces may therefore be deployed to improve economic security, as oil-supply shocks trigger price spikes that damage the US economy. In terms of economic-security risk, the Middle East is unique: the region's exports account for 25% of world consumption; its production and export infrastructure is highly concentrated; and it has been geopolitically volatile for far longer than it has had vast oil wealth. Furthermore, the oil exporters of the Gulf, especially Saudi Arabia, usually hold most of the world's spare production capacity. This raises the economic-security value of securing these countries, because spare capacity is the first line of defence against oil-supply shocks. Any disruption in Gulf oil exports is exacerbated by the fact that far less spare capacity is available to mitigate the loss of supply.

Importantly, American security guarantees have only covered the petro-monarchies of the Gulf, rather than all Middle East producers. Oil production from Iraq and Iran has been severely diminished by war and sanctions. Over the years, there has been a steady transfer of production from these states to the Gulf – that is, from war-torn countries to those shielded by the US.

## A global public good
Securing the oil producers of the Gulf is only one aspect of a broader set of policies and mechanisms for ensuring global oil-market security. Other measures include securing some sea lines

of communication and key transit points, and maintaining and coordinating large strategic oil stocks (through the International Energy Agency). Some of these measures reduce the likelihood of oil-market disruption, while others aim to mitigate the price impact of any disruption. Since the 1980s, the US has played a dominant role in securing the global oil market.

From an economic perspective, oil-market security has two peculiar characteristics. Firstly, the market makes it impossible to reserve consumption for those who pay for its security. Even if the US acts as security guarantor to Middle East producers and ensures freedom of navigation through the Strait of Hormuz, it cannot prevent other consumers from enjoying the benefits of that security for free. Economists describe oil-market security as 'non-excludable'. Secondly, China's 'consumption' of US-provided oil-market security does not reduce the amount of security available to America, nor to any other country. Such a good is described as 'non-rival'.

These peculiar characteristics stem from the deep level of integration in the oil market. Bilateral supply relationships do not determine availability or price for any importer. Geographical arbitrage has the effect of pooling all sources of supply. The interaction between global supply and demand, both in real time and in futures, sets one global price that balances the market at any given moment. Therefore, the disruption of a specific supply relationship is transformed by market arbitrage into a global price spike, inflicting the same amount of damage on all consumers. Conversely, if the risk of disruption in Middle East exports is reduced by foreign-policy shifts or military deployments, it is reduced for all consumers in the world, not just those who pay for these actions through taxation. Hence, the non-excludability and non-rivalry of oil-market security. Economists define a public good as one that is both non-excludable and non-rival. Accordingly, oil-market security is a global public good.

Theory and evidence suggest that public goods are not adequately provided by self-interested actors. Everyone has an interest in letting others provide a public good, in the knowledge they cannot be forced to pay for it once it has been produced. But few will invest in creating a good that cannot be reliably charged to those who consume it. As a consequence, public goods are often imperfectly provided, or not provided at all.

However, the US has not necessarily secured the global oil market out of altruism. A self-interested Washington would still secure oil exporters in the Gulf if it perceived that the cost of oil-market insecurity – the expected macroeconomic impact of oil-supply disruptions – was greater than that of its diplomatic and military commitments to the Middle East. In other words, if the value of a public good to a particular actor is high enough, the fact that others will benefit for free does not reduce that actor's incentive to produce it.

The main free-riders on American efforts to provide oil-market security have traditionally been European states and Japan, but emerging countries, particularly fast-growing Asian oil importers such as China, increasingly benefit from US guarantees. That said, Washington has sometimes been able to invoice consumers of the oil-market security it provides; for instance, in 1991 it asked Japan and Germany to provide funds for *Operation Desert Storm*, the American-led mission to repel Iraq's invasion of Kuwait.

## Would the US calculus change with oil independence?

As the US rapidly becomes much less reliant on internationally traded oil, and perhaps moves towards oil independence in the near future, could it lose interest in ensuring global oil-market security? It is unlikely to do so. Securing the Middle East makes sense as an economic-security policy because the American economy is vulnerable to price spikes triggered by oil-supply shocks. That risk does not correlate with the rate of US oil imports.

America could only disregard global oil-supply shocks if it was both isolated from global market arbitrage and oil-independent. Yet the US oil market is still tightly integrated with the global market. If there was a major disruption in the global oil supply, countries that were directly affected would look for substitutes on the spot markets for crude oil and refined products, triggering a worldwide reallocation of physical supplies, including exports from the US. The oil price would go up in America just as it would everywhere else. Even without the authorisation of crude-oil exports from the US, the country's export of refined products would be sufficient to ensure that it remained fully integrated with the global oil market and vulnerable to global price spikes. This is illustrated by the fact that, despite a 60% drop in US oil imports since 2006, American oil consumers still pay global market prices for oil products. Although the US has maintained its ban on crude-oil exports, its oil-supply boom contributes to the fall in global prices – another clear sign of direct and indirect market integration. Moreover, even if the American economy acquired direct immunity to global price spikes, it would still be indirectly exposed to a global oil shock through the harm done to its financial and trading partners in Asia and Europe.

Finally, rapidly declining US oil imports do not mean that the Middle East will become significantly less important to the global oil market. The share of global oil consumption accounted for by Middle East exports has been roughly stable for 20 years, at 20–25%. A number of factors, on the supply and demand sides, will determine the Gulf's market share, but this share is unlikely to change dramatically in the next decade.

It is therefore unlikely that there will be a major shift in Washington's economic calculus on Gulf security. The US will remain part of a global oil system to which the security of the Gulf states is essential, and part of a world economy vulnerable to oil-price shocks. The macroeconomic risk associated with global

Figure 3. **Middle East exports as a share of global oil consumption**

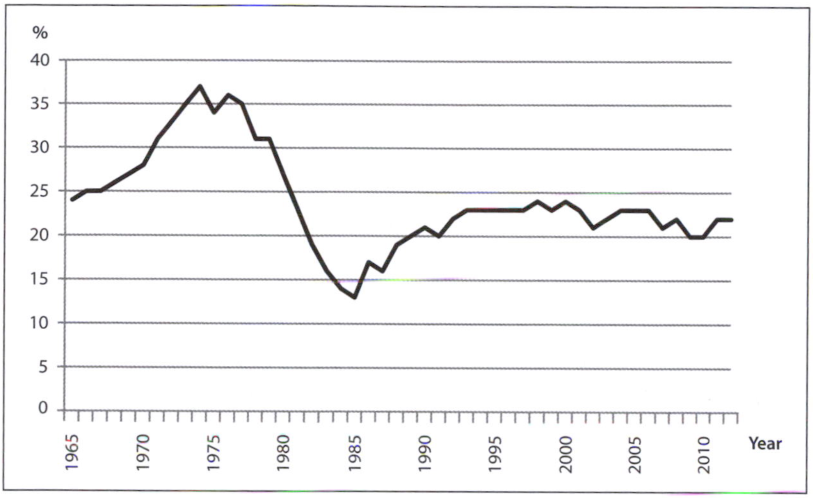

Source: BP Statistical Review of World Energy 2012

oil-price spikes will not be significantly reduced by the fall in US oil imports. Washington will likely remain willing to underwrite the security of the Gulf, even if China and other countries benefit for free.

## Oil-market security and American policy

The need to strengthen oil-market security is probably not the main driver of American strategy in the Middle East, let alone the sole rationale for Washington's approach. Arguably, oil-market security is only a by-product of a strategic posture largely determined by other factors, such as the security of Israel, the perceived threat from Iran, and the importance of the Middle East security umbrella to America's status as a global power.

These considerations are likely to prevent Washington from transferring the burden of securing the Gulf to Asian powers, especially China. If US policy is driven by a need to preserve influence, status and global reach in the eyes of a new strategic competitor, there is little risk that Washington will disengage from the region and force Beijing to assume control. In this sense, the logic of the public good is reversed: the closer China comes to replacing the US in the Middle East, the less willing Washington will be to give Beijing more say in the region's security affairs.

If the benefits to oil-market security are merely a side effect of America's strategic posture in the Middle East, economics matter much less than they otherwise would. The US might continue to provide this global public good even where it no longer makes economic sense for it to do so.

It is unlikely that the US will lose interest in providing security to the Gulf, forcing the so-called free-riders, particularly China, to take over. There is little chance that American policy on global oil-market security will fundamentally change, due to the fact that a reduction in import dependence provides no protection from the threat of global oil-price spikes.

America's security strategy in the Middle East, especially its military posture in the Gulf, may well develop in coming years, perhaps significantly. Essential security objectives could be achieved under new arrangements (which may involve a degree of participation by Asian and regional powers), allowing the US to move away from its role as the dominant provider of security. Yet such a shift would be a function of Washington's strategic decisions about the US political and military footprint in the Middle East; America's relationship with Asian powers; progress in negotiations over the Iranian nuclear programme; and perhaps severe budget constraints at home.

## Notes

[1] Morris Albert Adelman, *The Economics of Petroleum Supply* (Cambridge, MA: MIT Press, 1993), p. 545.